God Is on Your Side

"This isn't a pastor's advice on getting through it with flowery and clean platitudes. It's a broken vessel crying out in the wilderness. *God Is on Your Side* pulls readers into the pages of John, creating a new lived experience of what the biblical text really means. Josh doesn't shy away from tumultuous parts of his own story but gives personal testimony and sound theology for how Christ meets us in the gnarliest of places."

—BRENNA BLAIN, theologian and author of *Can I Say That?*

"Be warned: This isn't a typical Bible study on the book of John. Butler exquisitely sets the table for the reader to have a deep, vulnerable, hope-filled, and transforming conversation with God through Scripture. In our age of overwhelming disillusionment and discouragement, this book reminded me why the gospel of Jesus Christ is still good news. The love of Christ is the theme of the gospel of the beloved disciple. Let it be the song of your heart. This is what it means to have life to the full."

—NIJAY K. GUPTA, professor of New Testament at Northern Seminary and author of *Strange Religion*

"*God Is on Your Side* takes profound truths and paints them in majestic, moving images. Butler has the mind of a theologian but the pen of an artist, with his finger on the pulse of the mainstream world and a yearning to show you the heart of

God. Most important, he shares realities that he actually lives. Read this book—and everything he writes."

—JESSE LUSKO, lead pastor of Counterculture Church

"Joshua Ryan Butler's new book on John's gospel seamlessly combines literary and pastoral attentiveness. Whether John is new territory or an old friend, Butler offers fresh insight and will reassure you that God has indeed taken our side."

—PETER LEITHART, president of the Theopolis Institute
and author of *On Earth as in Heaven*

"We live in a world of constant comparisons and pressures that cause us to question our worth and value and sometimes doubt how much God is with us. *God Is on Your Side* is like refreshing medicine to remind us of the biblical truths that God is not only with us; he is for us and loves us far beyond anything we can possibly imagine."

—DAN KIMBALL, author of *How (Not) to Read the Bible*,
co–lead pastor of Vintage Faith Church (Santa Cruz),
and vice president of Western Seminary

"Like a rich balm to the heart, *God Is on Your Side* feels like sitting across from a trusted friend—someone who has walked through deep valleys and still clings to Jesus with a deep hope and fidelity. Josh blends profound theological depth with a pastor's care and a vulnerable honesty that refreshed me with grace and renewed wonder. As a fellow pastor, I was reminded again of Jesus's passion for me as his beloved: the reality that with him, *all you need is need.* Jesus is one who comes down to meet us, and he is the ladder that pulls us up into his loving arms."

—NASEEM KHALILI, pastor of community
formation, Imago Dei Community

"This is not just a book. It's a lifeline for the weary heart. In a world where everything feels stacked against us, Josh offers a timely reminder that Jesus is not against you—he is for you. With pastoral wisdom, theological depth, and vulnerable story-telling, *God Is on Your Side* will renew your vision of Jesus and his life-giving gospel."

—Rev. Ashish Mathew, lead pastor of Seven Hills Church

"This is a beautiful book. Butler's engagement with Scripture is rich and delightful."

—Justin Whitmel Earley, business lawyer and author of *Habits of the Household* and *The Body Teaches the Soul*

"We've all heard the well-known saying 'God is on our side.' But what does this actually mean? I'm grateful for the wisdom and theological attentiveness of my friend Josh Butler as he tackles a simple saying that has profound impact on our lives. In this book, Josh walks with us, pointing us to Jesus every step of the way. He keeps us centered on the story of Jesus and the Resurrection as proof of this eternal truth: God is on our side."

—Joel Muddamalle, PhD, theologian in residence at Proverbs 31 Ministries and author of *The Hidden Peace*

GOD
IS ON
YOUR
SIDE

GOD IS ON YOUR SIDE

HOW JESUS IS FOR YOU WHEN EVERYTHING

SEEMS AGAINST YOU

Joshua Ryan Butler

MULTNOMAH

Multnomah

An imprint of the Penguin Random House Christian Publishing Group,
a division of Penguin Random House LLC

1745 Broadway, New York, NY 10019

waterbrookmultnomah.com
penguinrandomhouse.com

A Multnomah Trade Paperback Original

Library of Congress Cataloging-in-Publication Data
Names: Butler, Joshua Ryan author
Title: God is on your side : how Jesus is for you when everything seems against you /
Joshua Ryan Butler.
Description: [Colorado Springs] : Multnomah, [2025] | Includes bibliographical references.
Identifiers: LCCN 2025008187 | ISBN 9780593445075 trade paperback | ISBN 9780593445082 ebook
Subjects: LCSH: Christian life
Classification: LCC BV4501.3 B9157 2025 | DDC 248.8/6—dc23/eng/20250508
LC record available at https://lccn.loc.gov/2025008187

Printed in the United States of America on acid-free paper

1st Printing

The authorized representative in the EU for product safety and compliance is Penguin Random
House Ireland, Morrison Chambers, 32 Nassau Street, Dublin D02 YH68, Ireland.
https://eu-contact.penguin.ie

BOOK TEAM: Production editor: Laura Wright • Managing editor: Julia Wallace • Production
manager: Katie Zilberman • Copy editor: Kayla Fenstermaker • Proofreaders: Bailey Utecht,
Lisa Grimenstein

Book design by Caroline Cunningham
Title page starburst: iiierlok_xolms/Adobe Stock

For details on special quantity discounts for bulk purchases, contact
specialmarketscms@penguinrandomhouse.com.

To my beloved sons, James and Jacob.

I am for you, even when everything else seems against you.

May you know in your bones that your heavenly Father is too.

CONTENTS

INTRODUCTION

On Your Side

Is God on my side? Is he really for me? It's easy to answer "Yes!" when life is going well. When your body's healthy, your bank account's full, and your best friends are by your side. It's harder to believe when life takes a turn for the worse.

It was harder to believe when my five-year-old daughter had a psychotic break and we spent ten days in the hospital, six months with specialists, and countless sleepless nights worrying that the girl we loved to the moon and back was gone forever. Or when our adopted son received a diagnosis that sparked our fear for his future.

It was harder to believe when my wife and I had the biggest fight of our marriage and went through months of intense counseling to work through significant issues.

It was harder to believe as a newer Christian when the girl I was hung up on for five years said no and I went on a forty-day hunger strike to challenge God on why he'd bring her into my life if it would end in such devastating heartbreak.

It was harder to believe when I went blind in my right eye and the doctors were concerned I'd soon go blind in my left eye too. Suddenly, I was afraid I'd never see my children's faces as they grew up or be able to read and write or be able to do my job and fulfill my sense of calling.

It was harder to believe when a trusted friend stabbed me in the back and dragged my name through the mud of our community and—though I tried to walk the cruciform path of Jesus and not retaliate—God didn't vindicate me as I hoped.

It was harder to believe when a major dream I thought God had given for my future, confirmed by multiple prophetic words from a variety of people over seven years, came crashing down, disorienting my sense of God's voice and direction for the road ahead.

It was harder to believe during a dark night of the soul when I first heard a sinister voice whispering that it would be better for everyone close to me if I weren't around.

In such seasons, I've found myself wondering, *God, are you really on my side?*

Friend, have you ever wondered whether God is really *for* you? This is, I'd suggest, the question beneath the question. The tension beneath our tension. When we're shaking with anxiety, laid low with depression, or groping in the darkness to discover whether it's really all worth it. When it feels like God has left the building.

In the wake of disappointment and loss, you can find yourself wondering, *Is my maker for me? Does my savior have my back? Is God committed to my good?*

Where do you go when you wrestle with such questions?

THE GOSPEL OF JOHN

There's a place I love to go when wondering whether God is on my side: the gospel of John. This beloved gospel is a favorite for so many people. "I run to [it] over and over again," my friend Brenna Blain says, "like a child running toward their favorite pair of arms."[1]

This gospel has powerful layers. While John is often the first book recommended for someone new to following Jesus, I'm still experiencing epiphanies after decades of reading it. John's waters are shallow enough for a baby believer to wade in and oceanic enough for scuba-diving Christians to explore for a lifetime.

I want to introduce you to some of these deeper layers. We're going to explore John's gospel throughout this book, focusing on the seven signs Jesus performs and the one-on-one encounters he has. As we'll see, John wants you to discover *yourself* in these stories. We'll also explore the Old Testament background that makes each scene pop in vivid Technicolor. This is the trick to uncovering the deeper layers of this gospel: When you see how Jesus fulfills the hope of the biblical story, you can experience more fully how he encounters you in the depths of your own life story.

Let me first explain what I mean—and don't mean—by God being on your side.

IN IT WITH YOU, FIGHTING FOR YOU, WORKING THROUGH YOU

John introduces us to Jesus as the Word made flesh, the Creator entering *our side* of creation.[2] Some people do spoken *word* poetry; God does spoken *world* poetry: speaking worlds into existence.[3] Jesus is the spoken Word who has entered our spoken world—the audio become visual—to find you and be with you forever. This means God is in it with us. Literally. You might feel like God's left the building, but in Christ, he has entered the building to be with you forever.

In Christ, he is *on your side* of creation.

John also introduces us to Jesus as the Lamb of God, the Innocent One who steps *onto our side* as the guilty, to die in our place.[4] Like that sponge I use when my kid spills spaghetti all over the floor, soaking up the mess until the tile is pristine again, Jesus "takes away the sin of the world."[5] This means God fights for you. Jesus has come to bear your guilt, to soak up your shame, to win you back. He isn't willing to let you go without a fight. He has gone the ultimate distance—all the way to hell and back—to be with you forever.

He is *on your side* in salvation.

One last image: John introduces us to Jesus as the ladder we need, with "angels of God ascending and descending" on him.[6] The risen Jesus brings his side of heaven *to our side* of earth. He wants to unite you to himself and make you like rungs on his ladder. This means God wants to work through you. Maybe you feel like you don't have purpose, yet God wants to dwell not only *with* you but also *within* you, to fill you with his Spirit and form you as his body. He wants to partner with you in bringing heaven to earth.[7] There's no greater calling than that.

He is *on your side* in restoration.

While writing this book, I heard a worship anthem that sings about God being in it with us, working through us, and fighting for us: "You're on my side. . . . God is not against me."[8] That's a good summary of John's introduction. If you struggle believing that's true, this book is for you.

ON GOD'S SIDE

Okay, here's what God being on your side *doesn't* mean. It doesn't mean he *picks* sides. It doesn't mean he'll make your fantasy football team win. It doesn't mean he'll necessarily back your argument against your spouse, endorse your candidate, or support your nation's battle against its enemies.

There's a famous Old Testament scene where Joshua asked the angelic commander of God's armies whose side he was on:

> Joshua went up to him and asked, "Are you for us or for our enemies?"
>
> "Neither," he replied, "but as commander of the army of the LORD I have now come."[9]

I'm on God's side, in other words. The real question is how we stand in relation to God. When Abraham Lincoln was asked whether he thought God supported his side of the Civil War, he wisely reflected, "Sir, my concern is not whether God is on our side; my greatest concern is to be on God's side, for God is always right."

The claim of this book is not that God *takes sides* (on a horizontal level) in our messy human spats but rather that God *comes down to our side* (on a vertical level) to encounter us in Christ and transform us in the midst of our mess.

God being on your side doesn't mean he endorses everything you do. Au contraire! Jesus came "full of grace *and* truth," John tells us.[10] Your savior shows up with both *grace* to save you from sin and *truth* to call out the sin he's saving you from.

Jesus confronts and challenges us. Yet even here, as theologian Karl Barth observes, God's "No" to our sin is embedded within his bigger "Yes" to our humanity—the very humanity he's come to rescue.[11] God's confrontation, in other words, unveils an even deeper sense in which he's on our side.

Even when Jesus confronts you, he's out to set you free.

THE ARTIST IS PRESENT

The world-renowned performance artist Marina Abramović put on *The Artist Is Present,* an exhibit at New York's Museum of Modern Art. For two and a half months straight, the Yugoslavian-born artist sat in the museum's atrium for seven hours a day, five days a week, and ten hours on Fridays.[12] People were invited to come sit across from her, one at a time, face-to-face, and look into her eyes as she looked into theirs.

People waited hours in line to be part of this unusual experience. Over the course of the exhibit, she sat with more than 1,500 people for a total of 736 hours and thirty minutes.

Here's the crazy thing: People were overwhelmed. As they sat with her, many were moved to tears, or their jaw dropped in awe, or a look of peace and serenity came over them. You can see photos of their expressions online.[13] After the initial awkwardness of sitting with a stranger in silence, they were moved by the experience of simply being seen.

There's something powerful to being seen.

In Christ, the Artist is present. You're invited in the pages ahead to sit across from the Artist who made the world—and who made you—and encounter his gaze. To lock eyes with Jesus, the God who entered the painting of his creation, on our side of the equation, to meet you where you're at, in all your mess and brokenness.

You're invited to see God seeing you.

Friend, God sees you. You were made to be seen. Maybe you feel ignored or unwanted. Perhaps you've been let down by those who were supposed to care for and protect you. Maybe people have only taken from you rather than giving themselves to you. Christ is different.

Maybe it's hard to believe God sees you right now. If you're having a hard time seeing the Artist, it's okay. I've been there too. I'll share more from my own dark nights of the soul in the pages ahead. Yet I believe God wants to encounter you not in spite of your pain but *through* your pain in a powerful way. Please stick with me.

Jesus approaches you not to take something from you but to give himself to you. Not with self-serving avarice but with life-giving love. He does more than look at you; he *sees* you. All of you. Your story and gifts, your desires and wounds, your trophies and scars. God sees all that lies beneath the tip of your iceberg, his Spirit searching beneath the surface like deep calling to the deep of your ocean floor. God cares about the whole you. Body and soul.

John wants you to see *yourself* in the one-on-one encounters of his gospel. These encounters are more than interesting historical vignettes. Each story is like a stained glass window of that scene, to look through into a greater heavenly reality in which you find yourself.

There's a moment in John's introduction when Nathanael, one of the original disciples, first encounters Jesus. He's astounded that Jesus saw him "under the fig tree" before they even met.

"How do you know me?" he asks.

We're not told what Nathanael was doing under the fig tree, but Jesus *sees* Nathanael before he comes to see Jesus. Jesus *knows* Nathanael before he comes to know Jesus. This is what draws him to worship Jesus.[14]

He sees Jesus seeing him. And it changes everything.

I wonder, Have you seen Jesus seeing you? He sees your situation, knows your backstory, is privy to the "fig trees" where you thought you were all alone. Maybe God feels like a distant stranger, Jesus an odd curiosity. But the gospel invites you to come close to the One who's already come close to you. Encoun-tering his gaze of divine love is what draws you to worship.

The Artist has entered his painting and taken a seat at its cen-ter, inviting you to pull up a chair. To look into the face of the One who made you, who knows you more deeply than you know yourself, and to see him seeing you. In his countenance, you'll discover the divine mercy and unwavering veracity that has long been set on you.

What would it be like to sit face-to-face with Jesus? To stare into the gaze of your Creator? What questions would you think? What stirrings would your heart feel? The pages that follow are an invitation to find out. To meet your maker, who calls you his masterpiece—a masterpiece worth saving.[15]

Is that too good to be true? That even when your world blows up, God is in it with you, fighting for you and working for your good? That even when you feel rejected, discarded, and alone, you can know in your bones that Jesus is on your side?

Then pull up a chair in front of the Artist, and let's find out.

GOD
IS ON
YOUR
SIDE

1

SET THE GPS

When You Don't Know Where You're Going

I remember the first time I had a suicidal thought. *Your family and friends would be better off if you weren't around.* I'd been through a season that felt like crucifixion: publicly mocked, humiliated, and scorned. I lost my reputation, network, job, stability, and community. Many of those close to me needed distance.

Yet I felt called to cruciformity. *Don't retaliate,* I sensed God saying. *Don't try to get even. I'm calling you to humbly endure.* But months later, the adrenaline I'd been running on wore off. I hit rock bottom.

I couldn't see a future.

What do you do when life's direction doesn't seem clear anymore? When your boss says you're fired, your spouse hands you divorce papers, or the doctor delivers a debilitating diagnosis? It can be easy to think you've hit a dead end.

Sometimes you need to reset your GPS.

We're going to Disneyland soon on vacation. Before we hit the road, I'll set the GPS. Once our family's bags are packed, gas tank's full, and seatbelts are buckled, I'll type in our destination.

If we get lost, this will reorient us toward where we're headed. When the kids ask for the thousandth time, "Are we there yet?" it will assure us we're getting closer.

This is true of any journey: It's good to start with the end in mind.

Jesus invites you to realign your GPS with his. In John 2, he shows us where his ministry is heading. It's a famous story, where Jesus turns water to wine at a wedding. At face value, we might misunderstand this as simply a display of his power. (*Cool party trick, Jesus!*) Yet Jesus is doing something much more here.

Jesus is giving us a sign of where his ministry is headed, a road map of the destination he's driving us toward. So buckle up: Jesus is taking us to a resurrection wedding. The road might get rough, but your journey's end is where the rivers run with wine, the celebration never ends, and you encounter your destiny in union with God.

RESURRECTION WEDDING

"On the third day," John opens, "a wedding took place at Cana."[1] *The third day of what?* Is John telling us this wedding takes place on the third day of the week? Or the third day of the year? No, weddings were often a week long back then, not a single day. And this wedding doesn't necessarily follow on the heels of anything earlier in the gospel.[2]

"The third day" may seem like an insignificant detail, but every detail in John's gospel is significant. As we'll see, John opens stories with clues like this to show us how the story fits into the bigger picture of Jesus's ministry. Which raises the question, Can you think of any other significant Jesus events that happen on the third day? That's right.

Resurrection.

This is a resurrection scene. Jesus's miracle here foreshadows what his rising from the dead will accomplish. On the second day, there was a funeral. On the third day, there was a wedding. On the second day, his body lay in a tomb. On the third day, he rose again. The second day looked like defeat. The third day saw vindication. On the second day, the enemy seemed to have won. On the third day, the devil learned you can't keep a good man down.

Our destination is a resurrection wedding. We live in the second day, when the nations are tearing apart at the seams. But the third day's coming, when every nation, tribe, and tongue will worship in reconciled glory. Right now, disease runs rampant. But at the resurrection, healing will go viral. Right now, you might feel alone and tempted by terrible thoughts. But, Christian, the day's coming when you will enter fully into union with God.

On the second day, the wine ran out and all we had was bathwater to drink. On the third day, the rivers started pumping merlot and cabernet. Why? To celebrate the King rising out of that grave. Why did he rise again? To marry his bride.

Jesus's destination is a resurrection wedding. This is helpful to remember when the road gets rough. When you've run out of gas and are stranded, exhausted and desperate, on the side of the road. Or when you've run out of wine . . .

WHEN YOU'VE RUN OUT

"They have no more wine," Mary tells Jesus.[3] This was embarrassing. Parents were expected to host an extravagant feast. Imagine: Your child has been looking forward to this big day their entire life. The whole neighborhood is watching; the social expectations are high. You don't want to let them down.

Have you ever run out? Tried so hard to meet expectations but felt like you have nothing left to give? Maybe you're worried this will mark your reputation forever. *God, I tried so hard to be what they wanted me to be—what I thought you wanted me to be—and I've got nothing left.*

Maybe you've run out of patience with your kids, or stamina with your roommate, and said things you regret. Maybe you've lost passion for your job, or endurance in your loneliness, and gone places for comfort and connection you shouldn't have. Maybe you've run out of hope and given in to despair.

Maybe you need someone to intercede for you, like Mary intercedes for her friend: *Jesus, do something!*[4]

"Woman," he replies, "my hour has not yet come."[5] Now, if I called my mom "Woman," she'd slap me. Yet while that can sound rude in English, it's a sign of respect in the original language—like calling her "Madam."

When Jesus refers to his "hour," he's talking about his crucifixion. This word is used throughout John's gospel to refer to the hour when Jesus is lifted up on the cross. So Jesus is essentially saying, *Mary, it's not yet time for me to reveal my glory—that is coming at the cross. But I'm going to give you a sneak preview right now.*[6]

A picture of his destination.

Jesus's turning of water to wine is a sign of what his crucifixion will accomplish. When you've run out, Jesus meets you with his fullness. When you've got nothing left to give, he gives you himself. When you feel lost and abandoned, sideswiped and stranded on the side of the road, he pulls up alongside and invites you to journey with him. He's got plenty of gas for the both of you, and he knows where he's going.

Jesus's presence doesn't always make the pain of your circumstances go away, but his promise can put it in proper perspective.

"I consider that our present sufferings are not worth comparing," the apostle Paul said, "with the glory that will be revealed in us."[7] You may currently be driving through the hostility and crossfire of a war zone, but you're on your way to a wedding with a trustworthy guide at the wheel.

And this wedding will have plenty of wine.

RIVERS OF WINE

If you hadn't noticed, Jesus makes *a lot* of wine. He has the servants fill "six stone water jars . . . each holding from twenty to thirty gallons . . . so they filled them to the brim."[8] Add it up: Jesus makes around 150 gallons—*that's 750 bottles!*—of wine. He takes it to a party where the guests are already lit (*they've been drinking for days!*). Jesus isn't the dude who shows up with a half-eaten bag of Doritos and some leftover KFC to contribute to the potluck. No, he drops in with a truckload of the best vintage in town!

You might envision a sour-faced Jesus throwing a wet blanket on your celebration. *Jim, was that joke really appropriate? Sarah, are you sure you really need another glass? Colby and Claire, yeah, you on the dance floor, make some room for the Holy Spirit!* That couldn't be further from the truth.

Jesus is the life of the party.

Jesus is out to enliven your life and embolden your celebration. Now, the point of this miracle isn't about getting wasted. Jesus isn't condoning anything inappropriate. But he wasn't crashing this wedding; the family *wanted* him there. They were right to request his presence. Jesus brings better things than we had on our own.

Still, why does Jesus make *so much* wine? *Really, Jesus? Isn't 750 bottles overkill?* This is where some Old Testament backdrop is helpful. The prophets foresaw a coming wedding when God would be united forever with his people.[9] When the Messiah came, the prophet Amos foretold,

> The mountains shall drip sweet wine,
>   and all the hills shall flow with it.
> I will restore the fortunes of my people Israel,
>   and they shall rebuild the ruined cities and inhabit them;
> they shall plant vineyards and drink their wine,
>   and they shall make gardens and eat their fruit.[10]

Similarly, the prophet Joel foresaw this messianic age of abundance:

> In that day
> the mountains shall drip sweet wine,
>   and the hills shall flow with milk,
> and all the streambeds of Judah
>   shall flow with water;
> and a fountain shall come forth from the house of the LORD
>   and water the Valley of Shittim.[11]

These passages are about more than just wine. They're about God restoring his people's fortunes, rebuilding their cities, and returning them from exile. They're about an end to the day of disaster and a revival of abundance in the land.

This day has arrived in Jesus.

That's why Jesus makes *so much* wine. It's not just a cool party trick; it's a sign the messianic age is here. It's a picture of the fuller kingdom restoration he's come to bring. Jesus arrives to restore the vineyards of his people, to make the mountains and hills drip with the best vintage, and to kickstart the wedding

SET THE GPS   9

party with a resurrection river that brings life to the land in vital union with God.

This raises a question, however: Where does this wine come from?

THE SEVENTH VESSEL

The six stone water jars, John tells us, were "for the Jewish rites of purification."[12] Jewish ceremonies used this water to wash away dirt and deal with impurity. These jars were for cleansing, dealing with things that defiled or were associated with decay and death.[13] Why does John include this detail? It points to the sacrificial death of Christ.

You used to get washed with water; now you get washed with wine!

In the Gospels, Jesus identifies wine with his blood. "This is my blood of the covenant," he says while holding up a goblet of wine on the eve of his death, "which is poured out for many for the forgiveness of sins."[14] Like the wine from the blood of the grape, Jesus's blood is *poured out* for purification ("the forgiveness of sins"). The miracle at Cana points to something powerful: Jesus's blood washes us clean.

Jesus has replaced the Jewish rites of purification in the old covenant (represented by the jars of water) with his blood of the new covenant poured out for the forgiveness of sins (represented by the wine).

Wait a sec, you might be thinking. *Are you reading too much into this? Is that what John really intends?* This is probably a good place to lay some of my cards on the table as to how I think we can best interpret John. First, most scholars agree John was the last gospel written. This means John can echo things written in Matthew, Mark, and Luke—like Jesus's institution of the Last

Supper, where he associates wine with his blood—without re-hashing all the details that were already in circulation.

Second, John loves symbolism. He calls this event a sign, meaning it points forward to something greater. As we'll see, all of Jesus's signs point forward to what his cross and resurrection will accomplish. They are symbols of a greater coming reality. Jesus is intentionally orchestrating the details of this sign to give us a symbolic picture, a living parable, of his gospel.

Finally, John's audience is the early church. Practices like the Lord's Supper and baptism were central to their gathering. John knows his audience is familiar with this symbolism.

Okay, back to getting washed by blood. That image may seem strange. *Wouldn't blood—or wine—stain your clothes? Isn't it almost impossible to get out?* But it points to a deeper theological truth: Jesus's atoning death is what washes away our sin and purifies us before God. As John says elsewhere, "The blood of Jesus . . . purifies us from all sin."[15] And the saints are those who have "washed their robes and made them white in the blood of [Jesus] the Lamb."[16]

Some people take ice baths to improve blood flow and decrease inflammation. Others take milk baths to help their skin feel softer and smoother. Yet if you *really* want to feel like new, the gospel says you need to take a wine bath! You need to experience the life-changing power of Jesus's love for you through the dynamic vitality of his blood shed for you. This purification can wash you spotless as his bride and unite his life with yours forever.

Another symbol: You'll notice there are six jars at the wedding. That's because the Jewish rites of purification were good but incomplete (seven is the Hebrew number of completion). Yet when Jesus dies, at the climax of John's gospel, water and blood flow from his side.[17]

Jesus is the seventh vessel.

Jesus turns water to wine through his death. He's crushed to make atonement for our sins through the wine of his shed blood. Jesus brings the purification rites to fulfillment. He provides a complete purification from sin: not through the rituals and regulations of the old system but through the power of his new covenant blood.

Jesus's blood is stronger than Dove soap. More powerful than Clorox bleach. You might fear you're too dirty. *If you only knew the mistakes I've made, the people I've hurt, the things I've said and done.* Yet this wine is potent enough to cleanse any stain you've got. You might worry there's not enough to go around, but Jesus made *150 gallons* to show there's plenty to cover you!

With God on your side, there's no mistake big enough, no crime bad enough, no reputational damage severe enough to keep you away from his love.

❊ ❊ ❊

A little secret: God turns water into wine all the time. Rain falls to the earth, soaks into the soil, and is absorbed by the vine. It eventually emerges in the grapes, which come bursting off the branches. With this miracle, Jesus is not contradicting nature but rather speeding up the process, through *himself* as the vine.

Yet there's one more crucial step in the process of making wine: You have to crush the grapes. Jesus is crushed to bring forth resurrection wine. His life poured out is what brings life to the world. That's how seriously he wants to cleanse you from your mistakes and regrets, to purify you from your failures and shortcomings.

So bring your dirty old rags to Jesus. Confess your darkest deeds and deepest fears. "There is a fountain filled with blood," the old hymn says, "drawn from Immanuel's veins." I used to think those were some crazy lyrics! But they point to this powerful theological truth: "Sinners, plunged beneath that flood, / lose all their guilty stains."[18] Let him wash you clean, dress you in his righteousness, and bring you to a wedding where he's saved the best for last.

BEST FOR LAST

Time for the finale. The servants take the wine to the head of the feast:

> The master of the banquet tasted the water that had been turned into wine. . . . Then he called the bridegroom aside and said, "Everyone brings out the choice wine first and then the cheaper wine after the guests have had too much to drink; but you have saved the best till now."[19]

This is a different kind of party. Usually you start with the twenty-year-old cabernet and the fifteen-year-old scotch. Then, once everyone's lit, you pull out the Two-Buck Chuck and Mike's Hard Lemonade. Jesus does it backward.

He saves the best for last.

This is a picture of the gospel. What Jesus brings is better than everything that's come before. His sacrifice is better than all the Old Testament sacrifices. His purification is deeper than the Jewish rites of purification. He can cleanse you more fully than any bleach, beauty exfoliant, or behavioral modification you've tried before. His wedding brings more joy than any wedding you've ever attended.

Compared with anything you've ever tried to manufacture meaning from, find fulfillment in, or cultivate contentment through . . .

Jesus is better.

We generally start with our best. On that first date, we dress to the nines and strive to make a good impression. Then, after twenty years of marriage, we flop our socks on the floor and pop that beer belly out. In our union with Christ, however, it's "further up and further in."[20] Things will keep getting better into eternity.

The master of the banquet is a picture of the Father. God the Father is pleased with the sacrifice of his Son. That's the deepest meaning of this final scene. Like the master of the banquet, God the Father presides over the wedding of his Son. He tastes the miraculous wine and declares to the bridegroom, *You've saved the best for last!* The Father savors the sacrificial love of his Son, poured out on the cross for his bride, and delightedly declares, *This is better than everything that's come before!*

This is the gospel. Jesus has offered a "once for all" sacrifice at "the culmination of the ages," in the words of Hebrews, "to do away with sin by the sacrifice of himself," making "perfect forever those who are being made holy."[21] Jesus's sacrifice brings forth the wedding day Isaiah foresaw, when God would "prepare a feast of rich food for all peoples, a banquet of aged wine—the best of meats and the finest of wines. . . . He will swallow up death forever [and] wipe away the tears from all faces; he will remove his people's disgrace from all the earth."[22]

This is the wedding of the Lamb.

Jesus's miracle at Cana is a *living parable* of the gospel. Famously, John doesn't include the parable stories highlighted in the other gospels. Why? I would suggest this is because John does something spectacular: He narrates Jesus's signs—the seven miracles he performs in John's gospel—as living parables, pictures of the gospel in motion. John does have parables; they're just not the *stories* Jesus tells but rather the *signs* Jesus performs.

To be clear, this doesn't mean John invents details, making them up for symbolic purposes. Rather, *Jesus performs these signs intentionally*, with details that set them up as living parables.

John, as the beloved disciple, is being faithful to Christ's intentions. He lived the longest and, as we saw earlier, wrote his gospel last. He had a lifetime to reflect on Christ's actions and to craft his narratives. He highlights details that help us look *through* these stories, like windows, to find ourselves in the greater realities they represent.

So where do we find ourselves in this living parable?

We are the bride. We gaze on Christ the Bridegroom, who loved us so much he shed his blood to wash us spotless for the wedding. We hear the voice of the Father, rejoicing in the sacrifice of his Son and his union with us as the church. We feel the presence of the Spirit, who unites us to Christ in this joyous celebration that will bring new life to the world.

DON'T STOP AT THE SIGN

On our upcoming trip to Disneyland, imagine we see a giant billboard a few hours outside Anaheim with a picture of our destination on it. I pull off to the side of the road, roll out a picnic blanket, and unpack sandwiches and soda from the cooler. I sit beneath the sign and yell out to the kids, "We're here!"

My kids would be confused and disappointed. They'd think I was crazy. The picture on that billboard is an image of where we're headed, but it's not the reality itself. We're still sitting next to the freeway. The moral of the story? Don't stop at the sign.

Keep going to the destination.

Jesus's miracle at Cana is a sign, not the destination. John says it's "the first of the signs through which [Jesus] revealed his glory."[23] Jesus is setting the GPS for his ministry. Water to wine is a picture of where we're headed. We disciples are like children in the back seat of his car, moving ever closer to the destination: our resurrection wedding.

So when I face a disheartening thought that knocks me off my feet, the first thing I try to do is look up. To recognize: *That's not the voice of God; that's the enemy.* I call my wife and bring the thought out of the dark into the light. I go to see my counselor, spiritual director, or doctor. I focus on the things I can control—like diet, sleep, and exercise. I seek Christ the Living Word in his written Word and the presence of his Spirit in prayer.

And I look beyond the sign toward the destination.

You're invited to a royal wedding. Don't stop at the billboard in Cana; set your eyes on the kingdom it points to. Jesus has come to cleanse you of your stains, to wash you white as snow and get you ready for the big day. Jesus pours for you a richer vintage than any wine you've ever tasted, a love more satisfying and sacrifice more satiating than anything you've tried before. Jesus has inaugurated a celebration that will go on into eternity, when we will discover that the best has truly been saved for last as we are united with God forever.

✸　✸　✸

When you're unsure where you're going, when you've lost your way, when life crashes into you and leaves you aimless and disoriented, do you know what I recommend doing? Set your GPS. Align with Jesus. If you need a place to start, check out Revelation 21. Set your sights on this destination he's bringing you to: union with him forever. You're on your way to a love that is stronger, a joy that is brighter, and a kingdom that is more secure than any you can imagine.

You're not simply invited to attend this wedding; you're invited to become the bride. On one side of the scene are the spectators: angels in a chorus of praise; the rocks, rivers, and rainforests that applaud the coming of the King; the whole of the new creation, which rejoices in this wedding that renews the world.

Yet we're not on that side of the scene. We're not in the throng of spectators with cameras outstretched to snap pictures of the spectacle. No, we're in front of the altar, hand in hand with the King. We're indwelt by the Spirit, who lifts the veil so that we can gaze on Christ before us, as we're brought into the home of the Father, who rejoices over us.

It's here, in this wedding at the end of the world—which is, more truly, the beginning of the world—that all things will be made new, including us, through our union with Christ. It's here, on the other side of the altar and the other side of eternity, that we will most fully experience the reality that, in Christ, has been true all along.

God is on our side.

2

BRING DOWN THE HOUSE

When Change Is Painful

The city is under attack. I'm in the back seat of an SUV, and my friend—I'll call him Kevin—is in the front passenger seat, when suddenly a missile slams into a building up ahead. The SUV swerves to go a different direction when a second missile slams into another building in front of us. We swerve again and head over a bridge across a river when a third missile slams into the other end of the bridge. The whole bridge wobbles, collapses, and crumbles. We're plummeting toward the water when, just before we hit, I wake up.

Now, sometimes I have a crazy dream because I had a bad burrito for dinner. But sometimes it feels like God. This was one of those. The driver of the SUV was a shadowy figure I couldn't see but who I could tell was God.

I prayed about the dream and sensed God saying, *Josh, everything familiar is going to come crashing down around you. Your job, stability, routines, and city. It's going to feel like you're falling into nothing, but I've got you.*

Years later, this dream would come true. A wave of attacks—

online, personal, professional—would lead to the dismantling of our church into ten separate churches, like a falling city. Kevin and I were driven out from a church we loved and had long sought to faithfully lead (we both sensed strongly God's leading us out). My job, home, stability, and community crumbled around me. My wife, Holly, and I left the city to move our family back to our hometown.

I felt like I was falling into nothing.

Yet I also sensed God was in the driver's seat. But if he foresaw this why would he not stop it? Why wouldn't he prevent the dismantling of a church I loved? Why would he let everything familiar collapse around me?

Sometimes God's got to bring down the house.

The phrase *bring down the house* originated in the 1700s, when applause in the theater—the quake of clapping and stomping in response to a stellar performance—was loud enough to pose a threat that the building might collapse. In the 1800s, the phrase became a joke in British comedy to call out an awkward silence: *Don't clap so hard. You'll bring down the house!*[1] Today we use the phrase for a performance that leads to thunderous applause.

In John 2, Jesus brings down the house. He gives a theatrical performance in the temple—turning over tables, whipping animals, driving out people—in a symbolic display of the temple's coming destruction. This is not buddy Jesus, meek and mild, but prophetic-fire Jesus with a holy flame. He's bringing down the house of God.

What do you do when change is painful? When Jesus shows up with confrontation rather than comfort, turning your life upside down? When the place where you once encountered God now seems to be crumbling around you? It can be easy to think God is against you, but what if this is part of his being more deeply on your side? What if he goes all bull-in-a-china-shop because he's willing to crash through your distance and crush your idols to get to your heart?

DEMOLITION GOD

Jesus isn't losing his cool in the temple; he's giving us a prophetic sign of what his death will accomplish. "When it was almost time for the Jewish Passover," John opens, "Jesus went up to Jerusalem."[2] "Passover" is John's way of saying, *You're about to read a crucifixion-themed story* (similar to how, as we saw in the last chapter, "the third day" is John's setup for a resurrection-themed story). At the climax of John's gospel, Jesus will go up to Jerusalem during Passover week to die as the Passover Lamb and atone for the sin of the world. Here John is giving us a Blue's Clue: This story is about to foreshadow that finale.

Jesus arrives in the big city and causes a scene:

> In the temple courts he found people selling cattle, sheep and doves, and others sitting at tables exchanging money. So he made a whip out of cords, and drove all from the temple courts, both sheep and cattle; he scattered the coins of the money changers and overturned their tables.[3]

Many people assume Jesus is angry with folks selling stuff in the temple. (*Get that bookstore out of the church lobby!*) But they're *supposed* to be selling stuff there. God knew it would be too difficult for his people to carry their offerings and sacrifices all the way to Jerusalem for the festivals. So in Deuteronomy, he made an accommodation:

> If the way is too long for you, so that you are not able to carry [your offering] because the place is too far from you . . . then you shall turn it into money and bind up the money in your

hand and go to [the temple] and spend the money for whatever you desire—oxen or sheep or wine or strong drink, whatever your appetite craves. And you shall eat there before the
LORD your God and rejoice, you and your household.[4]

The money changers and animals are supposed to be in the
temple courts. So what's the problem, then? Yes, Jesus could be
confronting dishonest practices of the day or the excluding of
God-fearing Gentiles from worship.[5] But there's something
deeper going on.

Jesus is bringing an end to sacrifice.

Jesus does a symbolic act. He's a prophet giving a dramatic
performance to symbolize the temple's coming destruction.
Here's where some Old Testament backdrop can be helpful
again. Such symbolic actions were common for the prophets:

- Ezekiel lay on his side for 430 days and ate food cooked
  over dung to symbolize the nation's sin and coming captivity.[6]
- Isaiah walked around naked to portray the people of
  Egypt and Cush being led away stripped and shamed.[7]
- Jeremiah smashed a clay jar outside Jerusalem's walls as a
  sign of the city's coming destruction.[8]

Jesus is a prophet in this line. He's like Banksy, creating an
unsolicited public art display. Or like an actor, giving a dramatic
street performance. Or like my dream, foreshadowing coming
destruction. All the disruptive actions of the prophets in the biblical examples above are similar.

In the words of theologian N. T. Wright,

Jesus' dramatic action in the Temple . . . was an acted parable
of judgment, of destruction. . . . [Jesus] was claiming pro-

phetic and messianic authority to pronounce judgment on the Temple.[9]

Jesus's actions interrupt the temple's daily sacrifices, where pilgrims bring their offerings to the priests and smoke arises throughout the day. Jesus is putting a kink in that hose, breaking the flow of the sacrificial system. That's what gets him into so much trouble.[10] Jesus's audience would have seen his disruptive actions as something like an attack on the White House, Wall Street, or Times Square—the symbolic center of the nation.

To attack the temple was to attack the world.

Of course, this interruption is temporary. The sacrifices resume soon after. So why do it? It's symbolic. Jesus's prophecy comes true within a generation of his death, when Rome destroys the temple and changes Judaism forever.[11] Throughout John's gospel, Jesus's confrontation with the religious leadership is a major theme, and this scene highlights the roots of that conflict.[12]

Jesus isn't blowing a gasket like Will Smith at the Oscars. No, his actions are premeditated and deliberate. It takes a while to make a whip out of cords. You can imagine the disciples: *Hey, Indiana, what are you planning to do with that whip?* The day before, Jesus inspected the temple and left for Bethany to make plans—so he's not flying off the handle in the moment.[13]

This isn't an emotional tantrum; it's a prophetic mission.

BULL IN A CHINA SHOP

Jesus isn't cleaning up the temple; he's tearing it down. Sometimes this event is called the cleansing of the temple. Yet Jesus is not like Marie Kondo, come to tidy it up and spark joy, but more like Dwayne "the Rock" Johnson, come to demolish it. He arrives not with a bottle of Formula 409 to make it shine but with a sledgehammer to raze it to the foundations.

Jesus is bringing down the house—only his audience isn't clapping.

Have you ever thought God came to clean up your life and been shocked to find he first came to tear it down? I love the song "24 Frames," where Jason Isbell croons,

> You thought God was an architect—now you know
> he's something like a pipe bomb ready to blow [14]

God will confront things we've built for appearances. We often want to use God as a contractor to tack on an addition to our life, yet he first comes to expose our faulty foundation.

You might be tempted to think, *If I follow Jesus, he'll give me the perfect spouse.* Then you discover he cares more about dealing with your emotional reliance on someone else for your sense of self-worth.

Or perhaps you assume, *If I'm faithful to God, he'll give me the perfect job.* Then you learn he's actually out to dismantle your false sense of security.

Maybe you hope, *If I walk with the Spirit, he'll heal my medical condition.* Then you realize there's a deeper soul surgery he's out to perform.

Or you assume, *If I read the Bible, God will reinforce my perfect political ideology.* Then you find he crashes your categories and confuses the assumptions you brought to the table.[15]

You might think, *If I pray enough, God will help me find the perfect church.* Then you come to understand your heavenly Father invites you to encounter him through your messy church family.

A year after our church's dismantling, Kevin and I met for coffee. We both saw the hand of God in the story. Even knowing all the brutal behind-the-scenes details, we both saw the prior year as an act of God's judgment on the church. Not in the sense of a vindictive "gotcha" moment. Instead, our church needed to face some deep-rooted problems, some skeletons in the backyard of our collective story, that had never been properly dealt with.

Some actors had truly bad intentions when they shot "missiles at the city," similar to how the Romans were unrighteous when they tore down Jerusalem's temple walls as Jesus's prophecy was fulfilled. Yet God had been up to something bigger in the situation—in Kevin's life, in mine, and in the ten churches that emerged from the aftermath. Something redemptive.

Jesus is hardcore, yet this is because he is for you *at his core.* He demolishes some things because he wants to build you up on a firm foundation. He cares more about your character than your comfort. More about your sanctification than your false security. More about your true heart than your temporary happiness.

He stands against your junk because he's standing up for your deeper humanity. Whenever Jesus drives out the dangerous things, he's making the sanctuary of your life a home fit for his presence. Even when Jesus turns over your tables—perhaps *especially* when he turns over your tables—God is on your side.

DIVINE RENOVATION

The temple leaders ask Jesus, "What sign do You show to us, since You do these things?"[16] Notice that word *sign:* This is the second time John uses the word in his gospel. Like with the wedding at Cana, we need to not stop at the sign but keep going to the destination. We need to look *through* this event toward his coming death and resurrection.

Jesus's actions in the temple are the second sign.

Scholars debate this, however, so let me show my work. The

temple leaders' question can be taken two ways: (1) What sign *are* you showing us by doing these things (i.e., *What's the point of your actions just now?*). Or, (2) What sign *can* you give us to prove your authority to do these things (i.e., *What gives you the right?*). I believe John intends *both* meanings. John loves double entendre, so he intentionally uses ambiguous language here that can be read both ways.[17] Then he connects the term *sign* with Jesus's response.

"Destroy this temple," Jesus responds, "and I will raise it again in three days."[18] That's an optimistic reconstruction timeline! Understandably perplexed, the Jewish leaders respond, "It has taken forty-six years to build this temple, and you are going to raise it in three days?"[19] *This guy's crazy,* they're thinking. This isn't *Minecraft.* Yet they miss something essential: They think he's referring to the building surrounding them, but he's actually talking about the temple standing and speaking in front of them.

"The temple he had spoken of was his body."[20]

Jesus is the true temple. He is the hot spot of God's presence, where heaven and earth meet and God enters most intimate communion with his people.[21]

Jesus's dramatic performance in the temple is a sign of his own coming crucifixion. As the Roman soldiers lash Jesus's body, they're tearing into God's dwelling place brick by brick. As the executioners hammer nails into his flesh, they're swinging a sledgehammer through the temple's sanctuary walls. When the pillagers divide his clothes, they're divvying up the spoils that adorned the temple. As the centurion thrusts the imperial spear into Jesus's side, this is the final blow that comes crashing into the sacred interior of his Most Holy Place.

Jesus is the temple torn down.

The Crucifixion is, from this angle, a demolition. As the curtain is torn and Jesus exhales his last breath, giving up his spirit, the glory departs the temple.

They have brought down the house of God.

Why does the old temple need to be demolished? This is another way of asking, Why does Jesus need to die? A powerful clue is found in the writing of Jeremiah, the Old Testament prophet, who foresaw God's coming judgment. Centuries earlier, he stood at the temple gates and confronted those entering:

> Will you steal, murder, commit adultery, swear falsely, make offerings to Baal, and go after other gods that you have not known, and then come and stand before me in this house, which is called by my name, and say, "We are delivered!"— only to go on doing all these abominations? Has this house, which is called by my name, become a den of robbers in your eyes?[22]

You're going to act like that, God's saying, *and then dwell in my house like nothing's wrong? You're living under my roof,* the heavenly Father's saying, *but not living by my ways.* We can't lie, cheat, and steal, then come sit on God's couch, watch his flat-screen, and help ourselves to anything in the fridge—while pretending nothing's wrong.

Jesus dies to bear the sin of his people. The problem is *much* bigger than a bookstore in the church lobby. The people are breaking all kinds of commands—six of the Ten Commandments are explicitly mentioned in the Jeremiah quote above—then hiding out in the temple like it's some kind of safe zone where they're untouchable. The place where they were supposed to dwell *with* God has become a place where they're hiding *from* God.

That's why it needs to be torn down.

HIDING FROM GOD

Are you hiding in a church building but living far from God? This won't do. Jesus cares about the purity of his people. He wants to make *you* a temple. He meets you where you're at but won't leave you there.

He's out for a divine renovation.

Imagine you hire a construction company to renovate your home. Yet, instead of fixing the broken window, they place a plant in front of it. Instead of removing mold, they slap a coat of paint over it. Instead of tackling the termites, they ignore the creepy crawlers dining on your dwelling.

At first, you might exclaim, "Wow, this renovation was less expensive than I'd thought!" Later, however, when the house is falling down around your head, you'll be upset at what a shoddy job they did. There's a cost to things being done cheap. You'll say they were a *bad* construction company.

Jesus is a good architect. He doesn't cut corners. You can trust him with your demolition because he's ultimately doing a renovation. Before the fresh paint, furniture, and plants can be added, there are some walls that might need to be torn down in your life, some cracks that might need to be repaired, some flooring or even a foundation that might need to be fixed.

Jesus is the firm foundation you can build your life on. If you're trusting in your health, it will eventually fade. Your money may run out. Your reputation might vanish with the snap of your fingers. But you can build your life on Jesus.

When Jesus calls you to come and die to yourself, it's so that you can live unto God.[23] As Jesus says later in John's gospel,

> Anyone who loves me will obey my teaching. My Father will love them, and we will come to them and *make our home* with them.[24]

God wants to make his home with you. This is temple language: the Father and Son dwelling with you by their Spirit living *in* you. As a house of God.

Sometimes Jesus calls you to changes that can feel threatening at first, but God cares about your foundation because he cares about you. Even when Jesus tears you down to the studs, it's so he can build you back even better and stronger in him. So you can be *with* him. You can take confidence that even when such change is painful, he's on your side.

Jesus wants to make you a living temple, built not with brick and stone but with flesh and bone. He wants to fill you with the wind of God, the presence of God, the glory of God. To make you a home for the living God.

Some people want to know how to get into heaven. Jesus flips the direction of movement: He wants to get heaven into you. He's not looking to tack himself onto your life as an addition; he's looking to renovate you from the inside out.

Jesus wants to make you a place where heaven crashes into earth, where the divine presence dwells in holy intimacy and sacred power, where you become a home for the Spirit and a house of prayer for all nations.

This is a major New Testament theme. "We are the temple of the living God," joined together as "living stones" who are "being built into a spiritual house" for God's presence.[25] The apostle Paul describes the church this way:

> Christ Jesus himself [is] the cornerstone, in whom the whole structure, being joined together, grows into a holy temple in the Lord. In him you also are being built together into a dwelling place for God by the Spirit.[26]

This is why Jesus had to die. The old temple had to be torn down so this new temple could be built up. The cornerstone was rejected so you could be accepted. The temple of his body was torn down so you and I could be built up in him. Jesus brought down the house so you and I could be brought into the house of God.

God's endgame isn't to get you into a building; it's *building you* into a home for his presence. God wants to dwell *inside* you! Jesus cares about your holiness because he's jealous for your wholeness—for you to be made fit as a house for God. So anything that's standing in the way? Kick it to the curb. Give your full devotion to Jesus. Build your life on the foundation of his love.

THE CRUCIFIXION AS DEMOLITION

Jesus tosses tables in the temple to prophesy his coming death. Don't stop at the sign; look forward to the destination. Check out how these images from John 2 foreshadow the cross.

When Jesus cracks the whip in the temple, he's enacting his own coming flogging, as cords will tear into his flesh. When he drives the sheep and cattle from the courts, he's showing that their sacrifices will no longer be needed, as the Lamb will now be slain. When he scatters the coins of the money changers, he's pointing to the day when he himself will be sold for thirty pieces of silver and provide the ransom for those held captive by the enemy.

John's language in this temple scene highlights what Jesus's death will accomplish. Jesus *drives out* everyone from the temple, a phrase with massive echoes of exile: when God drove out Adam and Eve from the garden, when he drove out Israel from the land, when the temple was torn down. At the cross, Jesus is himself driven out of the temple grounds and crucified outside the city.[27] The point: Jesus bears our exile, taking on himself the punishment for our sin and the destructive impact of our rebellion.

Jesus *pours out* the coins of the money changers, another phrase with massive overtones. The prophets associate the phrase *poured out* with divine anger at human evil.[28] As N. T. Wright summarizes, "the Temple would be destroyed by foreign armies, and . . . this event should be seen as the outpouring of [Yahweh]'s wrath upon his recalcitrant people."[29] The exile would continue until the cup of God's wrath was completely poured out, the prophets foretold, and the debt paid for the people's sin.[30] At the cross, Jesus drinks the cup down to its dregs, as the true temple is torn down by Roman soldiers, his vicarious humanity absorbing the triune God's justice against evil.[31] You no longer need to bring your coins to the money changers; the final sacrifice has been made. This is what brings our exile to completion so we can return home.

Jesus *overturns* the tables, a term that can also mean "overthrow" with a sense of destroying.[32] At the cross, Christ's body is overturned, this living temple overthrown, the house of God destroyed for our salvation. Yet the story doesn't end there.

Jesus rebuilds the temple in three days. He's the fastest contractor you've ever met. Construction projects often take *way longer* than anticipated, but Jesus meets his optimistic self-imposed deadline. "After he was raised from the dead," John tells us, "his disciples recalled what he had said [about the three days]. Then they believed the scripture and the words that Jesus had spoken."[33]

A SACRIFICE OF PRAISE

The risen Jesus is out to rebuild you. When change is painful, remember where he's taking you. His endgame is not demolition but renovation. Confronting patterns, removing idols, and calling you out of your vices are all part of a bigger plan to shape you into his image, to conform you to the character of his Father, to build you up as a temple for his Spirit. Holiness is for wholeness, to make you a home for the living God.

Jesus doesn't call you anywhere he hasn't already gone himself. He was torn down so we could be rebuilt in him. He bore our destruction to bring us renovation. How should we respond to such a great sacrifice? To such great love that would go so far to be with us forever?

Worship. We bring down the house. We sing loud enough to shake the rafters and quake the foundations of this whole old creation, until the rattling ramparts threaten to come crashing down at our feet. And then we sing some more. We erupt in praise with our voices and our lives. We offer the entirety of who we are as a sacrifice of praise. We bring down the house for him because he brought down the house for us. We worship him with everything we have and let our thunderous applause anticipate the encore that will echo throughout eternity.

When God will make his home with us forever.

3

BECOME THE BELOVED

When You Don't Feel Wanted

Jack broke his promise. Back in high school, he was dating my friend Melissa. Jack wanted to sleep together, so he made big promises and put on the pressure. He swore that he loved her. Was committed to her. Wanted to be with her forever. She didn't want him to leave and wanted to believe, so eventually she said yes. The next day, he broke up with her.

He broke his promise and broke her heart.

Where do you go when you feel unwanted? Rejection can lead you down some dark and dangerous roads. For Melissa, it led to a string of dysfunctional relationships. If you're facing the same thing, know you're not alone. Maybe you look for affection in the arms of another. Maybe you lower your standards and settle for someone who treats you like dirt.

Maybe you self-harm to feel something again or rely on substances to numb the pain. Maybe you turn to porn, the cheap rush of a façade that can't reject you. Maybe you isolate, protecting your heart by locking it in a cage where no one can break it again.

Melissa tried to get revenge by sleeping with a rebound, then dumping him to vicariously get back at the one who hurt her. She sought control, avoided trust, and established dominance in any new relationship to make sure her heart didn't get broken again.

Melissa eventually met Jesus and found he was able to minister to her pain. I share her story because in our passage for this chapter, John 4, Jesus encounters a woman who I imagine experienced some similar heartbreak.

The woman at the well is often misunderstood. She's had five husbands and is currently living with a man she's not married to. Some people assume this means she's a sexually promiscuous seductress. That's anachronistic, however. There was a strong double standard in the ancient world. Men could easily divorce their wives, not the other way around. So she's likely experienced a lot of broken promises.

This woman knows rejection. Probably tragedy too. (Maybe some husbands died.) Perhaps settling. (Why won't the guy she's now with marry her?[1]) She knows what it's like to feel dropped and discarded.

If you can relate, there's good news: Jesus is on his way.

FIRST ENCOUNTER

Jesus makes a pit stop in Samaria on his way to Galilee:

> Jacob's well was there, and Jesus, tired as he was from the journey, sat down by the well. It was about noon.
>
> When a Samaritan woman came to draw water, Jesus said to her, "Will you give me a drink?" . . .
>
> The Samaritan woman said to him, "You are a Jew and I am a Samaritan woman. How can you ask me for a drink?" (For Jews do not associate with Samaritans.)[2]

The well might seem like a passing detail, but it's significant. In the Old Testament, a well was where a groom first met his bride: Isaac's bride, Rebekah, was discovered at a well.[3] Jacob first locked eyes with Rachel, the love of his life, at a well.[4] Moses rescued Zipporah at a well, leading to their betrothal.[5]

The renowned Jewish scholar Robert Alter describes the well as a betrothal type-scene. Common in Hebrew literature, this type-scene includes the following five elements:

1. The future groom journeys to a foreign land.
2. There he encounters a girl at a well.
3. One of them draws water from the well.
4. The girl rushes home with news of the stranger's arrival.
5. A betrothal is concluded after he has been invited to a meal.[6]

Jesus's encounter with the Samaritan woman includes all five of these elements.

The point? John paints this scene as a picture of Christ's first encounter with his church. I want to be totally clear: Jesus isn't getting romantic with this woman. Rather, he intentionally orchestrates this encounter as a sign of a greater reality—true for all the people of God.

The well is where Christ meets his bride.

The place where a couple first meets is significant. Romeo and Juliet lock eyes at a dance. Tom Hanks is sleepless in Seattle until he meets Meg Ryan at the top of the Empire State Building. Jenny kindly offers Forrest Gump a seat on the bus next to her on his first day of school. Such iconic scenes of first encounters are emblazoned in our cultural memory.

I first met Holly at Old Laurelhurst Church. One Sunday morning, she sat down next to me. Our church plant rented this beautiful wedding chapel in the heart of Portland for our weekly gatherings. Its historic Spanish architecture boasts high vaulted ceilings that draw the gaze upward toward transcendence. Stained glass windows transport viewers to timeless scenes in the story of salvation. And its wooden pews are where I first sat next to my future bride.

This location holds a special place in my heart.

Where did you first meet Christ? How did you encounter him? What season of life were you in? How did he first capture your heart?

Christ meets his bride at a well. While on one level Christ's encounter with the woman of John 4 is totally platonic, on another level, John paints this scene with iconic details that draw the gaze upward, like the architecture of a cathedral, toward a transcendent truth for the church. John invites you to look through this scene, like a stained glass window, and find yourself in the timeless reality it portrays . . .

Our first encounter with Christ as his church.

BOUNDARY CROSSER

Let's see how Jesus fulfills each movement of the betrothal type-scene. First, the groom journeys to a foreign land. John tells us Jesus "had to go through Samaria."[7] Actually, he doesn't *have* to. There were alternative routes.

Jews and Samaritans hated one another. There was a racial component: Samaritans were part Jew and part Gentile (the product of intermarriage when Israel had been conquered centuries earlier). There was also a religious component: Samaritans accepted only the first five books of the Bible and had some strange spiritual practices (the product of syncretism with their oppressors' religion).

So good, upstanding Jewish boys looked down on Samaritans

as "half-breed pagans." This explains why the Samaritan woman responds incredulously to Jesus's question: "You are a Jew and I am a Samaritan woman. How can you ask me for a drink?" In case we missed it, the text highlights the tension: "Jews do not associate with Samaritans."[8]

Jews would *avoid* Samaritans, but Jesus *approaches* one. He "had to" go through Samaria—not because Google Maps says there's no other way but because he has a divine appointment at a well. There's someone he has to meet.

Jesus searches for his bride in unlikely places. He's playing pickup games on the dangerous South Side of Chicago, hanging out in the red-light district near the wasted at 2 A.M., vacationing in Colima, Mexico—the murder capital of the world. He goes places the upright and uptight don't like to go. Why?

Because he knows you're there.

Jesus finds you on the wrong side of town. He crosses boundaries many say he shouldn't cross. He pursues a people some say live in the wrong zip code, practice a muddled religion, belong to the wrong ethnicity, believe a confused ideology, have a stained reputation . . . Jesus could have gone *around* us, but he came *to* us. He stepped onto your side. He *had* to. Why?

Because he loves you.

The Samaritan woman is a picture of the church. Like her, the church is part Jew and part Gentile (a major theme in the New Testament[9]), we're from the wrong side of town, and we encounter Jesus as one who journeys from a distant land—all the way from heaven to earth—to meet us.

Jesus is the boundary crosser. There's no fence that can keep you from him. He's an Olympic athlete leaping over hurdles like they're speed bumps to get to the finish line of his people. Jesus has crossed every boundary to get to our side and make us his bride.

This raises a question: Are you *creating* dividing lines or *crossing* them? Let's be boundary crossers, like Jesus. Let's go to people who don't look like us, think like us, vote like us, post like us, or live like us. Let's sit down with them, like Jesus did at that well, and start a constructive conversation.

I'm not saying you shouldn't have convictions (I have strong ones). I'm saying you don't have to agree in order to love. I'm saying you shouldn't divide the church that Jesus came to unite. I'm saying it's powerful when you and I remember the only reason we are *in* the church is that Jesus crossed the greatest of boundaries to get to us.

THIRST QUENCHER

In the second and third movements of the betrothal type-scene, a conversation ensues and one person draws water from the well. Jesus tells the Samaritan woman, "If you knew the gift of God and who it is that asks you for a drink, you would have asked him and he would have given you living water."[10] Jesus is like, *If you knew who I was, you'd be asking me.*

Jesus is the fount of living water. So his asking for a drink is like Bill Gates asking, *Can I borrow ten dollars?* Or the Barefoot Contessa requesting, *Can you cook me a snack?* But the woman doesn't know this yet, so she responds,

> You have nothing to draw with and the well is deep. Where can you get this living water? Are you greater than our father Jacob, who gave us the well and drank from it himself, as did also his sons and his livestock?[11]

The well was an ancient fertility symbol. Similar to how a well could bring life-giving water to the surrounding land, so a bride held within herself the life-giving potential to generate new life. "You are a garden fountain," King Solomon sang to his queen, "a well of flowing water."[12] When a groom and bride met at a well, they hoped to give life together to an ensuing family.

It's worth mentioning here the painful reality of infertility. This is something many couples face and a common theme in the biblical story.[13] If this is part of your story, God sees you, knows you, loves you, and wants to walk with you through this difficult terrain. Whether or not you have children, there is a broader kind of fruitfulness Jesus has come to bring all of us as his people.[14]

Living water was an ancient term for rushing rivers and flowing streams. This water *moved*. It looked *alive*, with energy and vibrancy. Unlike ponds and puddles, which were stagnant—collecting dirt, leaves, feces, and disease—living water brought vitality to the land, with abundant crops and fresh drinking water.

Both wells and rivers were foundational for ancient life. One was below ground; one was above ground. Both brought life to the land.

Jesus is a thirst quencher greater than Gatorade. He's able to satiate your divine dehydration with the Spirit of God. He tells the woman,

> Everyone who drinks this water will be thirsty again, but whoever drinks the water I give them will never thirst. Indeed, the water I give them will become in them a well of water welling up to eternal life.[15]

We offer Jesus a sip from our Hydro Flask; he offers a rushing river in return. When he says the water he gives will become "a well of water" within us, that term "well" (*pēgē*) is the same one used earlier for the well they're meeting at. You may feel parched, but the Spirit of God can restore your reserves, pouring life into you until it wells up to overflowing.

Jesus offers you something greater than you could ever give him. Sometimes we get into Christianity thinking, *I'm going to give my life for God.* Then you realize, *He came to give his life for me.* It's great to want to serve God and do great things for him, but the Christian life starts in the other direction: He wants to serve you and do great things for you.

FIVE HUSBANDS

Jesus says to her, "Go, call your husband." She replies, "I have no husband." Then Jesus says,

> You are right when you say you have no husband. The fact is, you have had five husbands, and the man you now have is not your husband. What you have just said is quite true.[16]

Jesus knows what he's doing when he says, "Call your husband." (*Sneaky Jesus!*) The Savior doesn't stay at the surface; he digs into the depths. He's searching for your thirst. He's aiming for your heart.

You've had five husbands, Jesus says, *and the sixth won't marry you.*[17] She's been married a lot. She's likely been abandoned, abused, and betrayed; left widowed, wounded, and unwanted.

Jesus meets you in your tragedy. He sees you when your spouse walks away and you're left with a baby bottle to hold and bills to pay. He sees you when your loved one dies too soon and you're no longer able to hold them in your arms. The King of the universe sees your tears. He knows your parched heart.

He comes to meet you by the well.

On a symbolic level, the five husbands likely represent something more. In the Old Testament, *five* Assyrian cities colonized Samaria, bringing their idolatry and injustice with them.[18] Interpreters have seen the woman's five husbands as symbolizing the five male deities of these cities; Samaria had intermarried and integrated their foreign religious practices.[19] The prophets of the Old Testament regularly depicted the people of God as a spouse running after many lovers. Samaria, in particular, had cheated on God with a pagan empire. When Jesus picks a woman who's had five husbands, he picks a perfect representative for her people—and he does it to prove a point.

Jesus goes after a spouse with a checkered past.

We've cheated on God as the church. We've gone after other lovers—sex, money, power, fame—who've left us empty. We are Samaria, blending allegiance to God with devotion to idols. I don't know about you, but I'm a messy, cheating wreck. Actually, I do know that you are too—because we all are. "All have sinned and fall short of the glory of God."[20] We are all both victim and victimizer. Sinner and sinned against. We've not only endured tragedy but also committed treachery. We've made our bed and been left to sleep in it—embarrassed and ashamed. We've dug our own grave and faced a future in its darkness—alone.

Or at least this was our reality, until grace came along.

THE SEVENTH HUSBAND

Jesus is the seventh husband. The woman has had six lovers who've left her broken, wounded, and unfulfilled. But now, in this symbolic picture of the church, a seventh has arrived—and he's different. Similar to the six purification vessels at the wedding in Cana (with Jesus being the seventh, who brings them to completion), here the six men have fallen short, but Jesus, the seventh, is here.

The Maker has come to make her his bride.

Jesus reveals himself to her as Messiah. "I who speak to you am he."[21] This is the only time in John where Jesus comes right out and tells a worshipper this directly. The groom pulls back the veil to reveal himself to his bride. The church has a unique revelation of who Jesus is. This is what makes us the church: We *know* Christ intimately, having seen him for who he really is and accepted his invitation to be united with him.

Jesus meets the woman at the sixth hour, the same hour that—at the climax of John's gospel—he is crucified.[22] This little detail foreshadows the cross as the location where Christ will consummate his union most fully with his bride, united in death through the new covenant in his blood. We shall rest together in that grave so that we might rise together united in newness of life.

Jesus can fulfill you and bring your story to completion. Others may have taken from you, but he has come to give himself to you. He can satisfy your thirsty heart. He will never leave you or forsake you. Even when you're unfaithful, he remains faithful.[23] He delights to serve you, lay his life down for you, and bring you into life with him forever.

I proposed to Holly at Old Laurelhurst Church. I chose that place where we first met. I rented out the chapel one evening and tricked Holly into thinking we were on our way to meet friends nearby for dinner. When we swung by to "pick something up" for Sunday, she was shocked to discover hundreds of candles lighting up the sanctuary, the stained glass windows lit up from the outside, and a strings section playing orchestral music from the balcony.

"We're not supposed to be here," she said. "This is someone's wedding rehearsal."

"No," I responded, "this is for you."

Confused, she walked down the aisle with me until her eye caught the diamond ring at the front, glistening in the candlelight and surrounded by a dozen roses. Hand to mouth, she stumbled up the stairs, and I knelt to one knee and proposed.

She said yes.

The well is, similarly, where Christ is symbolically betrothed to his bride. It's shocking when you realize he's come not only to *meet* us but also to *marry* us. To be united with us forever as his church. You can feel like *I'm not supposed to be here. This ground is too holy.* Or *This is for someone else. He could never want me.* But Christ says, *No, this is for you.* He has come for the church, not as an abstract concept but as his people. Jesus wants to encounter you in all the particularity of your person and uniqueness of your story. He's not ashamed of you but comes to live with you in the light of day.

LIGHT AND DARK

The Samaritan woman contrasts with Nicodemus. In John 3, Nicodemus comes to Jesus "at night," in secrecy under the cover of darkness. In John 4, the Samaritan encounters Jesus "at noon," in the light of day. Light and dark are major themes in John's gospel. Darkness represents hiding, secrecy, and evil. ("Everyone who does evil hates the light, and will not come into the light for fear that their deeds will be exposed.") Light represents truth, transparency, and uprightness. ("Whoever lives by the truth comes into the light, so that it may be seen plainly that what they have done has been done in the sight of God.") The religious leader is hiding something; the rejected woman is vulnerable before Christ.[24]

Nicodemus's name means "victory of the people": from *nike* ("victory"), like the shoe brand, and *demos* ("people"), like democracy.[25] There are overtones of Israel's attempt to accomplish victory for the nation through worldly power, influence, and might—the pursuit of which will get Jesus killed.

The Samaritan woman is simply referred to as "Woman," a term John uses to highlight figures in his gospel as a type of the church.[26] She represents the church who will receive the victory *of God*—not of the people—with life through Jesus's death and the resurrecting water of the Spirit, which will flow beyond Israel to Samaria and the world.

Nicodemus is "a Pharisee," "a member of the Jewish ruling council," and his nighttime conversation occurs immediately after Jesus turns over tables in the temple.[27] He thus represents Israel's leaders who are in the dark and will "tear down this temple." While curious about Jesus, he is currently part of the old order that is passing away.[28]

The Samaritan woman, in contrast, represents those who will receive Jesus "in the light" in worship and obedience. This new movement of believers will be built up as his new living temple. The woman's next question highlights this temple theme: "I can see that you are a prophet," she says. "Our ancestors worshiped on this mountain, but you Jews claim that the place where we must worship is in Jerusalem."[29]

"This mountain" is temple imagery. Samaritans worshipped on Mount Gerizim, but the Jews claimed the proper place to worship was in the Jerusalem temple on Mount Zion.[30] Jesus affirms the history of the Jerusalem temple, saying, "Salvation is from the Jews," but he makes clear a new day is dawning:

A time is coming when you will worship the Father neither on this mountain [Gerizim] nor in Jerusalem. . . . The true worshipers will worship the Father in the Spirit and in truth, for they are the kind of worshipers the Father seeks.[31]

Jesus is the true temple; the church is the new mountain. This is where true worshippers gather in Spirit and truth. Our worship isn't bound by geographic location; the church is booming everywhere across the earth. The Samaritan woman represents the bridal people of God, his new and living temple, who will expand beyond Jewish boundaries to every nation, tribe, and tongue.[32]

Jesus calls you to worship not in flesh but in Spirit. You don't have to work yourself up in your own strength. You can rest in the grace of his gospel and respond to his extravagant love for you.

Jesus calls you to worship not in fakeness but in truth. You don't have to pretend around him. You can get honest with him and respond to the veracity of his character, seeking to align your life with the reality of his.

As we worship Jesus, the exalted King of heaven and earth, we are "being built together to become a dwelling in which God lives by his Spirit," which "is joined together and rises to become a holy temple in the Lord" as "his body, the fullness of him who fills everything in every way."[33] We become a mighty mountain, the home of true worship on the earth.

TELL THE TOWN

In the fourth movement of the betrothal type-scene, the woman rushes home with news of the stranger's arrival. Similarly, here in John 4, "leaving her water jar, the woman went back to the town and said to the people, 'Come, see a man who told me everything I ever did. Could this be the Messiah?'"[34]

The Samaritan woman shares the news of Jesus's arrival. She embodies the church's evangelistic calling. We proclaim the good news, running through the neighborhood to declare what

Christ has done for us. This is no dreary duty but a joyful overflow of excitement at the One we've found.

When someone gets engaged, you don't have to *convince*
them to tell the story. You *can't stop* them from sharing the good
news. They post it on their socials, delight in the details, and tell
everyone they can. They set up dinners to introduce their friends
and family to their fiancé.

When Christ overwhelms your life, you want to shout it from
the rooftops: *Come and see the One who knows me from the inside out and invited me into union forever!*

We're excited to tell the town.

The Samaritans are excited to meet Jesus. "We no longer believe just because of what you said; now we have heard for ourselves, and we know that this man really is the Savior of the
world."[35] They encounter Christ as the one *their* hearts were
made for too.

Some people look at sharing their faith as a chess match,
where you compile your arguments and strategies to beat your
opponent. But I'm convinced it's more like setting someone up
on a blind date, where you believe this person really is best for
them so you highlight how the special someone fulfills their
deepest desires.[36] The goal isn't simply to convince the head.

It's to ignite the heart.

Jesus is truly best for them. He can satisfy their deepest long-
ings. They have wells they've been running to day after day—we
all do—in an attempt to quench their divine dehydration. Yet
Christ can slake their thirst with his Spirit. ("The water I give
them will become in them a spring of water welling up to eternal
life."[37]) His living water can refresh them more than an iced tea
on a summer day; it's sweeter than soda and more celebratory
than champagne. The church is a people whose thirst has been
quenched by Christ.

Jesus is invited to stay in the Samaritan town for two days. This fulfills the fifth and final movement of the betrothal type-scene. While there is no explicit mention of a meal, it's assumed in their hospitality. Plus, Jesus tells his returning disciples, "I have food to eat that you know nothing about" (referring to the Samaritan woman's conversion). He then huddles up with his disciples to talk about the harvest (which segues into the conversion of the Samaritan town).[38]

The betrothal meal is transposed into a symbol of new people encountering, trusting, and receiving the Messiah.

ROLL THE STONE

How did Jesus provide living water for his bride? He rolled the stone away. Let me explain.

John echoes language from Old Testament betrothal scenes. When Jesus sits down by the well, this echoes Exodus 2:15, where Moses sat down by a well—and proceeded to rescue his bride.[39] When Jesus asks, "Will you give me a drink?" this echoes Genesis 24:17, where Rebekah was asked the same question—and proceeded to get engaged to Isaac.

Yet this scene takes place at *Jacob's* well. There's a powerful echo here: When Jacob got to the well where he would meet Rachel, he encountered a problem. A stone was over the mouth of the well. "The stone over the mouth of the well was large."[40] That big boulder looked intimidating, but when he saw Rachel, his jaw dropped and he fell head over heels in love. So what did Jacob do?

"He came near and rolled the stone away."[41]

Church, how did Jesus—the Greater Jacob—provide living water for his bride? He *came near* to us when we were thirsty. When we were wounded, unwanted, and rejected. When we were dead in our trespasses and sins. He drew so close that he entered our condition—proclaiming "I thirst!" on the cross and going all the way into the grave.[42]

Yet he didn't stop there; he rolled the stone away.

That big boulder looked intimidating. It would've been easier to stay at a distance. He prayed in Gethsemane, "If there be any other way . . ."[43] Yet when he looked upon his bride, his jaw dropped in awestruck love. He went to the cross for the joy set before him, entered that tomb to conquer it from the inside out, and on the third day rolled the stone away.

In risen power, Jesus brought forth a river of life-giving water for his bride. Jesus is the Resurrection and Life, who has unleashed his resurrecting Spirit for the church. (In chapter 7, we'll see John continue this theme, as Jesus "blows the dam" to bring forth a river of life. In chapter 12, we'll see how Christ's empty tomb has become a holy place, emanating resurrection power.) Jesus shares his vital presence with you to quench your deepest thirst, saturate your heart, and bring all that is dead in you to life.[44]

You can drench your desires in the all-consuming love of God.

Jesus is the boundary-crossing, thirst-quenching, stone-rolling seventh husband. He is the One your heart was made for. Worship him in Spirit and in truth. Bring him all of who you are. Don't bring him your fake or your superficial. No, bring your true condition before him. Bring him your questions. Bring him your thirst. He already sees it and wants to meet you there. The trick is vulnerability and transparency. This is how we open ourselves to the streams of his Spirit, making ourselves receptive to the rushing river of his presence. He can fill your parched heart to overflowing from within, until it bubbles up like a spring welling to eternal life.

GO BACK TO THE WELL

That first Sunday at Old Laurelhurst Church, when Holly sat down next to me, she heard God say, *That's the guy you're going to marry.* It freaked her out! She had been mistreated by past boyfriends and just come out of a four-year abusive relationship. She was new to Jesus and wanted nothing to do with men. For six months, she avoided me like the plague.

When we later began dating, she grew nervous I'd start acting like the other guys from before. She worried a dark side would come out. She wanted to preemptively quit the relationship to prevent that from happening. She wanted to avoid getting hurt again.

Yet she'd remember the first time we met, going back to that word God had spoken. It gave her the courage and confidence to keep moving forward, the assurance that it was worth stepping out in trust, that it was better to pursue vulnerability in a secure environment than to harden her heart against the possibility of loving again.

Now, I know it's unusual for God to say, *That's the person you're going to marry.* Holly wisely waited to tell me until after we got engaged (so it didn't put an awkward pressure on our relationship). She thinks God gave her that unique experience to help her see our relationship through.

When it comes to our relationship with Christ, Holly's experience points to something powerful. If you feel haunted by your past, if you're worried about being unwanted, if you experience fear in your relationship with God, go back to the well—back to that place where you first met, where you locked eyes, encountered Christ's love for you, and heard him call you his own.

There at your meeting place, you'll find that you're more wanted than you ever dared dream, that Christ is more committed to you than you could have imagined. He is *for* you, he will never leave you or forsake you, he will be with you through thick and thin, in good times and bad, in sickness and health, and not even death will be able to separate you from his love. There at the well, you can step back into your true identity.

You can become the beloved.

4

ENDURE THE HARDEST MILES

When Jesus Answers Only Half Your Prayer

I was going blind. In March 2020, I noticed a gray blur in the center of my vision. My doctor thought it was a cataract, so we scheduled surgery to put an artificial lens in my right eye. After the surgery, however, the gray patch was still there. We looked deeper and discovered the problem was not with my lens (at the front of my eye) but with my retina (at the back of my eye). I was diagnosed with a rare condition for my age.

I was now legally blind in my right eye. The doctor told me the condition was incurable and to prepare myself: Depending on causation, my good eye's vision might soon deteriorate as well.

I was losing my vision. Fear drove me to my knees in prayer. I begged God to be with me and heal my sight. I felt a strong awareness of Christ's presence (*Check!*) but no assurance that he would spare my sight (*Ugh . . .*).

That year felt like a marathon. On top of leading our church through a pandemic and our family through quarantine, the deepest challenge I faced was an intimate and personal one: the fear of losing my vision. I tried to retain hope, but, especially by the end of the year, my spirit was lagging. I was exhausted.

The hardest part of a marathon is the last six miles. In the first half of the race, your adrenaline is pumping, your mind is hopeful, and your body is full of energy. In the second half, however, your energy lags and your legs become exhausted. Then, in the last six miles, the mental battle begins.

Your energy runs out and you hit the wall. This is where you begin to think, *I've got nothing left; I can't do this* (even though your body actually can). As my marathon-running friend Andy says, "A marathon is a 10K race with a twenty-mile warm-up." Meaning, the *real* part of the race is this final stretch, where the challenge is more mental than physical.

The hardest part is the battle within.

Maybe you're in the last six miles of a marathon right now. A long-lasting season of difficulty, loss, or fear. Where you find yourself physically depleted, emotionally exhausted, and mentally worn thin. Maybe you just want to quit the race because there's no one on the sidelines cheering you on and you can't yet see the finish line on the horizon.

There's hope, friend. In John 4, we're introduced to a runner who finishes his marathon well. A royal official travels about the length of a marathon to see Jesus. The last part of his journey is harder than the first. The battle is more mental than physical: He has to trust Jesus with his dying son. Let's lace up and learn how to lean in when we're lagging, how to press forward and trust Jesus in our hardest miles when it feels like we've got nothing left.

HALF THE ANSWER

To set the scene, John references *the third day* ("after the two days") and *Cana* ("where [Jesus] had turned the water into wine").[1] This echoes John 2, when Jesus gives a sign of resurrection on the third day of the wedding in Cana. Before we even hear of the official's dying son, who needs to be raised from the brink of death, John is giving us another clue: We're about to see some resurrection.

> A certain royal official . . . went to [Jesus] and begged him to come down and heal his son, who was close to death.
>
> "Unless you people see signs and wonders," Jesus told him, "you will never believe."
>
> The royal official said, "Sir, come down before my child dies."
>
> "Go," Jesus replied, "your son will live."
>
> The man took Jesus at his word and departed.[2]

The royal official begs Jesus for two things: (1) Come down, and (2) heal my son. Yet Jesus answers only half his request. He grants the second half ("Your son will live") but not the first ("Go"). In other words, *I'm not going with you.* Why is this significant? The official has to step out in faith.

Have you ever had Jesus answer only half your prayer? Walk alongside you but not take away the threat? Journey with you in the valley but not dispel the shadow of death?

"God, give me peace and financial stability." *How about I give you peace in these uncertain financial times?* "God, bring my adult child back to you, and make me a better parent." *How about I grow your ability to walk in my grace and trust me in this season of your child's life?* Or maybe you find yourself asking, like Augustine famously prayed as a young man, "Give me chastity . . . but not just yet."[3] I imagine God smiling: *How about I give it to you now?*

I often find myself praying, essentially, "God, give me resurrection, but take away the cross. Give me your power, but take away the pain." Yet God often wants to carry us *through* the cross to resurrection on the other side. He often wants to give us his power and presence *in the midst of* the pain. Why?

He's building our trust.

BUILDING TRUST

Why doesn't Jesus go with the royal official? He's building his trust. Let me explain. Jesus's initial response can seem a bit harsh: "Unless you people see signs and wonders . . . you will never believe." Is Jesus rebuking a scared parent for seeking the healing of their child? No, that's not what's happening. The word he uses is plural, so we get the translation "you people." Jesus is calling out the crowds who are only looking for fireworks.

This official *does* trust Jesus without seeing signs or wonders. He believes what he can't yet see. Jesus knows what's in this official's heart and, I'd suggest, is setting him up to put his faith on display.[4]

What if God desires something deeper than the outcome? What if he places a higher priority on your relationship with him? What if his endgame is more about intimacy than income? His presence more than your prosperity? What if it's not just about the healing we want but about our heart that he wants? What if the ultimate healing of your heart is found through intimacy with him?

That's what building trust is all about.

The royal official is an exemplar of faith. Jesus critiques the crowds to contrast his faith. There's a similar story in another gospel, where Jesus responds to a Roman centurion: "With no one in Israel have I found such faith."[5] This royal official is also likely a Gentile.[6] So Jesus is contrasting the unbelief among his own people ("A prophet has no honor in his own hometown," the story opens[7]) with the faith of this outsider.

The outsiders get it; the insiders don't.

This is a theme in the gospel. Religious leaders like Nicodemus are confused and missing it, while a Samaritan woman is captivated and her village welcomes Jesus in. The high priest of Israel has Jesus crucified, while a Roman centurion declares, "Surely this man was the Son of God!"[8] The polished and put-together push Jesus aside, while the prodigals and prostitutes press into the kingdom.

"He came to that which was his own, but his own did not receive him," John foreshadows in the introduction to his gospel. "Yet to all who did receive him . . . he gave the right to become children of God."[9]

You might feel like an outsider, like you don't fit in the religious club you grew up in or the cultural lines drawn around you. You might not have the credentials or the clout you think you need to get God on your side. Yet Jesus levels the playing field. All you need is trust.

Faith is available to everyone. You're invited to come to the One who's already come to you. Who's crossed from heaven to earth to find you. Who's gone to the cross to be with you forever. Bring him your deepest heart-cry prayers. Listen for his voice and take him at his word. Believe even when you can't see.

THE JOURNEY HOME

Just because you trust Christ enough to take him at his word doesn't mean the second half of the marathon isn't hard. I wonder what the official's journey home was like. He traveled a few days on the return trip from Cana back to Capernaum. On foot. That's a long time to think.

What crossed his mind as he looked toward the horizon? Did he wonder if his son was dead? If he had missed being with his child in those final, fearful moments? A final chance to hold his hand, stroke his head, and say goodbye?

What would his wife say? *You were supposed to bring Jesus with you! That was the whole point. You failed in your journey, and now our son is gone.*

What did it cost the official to take Jesus at his word? I imagine the battle was mental rather than physical on that final stretch of road. Because the hardest part of a marathon is the last six miles.

When I thought I was going blind, I battled a variety of fears: *What if I won't be able to see my kids' faces as they grow up?*

What if I won't be able to read or write, two of my favorite activities?

How will I preach or teach or do my job?

I soaked in every sight of my children that I could. I studied their faces, seeking to imprint them as firmly as possible on my memory. I extrapolated what they might look like as they grew older. I knew I would still be able to hold them close, but I wanted a vision of them to carry me forward into the potential tunnel of darkness that lay ahead. Frequently, as I gazed on their precious faces, my eyes welled with tears.

My sense of calling felt threatened. While people with blindness live full and meaningful lives, I wondered how I would relearn to navigate daily parts of my job. Writing notes and outlines for preaching and teaching. Interpreting the subtle expressions on people's faces in pastoral counseling. Reading books—and underlining the heck out of them—a habit that's shaped my thinking and writing.

I grieved the loss of sight I'd already sustained. The distraction of double vision every time I looked into the distance. The blinking lights, like a halo of glitter, around every person I saw.

The difficulty falling asleep with electric crackles flashing whenever I closed my eyes.

"Jesus, come with me," I found myself praying, "and heal my sight."

FROM "WHAT IF" TO "EVEN IF"

Jesus answered only half my prayer. *I'll go with you,* I sensed him responding, *but I'm not going to let you know yet whether you'll be healed.* Ironically, this was the opposite half from his answer to the official. But the point was the same. *Do you trust me?* I sensed him asking. This was the response of my savior to my fear-filled, anxiety-ridden, heart-wrung prayers of that year.

And my heartfelt cry was "Yes, I trust you. Yes, but . . ." *If you love me, why won't you heal my sight? If you've given me a calling, why won't you give me what I need to do it? If you're on my side, why do you seem to withhold what's in your power to give?*

I hit the wall, where my battle became more mental than physical. My situation exposed layers beneath the surface of my life. Depths previously unseen by me but known by him. I sensed the Great Surgeon peeling back the layers, his divine retina gazing upon the depths of my heart, his voice calling out like deep calls out to deep: *Do you trust me?*

Yes, I trust you.

God began moving me from "what if" to "even if." From *What if I lose my sight?* to *Even if I lose my sight, I will trust you.* From *What if my worst fears happen?* to *Even if my worst fears happen, you have my heart.* From *What if everything unravels around me?* to *Even if "the earth give way and the mountains fall into the heart of the sea," I will trust you.*[10] Job 13:15 became my theme verse for that year: "Though He slay me, yet will I trust Him."[11]

That's the kind of cruciform, all-in trust Christ calls us to. And he doesn't call us somewhere he hasn't gone himself. In Gethsemane, he surrenders to his Father with sweat drops of blood: "Not my will, but yours be done."[12] His final words on the cross are a blood-drenched cry of surrender: "Father, into your hands I commit my spirit."[13] Though he is slain, he yet trusts his Father.

Even in death, he believes God is ultimately on his side.

When it came to my family, I found myself trusting there would be an intimacy and warmth together, regardless. When it came to my vocation, I found myself trusting that if God called me to it, he'd give me what I needed (and if he didn't call me to it, I wouldn't need it). When it came to my future, I found myself trusting that my Father would go with me and that would be more than enough.

The timing was a bit ironic: I lost my vision in 2020 (*lol!*). Yet God cultivated a deeper vision in me that year: the ability to look beyond my circumstances toward the broader horizon of his goodness. My eyesight eventually stabilized. A year after the initial loss of vision, I came out of the woods with no immediate risk of further deterioration. My good eye is in great condition and stable. Before I reached that finish line, however, I learned to trust where he was taking me.

What is Jesus inviting you to trust him with today? Maybe it's your precious child who has walked away from the faith or is heading down a dangerous road. Maybe it's your health condition or—like the official's son—the terminal diagnosis of someone you love, where the wound of losing them seems too painful to imagine. Maybe it's letting go of the what-ifs you keep forecasting for your future and declaring, "*Even if* the worst-case scenario happens, God, I'll trust in you."

Whatever horizon you're walking toward, Jesus invites you to trust him on the journey. The last six miles may be tough, but the finish line is coming.

THE FINISH LINE

As the royal official approaches his home, he receives news:

> While he was still on the way, his servants met him with the news that his boy was living. When he inquired as to the time when his son got better, they said to him, "Yesterday, at one in the afternoon, the fever left him." Then the father realized that this was the exact time at which Jesus had said to him, "Your son will live." So he and his whole household believed.[14]

At the finish line, the official finds Jesus has been faithful. I imagine it's sunset as he turns the last bend on the home stretch of his marathon. The servants run out to welcome him, like friends cheering from the sidelines. On this final leg of his race home, they shout out the news: *Your son is alive!*

Can you imagine the joy and relief? The father's heart for his beloved son? Their embrace, drenched in his sweat and tears? Can you imagine the feast and celebration? The whole household partying it up into the night? Can you imagine the wonder and awe in town as the news spreads about Jesus?

When? the awestruck father asks.

Yesterday, one in the afternoon.

The very moment Jesus speaks is the moment his son is healed. The eternal Son who spoke the world into existence speaks life into the man's dying son. Jesus's word is powerful. When he speaks, sickness is healed, chains break, demons flee, mountains move, light shines, and dead folks waltz out of their graves.

A GREATER PROPHET

This story has a significant Old Testament backdrop: the prophet raising a dead son to life. Both the great prophet Elijah and his protégé, Elisha, resurrected a dead child.[15] Elijah was rejected by his own people, yet welcomed with hospitality by an outsider. Similarly, John opens this story: "A prophet has no honor in his own hometown."[16] Like the great prophet of old, Jesus has been rejected on his home turf but is about to be welcomed by an outsider.

There's an important difference between these stories, however: Unlike Jesus, both Elijah and Elisha needed to be physically present to accomplish the healing. Elisha sent his staff with his servant to accomplish the miracle, but the staff wasn't enough to heal the boy. The prophet had to be physically present. This contrast highlights Jesus's status as a greater prophet who can speak life into the child from a town many miles away.

Another difference: The mother refused Elisha's plan to not go with her. "As the LORD lives and as you yourself live," she responded, "I will not leave you."[17] So the prophet accompanied her home to accomplish the healing. This contrast highlights the faith of the official, who trusts that the word of Jesus is powerful enough to raise his son to life, even if Jesus isn't physically present.

Jesus is a greater prophet.

The most powerful part of this Old Testament backdrop is *how* the dead son was raised to life. In both the Elijah and the Elisha stories, the prophet stretched his living body on the dead body of the son—a sign of identification and solidarity—and God's life-giving presence was imparted to the dead:

[Elisha] went up and lay on the child, putting his mouth on his mouth, his eyes on his eyes, and his hands on his hands. And

as he stretched himself upon him, the flesh of the child became warm. . . . The child sneezed seven times, and the child
opened his eyes.[18]

Like God breathing into the lifeless body of Adam in Genesis 2, exhaling to fill his lungs with divine breath until his eyes
opened to behold the face of God, so here the prophet—a representative of God—identified with the lifeless body of the dead
son and exhaled the divine presence so that the corpse might
inhale heaven until his body grew warm and eyes opened.

This is a picture of the cross. Jesus is the greater prophet who
stretches out on those wooden beams to identify with us in our
condition. He puts his eyes on our eyes, seeing us in our desperate estate. He puts his wounded hands on our hands, feeling the
torment of our pain. He puts his mouth on our mouth, exhaling
his final breath that we might inhale the wind of heaven. He
entrusts himself to his Father that we might be embraced as
children of God.

In John's gospel, the official's dying son is healed at the seventh hour (one o'clock), the same hour that Christ will later
die.[19] This detail foreshadows why the official's son can be raised:
because the greater royal Son will die in his place—and in ours.
When Jesus brings his atonement to completion (remember,
seven is the number of completion), he will raise us from the
power of death.

This healing is a sign of our resurrection.

Jesus's solidarity is our salvation. "By his wounds we are
healed."[20] His sinless and spotless union with us in our decay and
death is what overcomes the grave. His presence imparts prox-
imity to his divine Spirit, breathing life into our dead bodies and
opening our eyes to behold the face of God.

Jesus may not have been the prophet his hometown wanted,
but he's the greater prophet we all need.

GOD ALWAYS HEALS

The royal official's son raises an important question: Why do some people get healed and not others? This can be a painful topic. My friend Beth was miraculously cured from cancer, while the same disease devoured the days of five devout friends. A church member, Cameron, was cured of multiple sclerosis and Lyme disease through prayer, while another faithful church member, Daniel, still faces the gradual deterioration of his body from MS.

Why did our prayer team see an end to Stephanie's five years of tremors, a child given to Aaron and Claudia after years of infertility, and a screeching halt brought to Nick's leukemia, while Joanna still endures debilitating depression, Matt and Leah lost their precious baby, and Helen's memory continues to fade from Alzheimer's?

Why was the royal son raised, when other parents buried their children in Galilee that year? It's a heart-wrenching question: Why some and not others?

My favorite response comes from pastor Andrew Wilson, who wisely asserts that the question is not *if* God will heal but *when*. The resurrection means healing is coming—for us and our world.

Wilson has wrestled with this tension in his own life, witnessing the miraculous healing of many people in his church, while seeing prayers for his own children's medical conditions go unanswered. Yet he's found hope in the resurrection.

Resurrection is the horizon that this marathon of history is running toward. Sometimes we get advance signs of that future in our own homes today. We're invited to pray boldly—to beg Jesus like that ancient father did—for the "not yet" to break into the "now." *Jesus, heal my child.* We seek signs of the kingdom that foreshadow the resurrection to come.

God answers such prayers in four ways. As Wilson observes, sometimes God heals through the body's immune system (a powerful, divine gift embedded in our being). Sometimes God heals through the expertise of doctors and the power of modern medicine (like he did for my young daughter years ago—*Thank you, God!*). Sometimes God heals through prayer (like in the stories I mentioned above).

Yet even when all these fail, you can be confident in the fourth way God heals: resurrection. This future is assured. When the trumpet sounds, the dead will be raised in the twinkling of an eye, never to perish again. On that day,

> Corrupted bodies become incorruptible; sickness and affliction will never again befall them. The sterile smell of the operating room corridor is no more. . . . Every deaf ear is unblocked, every damaged limb is repaired, every blind eye sees. . . . Nobody cries, except with joy.

I love that. God says "Yes" or "Not yet," but God always heals.[21]

The finish line you're running toward is resurrection. That's the horizon where your true home is found. You don't have to believe the health-and-wealth preachers who claim God will heal you if you just have enough faith. You don't have to follow the skeptics who deny God can heal you now or the cynics who despair such healing will ever come. You can keep running toward Jesus, praying to the One whose word is powerful and who will meet you at the finish line.

Even when you're limping and dead-dog tired, take heart. When you cross that finish line, you'll discover—like that ancient official did so long ago—Christ is faithful. Your hope is in the risen Son.

THE RISEN SON

Not only does Jesus raise the dying son; he is also the dying Son who is raised. John tells us this miracle is the second sign Jesus performs at Cana.[22] Like the first sign at Cana (water to wine), this second sign is also a *living parable* of the gospel.

The son "close to death" (*ēmellen apothnēskein*) is a picture of Jesus. Later in John's gospel, that same term is used multiple times to describe Jesus's crucifixion.[23] The phrase is associated with the power and significance of Jesus's death. Of course, unlike the official's son, Jesus has agency in approaching this fate. ("No one takes [my life] from me," he declares later in John. "I have authority to lay it down and authority to take it up again."[24]) Yet like the bridegroom rejoicing with the master of the banquet over the new wine in the wedding at Cana (see chapter 1), this second miraculous sign at Cana ends with a picture of joyous resurrection.

Jesus is the royal Son who gives his life at the cross and is raised into the embrace of his heavenly Father.

God is a Father whose Son goes down to the brink of death—and beyond—carrying our infirmity into the grave.[25] God is a Father who gives his only begotten Son that we might have life in him forever. God is a Father who raises his royal Son on the third day to reign with him in their kingdom forevermore.

There are differences, of course. Our heavenly Father doesn't have to travel to seek healing from someone else (he is the one who will raise his Son from the grave). He isn't pulling his hair out on Holy Saturday (he knows what Sunday holds). Yet the climactic closing scene of this living parable points to the Father who extravagantly loves his Son with an undying affection, receiving him back from the grave. It's a picture of the Resurrection.

A father embracing his risen son.

The servants who announce the good news of the risen son are a picture of the disciples. They will run forth and proclaim the One whose tomb lies empty, with linen clothes discarded, now blazing in radiant glory. They will celebrate the resurrection embrace of the Son and the Father, who welcome all who will come to the riotous feast of their household, as daughters and sons of the King.

That's the finish line we're heading toward. That's where we'll party it up with the royal Father who rejoices over his risen Son. That's where we'll be greeted by angels announcing that what we've lost has been made new. That's where we'll join the whole household of daughters and sons, raised to life to rejoice with the Father forever.

You're not there yet, but you can be confident on the way.

Christ has given you his word.

5

RISE UP

When You're Stuck and Can't Get Out of Bed

Our daughter was hospitalized at five years old with an extreme health condition that led to ten days in the children's hospital, a barrage of tests, and six months with specialists. It was the scariest time of our life as we wondered whether our daughter would ever rise up and be the same.

At the end, we were simply grateful for her recovery. But I also had a low-paying ministry job, we had three young children, and we weren't sure how we could crawl out of the financial hole we now found ourselves in.

What do you do when you're stuck and can't get out of bed? When you feel overwhelmed by a depression you cannot lift, a dread you cannot shake, a debt you cannot pay?

We had massive medical debt. We'd never met David, but he heard of our daughter's situation through the grapevine. When a friend of a friend shared our story, he called us up and offered to pay the full amount of our medical debt. We were blown away. As we later learned, he simply loved Jesus and was on the lookout for situations like ours to help with. He loved to walk around paying the debts of people in difficult situations.

We were so grateful. He gave us a hand when we were trapped by the weight of a debt we couldn't get out from under. With his assistance, we were able to rise up and return home light and free.

David asked, "Can I help you?" We simply said yes.

"Can I help you?" is an interesting question. Tone matters. Depending on the inflection of someone's voice, those four simple words can communicate . . .

- *A genuine offer of assistance:* The smiling staff member behind the counter greets you, "Welcome to McDonald's. Can I help you?" Or your best friend with a truck offers, "You're moving this weekend. Can I help?"
- *Annoyance at an intrusion:* The annoyed subway rider catches you looking over his shoulder at the newspaper he's reading: "Uh, excuse me. Can I help you?" Or the prom queen confronts you as you intrude on her high school social circle: "Uh, can we help you?"
- *A plea for someone's best:* A parent offers to cover the cost of rehab for their adult child, caught in the throes of addiction: "Please, son, I love you. Can I help you?" Or a stranger calls and unexpectedly offers to pay a distraught family's medical debt.

It's good to not confuse these three tones. For example, the guy who develops a crush on his barista might mistakenly think she's using tone 3: *She cares so much about me! She always smiles at me, wishes me a good day, and serves me coffee.* But she's actually using tone 1: *Dude, that's her job! She's just offering to help.* And the misunderstanding can lead her to use tone 2: *Uh, you made this weird. Can I help you?*

In John 5, Jesus uses all three tones. He asks, *Can I help you?* Yet he is giving one person a genuine offer of assistance, calling another crew to mind their own business, and pleading with all of us to let him pay the debt for our healing and raise us up into our best future with him.

That's what Jesus offers *you* in this famous passage: a plea for your best.

AN OFFER OF ASSISTANCE

Jesus goes up to Jerusalem for one of the annual festivals. He arrives to find someone in need:

> Now there is in Jerusalem near the Sheep Gate a pool, which in Aramaic is called Bethesda and which is surrounded by five covered colonnades. Here a great number of disabled people used to lie—the blind, the lame, the paralyzed. One who was there had been an invalid for thirty-eight years. When Jesus saw him lying there and learned that he had been in this condition for a long time, he asked him, "Do you want to get well?"[1]

When Jesus visits the big city, he doesn't beeline to Hollywood's red carpet to hobnob with the rich and famous under the bright lights. No, he heads backstage to help a man who's been paralyzed for thirty-eight years—longer than Jesus has been alive. Like our daughter in the hospital, he's unable to get up from his bed.

This scene takes place "near the Sheep Gate." John is intentional with this detail. This starts a new section of his gospel that will end with Jesus declaring himself to be the Good Shepherd and gate for the sheep.[2] The hospital infirmary here is like a herd of hurting sheep around a pool, and there's one who can't get to the water. Jesus has come to bind up the broken and bring living water to the sheep.

Dr. Dwight Peterson, a paraplegic theologian, says that in the ancient world we should imagine that a man with a condition like this probably smells. He can't wash up or clean his own feces. Likely, no one wants to be around him.[3]

Jesus asks him, "Do you want to get well?" In other words, *Can I help you?* This is tone 1: Jesus gives him a genuine offer of assistance. At first glance, it's a strange question. *Of course the dude wants to be healed!* Who'd turn that offer down?

So why does Jesus ask? Jesus's question gives this man agency. All his life, he's had no real voice. He's been a needy beggar in the shadows. Thought of as a recipient but not an agent. I wonder how long it's been since someone's even talked to him. Jesus *sees* him, however. And Jesus is on his side. The Artist is present, setting up a chair across from the man and asking him a question, inviting him to see himself being seen—and respond.

The man is given a voice.

When I worked in Vietnam, I loved to visit a print shop in Hanoi run by youth with disabilities. Their joy was palpable and infectious. They told me they used to live in the shadows. There's still stigma around disabilities in Vietnam, so families often kept them isolated in the back room of the house. They were alone and ashamed, feeling like they had nothing to contribute to their families and community.

Then Vietnamese Christians started local businesses—including this chain of print shops—to train and employ people with disabilities. To bring dignity and combat stigma. To give them a voice.

The youth told me they loved being able to contribute to their families. Many were now given the seat of honor at the dinner table. (Some now brought more income to the family table than their parents!) They loved interacting with customers. They were seen not as projects but as people, with something to contribute to the community.

If you have a disability, you need to know *we need your voice!*
Our church families aren't whole without you. Maybe you've
faced seasons when you felt hidden in the shadows or were
treated as a project, but Jesus is on your side. He cares about
your voice, your contribution, the gifts you've been given to
bring to the family table.

When you see him seeing you—when you behold the glory of
God in the face of Christ—he invites you to be not simply a *recipient* in the Father's family but a *participant.* His goal is not
just to *heal* you but to *hear* you. To draw out your voice. To let
you get to know his. To know you.

LIFE UNDER THE LAW

Thirty-eight years. That's how long this man has been stuck
there. Is there anywhere else in Scripture that this number appears? Yes. Deuteronomy 2:14 tells us "thirty-eight years passed"
from when the people of Israel began their wilderness wandering until "that entire generation of fighting men had perished
from the camp." That's our Old Testament backdrop for this passage.

Israel was unable to enter the promised land for *thirty-eight
years* because of their rebellion. They wanted to rise up through
the waters of the Jordan and enter their inheritance, but under
the weight of the law, they were like a paralyzed man unable to
rise up into healing and restoration.

The early church saw in this paralytic a picture of Israel under
the law. The commentator William Barclay observes how, in this
ancient reading,

The *man* stands for the people of Israel. The *five porches*
stand for the five books of the law. In the porches, the people

lay ill. The law could show people their sin, but could never mend it; the law could uncover people's weaknesses, but could never cure them. The law, like the porches, sheltered sick souls but could never heal them. The *thirty-eight years* stand for the thirty-eight years in which the Jews wandered in the desert before they entered the promised land; or for the number of the centuries they had been waiting for the Messiah.[4]

Wow! I'm not sure about you, but my mind is blown. Scholars today are often suspicious: *Oh, there go those early-church fathers reading into things again!* Not so fast. I believe this reading is amazing, beautiful, and true to John's intentions. Let me make a few observations on why.

First, John regularly uses characters as representatives for greater themes. Nicodemus represents Israel's religious leadership, who need to be born from above. The Samaritan woman represents the church as the bride of Christ. Similarly, this paralyzed man represents Israel under the curse of the law—whom Jesus has come to heal. Such symbolism runs with the grain of John's style.

Second, John regularly uses numbers symbolically. There are famously seven signs and seven "I am" claims in this gospel. There is symbolic value to the seven titles the disciples and John the Baptist ascribe to Jesus (John 1), the six water jars (John 2), the five husbands (John 4), the twelve baskets of leftover bread (John 6), and the 153 fish caught by the disciples (John 21).

Thirty-eight is a very specific number. John doesn't round it up to "around forty." Elsewhere, he doesn't highlight how long someone has been ill; that he does here suggests intentionality.

This intentionality is true of the five colonnades as well. These were porticoes supported by pillars under which people could congregate. This is a fitting image for the Law under whose covering the people of God were assembled in the wilderness.

Third, this new section of John is set against the primary backdrop of Israel's wilderness wandering. The upcoming chapters echo God's provision of manna in the wilderness (John 6), God's provision of water in the wilderness (John 7), God's guiding light in the wilderness (John 8–9), and God shepherding his people in the wilderness (John 10). Such wilderness imagery saturates this section of John.[5]

The paralyzed man sets up this section as a picture of Israel in the wilderness.

Jesus's question "Do you want to get well?" becomes a question not only to the invalid (for whom the answer seems obvious) but also to his interlocutors (where the answer isn't so obvious). Do they want Jesus to make them well? The rest of John 5 will highlight the Jewish leaders' opposition to Jesus, who has come to deliver Israel from their new wilderness.[6] For Israel's leaders, at least, the answer seems to be no.

This is also Jesus's question to us. When you were stuck under the weight of the law, unable to rise up in your own strength and enter the kingdom of God, Jesus came and found you. He brought grace, not based on your performance. His question isn't "Are you good enough to get into my kingdom?" It is, rather, "Will you let me heal you?" *Do you want to get well?*

LAW OR GRACE?

I once couldn't get out of bed. I was depressed and heavy with fatigue. No amount of sleep could cure my exhaustion. I wanted to be present to my wife and children but had trouble mustering the strength. (This was the season I mentioned earlier, when I first faced a suicidal thought.) My dreams lay in tatters around me, and I kept rehashing the series of events that had led me there. I was stuck in a perpetual doom loop of relived memories.

Was I wrong, or was I wronged? Was I being persecuted for something good or punished for something bad? Could I have done something differently? Would that have changed the outcome? Did God call me a good and faithful servant, or had he pulled the Jenga block that sent it all tumbling down?

Without realizing it, I was analyzing myself under the categories of law. I was evaluating my ability to perfectly conform to standards of good and bad. I was trying to discern whether these were distorted expectations from my social circles or holy regulations from the perfect will of God.

There were, in retrospect, things I would have done differently. It became easy to criticize every minor misstep under a microscope. To overanalyze every shortcoming and beat myself up over the past. Then I sensed Jesus asking a pivotal question . . .

Are you going to live by law or by grace?

Law or grace? Do I really believe that life is about my performance? That God's approval rides on my perfection? That my belonging hinges on my intelligence or influence?

Or is my ultimate destiny determined by the glorious cataclysm of capital-G Grace? That disruptive explosion of the Divine Healer who intrudes on my scene? Who meets me in my wilderness and extends his hand in a genuine offer of divine assistance, to raise me up with him into new life? When I'm stuck on the mat of my own shortcomings and failures? When I feel like a disappointment and no one wants to be around my stench?

Can I help you?

Yes, Lord, yes! I want to be healed! I want a life driven by grace, not law—by your mercy rather than my performance. You lived the perfect life I haven't lived, you died the death that was mine to die, and, now risen, you extend your hand to raise me up out of that grave to be with you forever. In your acceptance I'm able to accept myself—warts and all. My belonging is found in your perfect and eternal love.

Now, when it comes to depression, I don't want to give the impression that you should just try to pray it away. I also got counseling. I saw my doctor and got on medication. I exercised and watched my diet. These all helped me deal with the distress. But the deepest thing my heart needed to encounter was the Savior who met me in my lowest place, not with law but with grace, with mercy in his eyes and welcome on his face.

The God who is on my side.

This good news is for you. You couldn't get to the healing, so Jesus brought the healing to you. Jesus found you pinned to the mat by the law and down for the count. When you were stuck in the stench of your sin, unable to cleanse yourself, he came to wash you with his mighty love. When you had made your own bed, dug your own grave, he came not to condemn but to save. When you were lying down in your transgressions, unable to rise, he came and surprised you with grace.

Jesus asks you, "Do you want to get well?" Notice that word *want*. He's out for your desires, coming after your heart. He's not content to control your behavior; he wants to renew your affections and activate your agency from the inside out. Jesus wants more than to simply give you a voice or mobilize your legs; the Great Physician has a divine defibrillator and wants to jump-start your heart.

Will you let Jesus heal you? The answer should be obvious. He's giving you a genuine offer of assistance. Don't live by law; live by grace. Don't rely on your performance; rely on his presence. When he asks, *Can I help you?* why would you resist it? How will you respond?

AN ANNOYING INTRUSION

"Get up, take up your bed, and walk," Jesus says. "And at once the man was healed, and he took up his bed and walked."[7] Pretty cool, right? Only some people aren't happy about it:

> The day on which this took place was a Sabbath, and so the Jewish leaders said to the man who had been healed, "It is the Sabbath; the law forbids you to carry your mat." . . .
>
> So, because Jesus was doing these things on the Sabbath, the Jewish leaders began to persecute him.[8]

The religious leaders reprimand the man: *It's the Sabbath; you're supposed to be resting.* I imagine him responding, *Dude, I've been resting for thirty-eight years.*

They also persecute Jesus. As the nosy perfectionists crowd in to question his actions, Jesus defends himself: "My Father is always at his work to this very day, and I too am working."[9] In other words, *I'm about my Father's business, so mind your own business.* The Messiah's response is essentially, *Excuse me. Can I help you?* This is tone 2: annoyance at an intrusion.

I love this: *feisty* Jesus. Poking the bear. Provoking a confrontation. Jesus is *intentional* in doing this sign on the Sabbath. He could've waited a day. He could've just healed the man without ordering him to pick up his mat. He knows what he's doing; he's picking a fight with the religious leaders.

You might see Jesus as a pushover, afraid of a standoff, avoiding difficult conversations. That's a figment of our cultural imagination. Jesus has a soft heart *and* a steel spine.

Now, let's not be too hard on the religious leaders. You'll often hear, *They were just being legalistic and adding things to the law!* But before we rush to judgment, the Old Testament gives some warrant to their case. In Numbers 15, someone was stoned for carrying sticks on the Sabbath—*sticks!* In Jeremiah 17, God warned the people "not to carry a load on the Sabbath day or bring it through the gates of Jerusalem." Nehemiah reprimanded the people when they *did* carry things around on the Sabbath.[10] Plus, Jewish tradition was not cold-hearted. They made exceptions for life-threatening emergencies.

And notice Jesus's defense: He doesn't pretend he's not working. He doesn't say, *Oh, this? This is child's play; it doesn't take any effort from me.* No, he says, "I too am working." What? Jesus acknowledges he *is* working on the Sabbath. This passage is difficult to understand. Theologians wrestle with it, but hang with me for a minute because it's important.

Jesus is making a claim to his unique identity. His defense focuses not on his actions but on his identity as the Son of the Father. Jesus moves their attention from *when* the healing takes place (the Sabbath) to *who* the healer is (the Son). *That's* why he heals this man on the Sabbath. His whole sermon that follows in John 5 is on his unique identity as the Son. His Father, who "is always at his work," *creates* through the Son, *redeems* through the Son, and *does all his other work* through the Son.

Unique offices in Israel were exempt from Sabbath restrictions. Priests worked on the Sabbath. (Think of your pastor working on Sundays; it's not exactly the same thing, but you get the picture.) Jesus is our Great High Priest and "Lord of the Sabbath."[11]

Jesus is like the CEO of a company entering a secure wing of the building. When security doesn't recognize him, they stop him and ask for identification. *Excuse me, sir. You can't go back there. It's off limits!* Then he pulls out his ID badge, revealing that he's the CEO. *Oh, it's you! Sorry, sir. Go on ahead.*

Jesus has a unique 24-7 pass to all of creation. He's the Son of the Father, the owner of the company. They run things together, like a family business. The Father has put Jesus in charge. As the chief executive officer, he executes his Father's will. When Israel's leaders—the middle management, whom God's entrusted with stewarding the family company—stop Jesus to ask for his credentials, he whips out his badge and barges forward.

Are there areas of your life you think Jesus shouldn't have access to? Areas you keep off limits to the eternal Son of God? Maybe it's your spending habits, your sex life, or your social media practices. The gospel says Jesus has authority to get into *all* your business. When you make him Lord of your life, you're acknowledging he's the boss.

Do you have time restrictions for Jesus? Maybe you restrict the Son of God to Sundays—the opposite problem as those religious leaders—thinking he should work only one day of the week. Maybe you keep Monday to Friday for yourself, seeing your job as a secular necessity for a paycheck rather than a sacred opportunity to contribute to the flourishing of God's world. Maybe you keep Saturday night for yourself, thinking debauchery is okay if you give him Sunday morning.

When Jesus draws close, don't tell him to mind his own business. Don't give him the annoyed tone: "Excuse me. Can I help you?" Instead, receive his generous offer of assistance: "Please help me, Lord—I need it!" Cry out to him in faith: "Lord Jesus, have mercy on me, a sinner."[12] When he stands at the door and knocks, fling that thing wide open and give him access to it all.

What would it look like to give Jesus all-access authority this week? To say,

Yes, Jesus, get into all my business. Do your mighty work. Do the Father's will in my life. Make me a home for your holy presence, on earth as in heaven. Every room is yours: every thought, every decision, every desire. I hold nothing back and give you access to it all.

This is where life is found.

PRACTICE RESURRECTION

The raising of the paralyzed man is a picture of the resurrection. At the climax of John 5, Jesus launches into a sermon.[13] Similar to how this man heard Jesus's voice and rose up from his mat, "a time is coming . . . when the dead will hear the voice of the Son of God and those who hear will live."[14] This miracle is the fourth sign in John's gospel. *Don't stop at the sign,* Jesus is saying. *Keep going to the destination.* The sign is a billboard advertising your coming resurrection.

You and I are the paralyzed man. We were stuck on the mat in the stench and stigma of our sin, suffering, and shame. We were decaying in the desert of our fallen condition, unable to arise in our own strength and enter the promised land of God's kingdom. We were on a trajectory toward death, where we'd be stuck in the grave, powerless to pull ourselves up by our performance into the presence of God.

Yet One more powerful than death is here. He is stronger than your sin, suffering, or shame. All he has to do is speak his word of grace and the lame walk, the captives are freed, the poor rejoice, the blind see, and the dead arise. Jesus has been given all authority in heaven and on earth, and he uses it to raise you into newness of life.

When Jesus proclaims, "Rise up!" we will all get out of our graves. This is good news—gloriously good news—but also a warning. He continues:

A time is coming when all who are in their graves will hear his voice and come out—those who have done what is good will rise to live, and those who have done what is evil will rise to be condemned.[15]

Jesus says we face a danger graver than the disability of our bodies; there is a judgment to come that will expose our souls. This helps explain why Jesus tells the healed man, "Stop sinning or something worse may happen to you."[16] He's not implying that the man was disabled because he did something wrong. (Jesus clearly confronts this false assumption in John 9.[17]) But Christ calls us to live well the new lives we're given.

We're called to practice resurrection.

Christ has come to set the world right. This is a good thing; our world needs justice and mercy. We need the wrongs of history to be righted and the sin that destroys to be done away with. Yet like this man rising from his mat, we will rise from our bed in the grave to face the mercy and justice of God in the face of Christ. This gives rise to Jesus's call: *Go and sin no more.* Prepare for new creation.

This is the third and final version of *Can I help you?* It's the voice of the Father pleading with you as his child to leave the dark backyard of pride and self-sufficiency to enter the light and celebration that welcome his prodigal children home.[18] This is the voice of Jesus, your compassionate older brother, pleading with you as his sibling caught in the throes of addiction to enter his divine rehab. This is the voice of the Spirit pleading with you to leave behind the self-reliance that alienates you and reattach to the God you were made for.

We're called to live in the light of God's love. Mortify the evil in your life; put to death its death-dealing ways. "Be killing sin," as the old Puritan John Owen puts it, "or it will be killing you."[19]

The love of Christ compels you to pin your wickedness to the mat, roll it up inside, and bury it there. Foreshadow the new creation, permeated by the love of Christ, by living into his grace *and* truth.

Practice resurrection and live into the love of God.

A BETTER REST

Jesus's miracle is a living parable of his own death and resurrection. When he was pinned to the cross, he was pinned to your mat under the weight of your sin. He bore the curse of the law to extend the power of grace. When you were stuck, paralyzed under the dominion of death, Christ did for you what you couldn't do for yourself. He lay down in the grave and made his bed there. Yet it couldn't keep him down . . .

Jesus picked up his bed and walked.

Jesus got up. Having extinguished the curse of the law, Jesus rose with the blessing of grace. He inaugurated the Sabbath rest of the new creation. He now holds power over the grave that once held power over you. The death grip that once pulled you down grasps you no longer; you are now pulled up by his grip of grace into life. What you couldn't do in your own strength, he offers in his.

Baptism is where you are united with Christ in his death and resurrection. "In early Christian art," William Barclay says, "a man is often depicted as rising from the baptismal waters carrying a bed upon his back."[20] That's because the pool of Bethesda in this story is a picture of baptism. *Bethesda* means, literally, "house of mercy."[21] There is water of mercy in the house of God. Like this man, however, you couldn't crawl or carry yourself there. You couldn't get to the living water, so Jesus brought the living water to you.

Like this man waiting for "an angel of the Lord [to] come down and stir up the waters," you and I need more than a bath; we need a baptism.[22] We need the God of angel armies to descend on the waters and stir them with sacred power. We need the presence of the Holy One to sacralize them into a baptismal stream, to consecrate them as a sacrament, and to raise us up through them into new life—born from above.

We need more than just water; we need "water and the Spirit."[23] Like the Holy Spirit hovering over the primordial waters of Genesis 1, preparing to separate them and bring forth creation . . . Like God's holy wind blowing to separate the Red Sea and deliver ancient Israel into freedom from their slavery . . . Like the ark of God's presence descending into the Jordan to stir and part the waters so God's people could leave the wild and waste of their thirty-eight-year wilderness and enter their promised-land destiny . . . Like the dove descending on those same Jordan waters to anoint Jesus as he rose up from that baptismal pool to bring forth new creation . . .

We need water and the Spirit.

God's sacred power delights to descend on the waters. This power is from above, for those who know they can't make it on their own. A close friend critiqued me when I was baptized: "God is a crutch," he said. "Christianity is just for weak people who don't have the strength to make it on their own."

But I knew the truth: "Christ is not my crutch," I responded. "He's my stretcher!" I don't just need a little bit of help; I'm laid out flat on my back and need resurrection. I need his grace to carry me, his strength to raise me up out of this grave.

Baptism is not a push-up. You don't lower yourself into the waters by your own strength, then push yourself back up. No, you are lowered backward into the waters, a sign of your surrender as you identify with Christ in his death. Then you are raised by another (who represents Christ to you) pulling you up from the pool by *their* strength, a sign of Christ yanking you out of that grave through the power of his grace.

In baptism, the God who is on your side raises you onto his side. The Christ who entered into your death raises you with him into newness of life. When Jesus tells the paralyzed man to pick up his mat and walk, one commentator observes,

> The man might well have said with a kind of injured resentment that for thirty-eight years his bed had been carrying him and there was not much sense in telling him to carry it.[24]

But he trusts Christ and carries his bed away. You can too.

In Christ, you can now carry those things that once carried you. You no longer need to make your bed in patterns of behavior that lead to destruction. You are no longer confined to sin and the grave. Christ stirred the waters by his Spirit to wash you in his mercy and anoint you with his presence that you might rise in resurrection and live victorious with him.

Where are you tired today? Not just sleepy but *exhausted*? Maybe the world has worn you down with expectations you just can't measure up to. Maybe your greatest efforts never seem to please the people who rely on you (*whining children, anyone?*). Maybe it's the twenty-four-hour news cycle of a society constantly on fire. Some days? It's hard to get out of bed. Easier to pull the covers over your head.

Yet like a cosmic alarm clock blaring, the Lord of the Sabbath has come to raise you up. Ironically, he awakens you *into rest*. He calls you out of your slumber, off your mat, up from your grave—into newness of life with him. He calls you out of thirty-eight years of slogging through the wilderness to feast with him in the land of milk and honey. He calls you to be washed in those baptismal Jordan waters through which you come home to him.

You no longer rest on that mat; now you rest in Christ.

This rest is deeper than just taking a nap. It's a deliverance into your destiny, free from your struggle and striving, into the wholeness you were made for.

Jesus's question is simple: *Can I help you?* This is the question posed by grace. It excavates beneath the mappable geography of your behavior into the subterranean territory of your heart. It reaches beyond what you do to what you love. Into the realm of your affections and desires. *What do you want?* Jesus interrogates your inner world to draw you out into his new creation. He wants to jump-start your heart and raise you up with him into his kingdom. *Will you let me heal you?* His question is an earnest plea for your best.

Will you say yes?

6

FEAST IN THE WILDERNESS

When Your Soul Is Starving

I once stopped eating for forty days. You might call it a fast, but it was more like a hunger strike. I was angry at God. *Why?* you might ask. I had been hung up on the same girl for five years. Here's the story in a nutshell:

- Year 1: I expressed how I felt only to learn she had just started dating somebody else.
  (*Embarrassing.*)
- Year 2: I waited to see if their relationship would last.
  (*It did.*)
- Year 3: They were still dating but not engaged, so I threw a dramatic Hail Mary pass to make my feelings known.
  (*Unrequited.*)
- Year 4: I tried dating other people to get over it, but she was like Conor McGregor, and her memory KO'd every would-be competitor.
- Year 5: I beat myself up for a while, then turned my anger toward God.

God, I'm not eating until you show up. I wondered why I was still hung up on the same girl after five years; it felt pathetic. I wondered why God had brought her into my life if he knew I'd fall so hard for her and not be able to get back up. Was he against me? I wondered how long I could go without food. I dug in my heels, subsisting on my anger at the God I didn't understand . . .

Where do you go when your soul is starving? When you hunger for more than bread? When you crave meaning and connection and are famished for a revelation from God?

In John 6, Jesus makes a carb-loaded meal: all the bread the crowds can eat. Some diets try to restrict carbs. (*Paleo and keto left me very hungry.*) Jesus puts them at the center of his meal plan. Let's look at his fifth sign: feeding more than five thousand people with a few loaves and fish. This is more than a display of his power; it's a picture of what he's come to bring *you* through his cross and resurrection.

BETTER BREAD

Jesus is surrounded by large crowds of followers, so he asks Philip, "Where shall we buy bread for these people to eat?"[1] There's no In-N-Out Burger nearby, so the disciples jump immediately to logistics: "It would take more than half a year's wages to buy enough bread for each one to have a bite!"[2] Andrew highlights their meager resources: There's "a little boy" with "five little barley loaves" and "two little fish." (Notice the repetition of that word *little*.) "How far will they go among so many?"[3]

They're trying to feed a football stadium with a Happy Meal.

The disciples focus on *how* to fix an impossible situation; Jesus wants them to look to *who* can fix an impossible situation. They're looking in the pantry at their sparse ingredients, but they've got the Bread Maker with them.

It's like that show *Chopped,* where amazing chefs are given a basket of crazy ingredients. "Here's a Twinkie, some arugula, Spam, and whipped cream." Yet they're somehow able to turn it into an amazing meal.

Jesus is the ultimate *Chopped* chef. You might not have the time you wish you had to lock in with those kids you're trying to raise, or the training you think you need to study the Bible with others, or the treasure you'd prefer to have to bless someone in need around you. Yet something powerful happens when you take the little you do have and put it in the hands of the Savior. He can make a crazy good meal with whatever you've got to bring.

Jesus can do a *lot* with your *little.*

Take heart. The power's not in the greatness of the materials you have on hand; rather, it's in the hands of the Master Chef who can make something great with what you have. Jesus says, *Stop focusing on how much you have; start looking to who I am.* He can make a feast from your famine.

John highlights an important Old Testament backdrop to this scene: God feeding Israel manna in the wilderness. Like Moses leading God's people out of Egypt, so Jesus "crossed to the far shore of the Sea of Galilee," and "a great crowd" who "saw the signs he had performed" "followed him" to that remote area. Like Moses then ascended Mount Sinai with the elders of Israel to meet with God, so Jesus "went up on a mountainside and sat down with his disciples."[4] There are more Moses echoes all over this story.[5] The point? Jesus is a greater Moses.

Moses was the opener; Jesus is the headliner.

Similar to how Moses fed the masses with manna from heaven, Jesus is about to feed the crowds with bread from heaven. As a greater Moses, Jesus is a faithful and trustworthy guide to lead you to the promised land of God's eternal kingdom. But first you have to face the wilderness.

Jesus "made" the people "sit down," and "there was plenty of grass in that place."[6] That's more than comfy seating; it's an allusion to Jesus being the Good Shepherd who "makes [you] sit down in green pastures."[7] Jesus can "prepare a table before [you] in the presence of [your] enemies,"[8] where you can sit down, stretch out, and relax in his presence. He's got you.

The "five thousand men" in this miracle arguably carry echoes of a military battalion in the wilderness, getting prepared for entry into the promised land.[9] Jesus fills you up to prepare you for his offensive against the powers of darkness in the world.

After Jesus distributes the bread and fish, everyone eats as much as they want. There's plenty to go around, with baskets of bread left over.[10] Jesus isn't one of those froufrou restaurants with skimpy portions, where you spend $150 and walk away hungry. When Holly and I were dating, we went to a fancy new restaurant everyone was talking about. The portions were so tiny—and expensive. After paying the (extravagant) bill, we left and drove through Burgerville.

I used to think restaurants were being generous when they served so much chips and salsa. (*I'll eat you out of business!*) Now I realize they know a secret: Carbs fill you up.

Jesus may be divine, but he doesn't hold back on the portions. He fills you up. He cares about both your *physical* and your *spiritual* needs.[11] He wants to meet your deepest cravings.

A TEST IN THE WILDERNESS

Okay, back to Jesus's question for Philip: Does the Savior ask him for a plan because he's out of ideas? No. "He asked this only to test him, for he already had in mind what he was going to do."[12] Jesus is testing the disciples, like God tested Israel with hunger in the wilderness. Moses told Israel,

> Remember how the LORD your God led you all the way in the
> wilderness these forty years, to humble and test you in order
> to know what was in your heart. . . . He humbled you, causing
> you to hunger and then feeding you with manna . . . to teach
> you that man does not live on bread alone but on every word
> that comes from the mouth of the LORD.[13]

The wilderness was a test. God knew what he was going to do,
but he wanted to sift his people's hearts. Would they trust him,
look to him, keep his commands? The goal was *humility:* to trade
self-reliance for God-reliance. The test involved *hunger.* How
would they survive in the desert with no grocery stores or credit
cards to cover the cost?

Would they stop asking *how* and start asking *who*?

We fail this test all the time. How many times have I hit a hard
spot and immediately thought, *God's left the building*? I can break
trust at the first sign of trouble and assume I'm all on my own.

When things get tough, do you turn first to *how* or to *who*?
Do you throw your hands up in despair or seek God in prayer?
Is your first instinct to focus on how much you have or on the
Lord who has you? We are so often like Israel and the disciples,
fixated on the impossibility of our circumstances instead of the
compassionate presence of Jesus, our guide.

Twice in John 6 the crowds grumble against Jesus.[14] In the
original language, that word *grumble* is a funny one that imitates
an animal sound (*goggyzō*). It means "to show 'smoldering discontent' . . . droning on in a low, constant murmur,"[15] like the
Israelites grumbling against Moses in the desert:

> If only we had meat to eat! We remember the fish we ate in
> Egypt at no cost—also the cucumbers, melons, leeks, onions,
> and garlic.[16]

Israel was ready to go back to Egypt. To slavery. All because they were hungry. They would have gladly traded their freedom for food.

The crowds grumble against Jesus, like they grumbled against Moses. Have you ever grumbled against Jesus? When he hasn't met your expectations? When your soul is starving and you're not sure how to fill it? When it feels like he's abandoned you in the desert? It's easy to succumb to "smoldering discontent." To consider going back to Egypt.

I grumbled against God during that hunger strike. *Why did you bring her into my life if you knew my heart would get broken like this? It's pathetic that I'm still hung up on her after five years—and where are you? I'm craving an answer, and it feels like you've abandoned me in this desert of desolation.*

Gradually, the Lord turned the attention back toward me. Two to three weeks into the fast, he began revealing the idol I had made of romantic relationships in my life. I had said, *God, I'll follow you anywhere. I'll do anything. I'll give you everything.* Except this area. I didn't trust God with it, so I deadbolted this one room in my heart and refused to open the door to him.

God revealed ways I had wounded people in past relationships. There was a cost to my idolatry. A cost others had paid. The arrow of accusation was redirected toward my heart.

I realized the thing I had been most drawn to in her was her love for Jesus. She was the first girl I encountered, after I became a Christian, who loved Jesus so deeply, whose face lit up when she worshipped, who cared immensely for justice in the world, whose heart broke for the things that break God's, who was a good and faithful friend to those in her life. I realized the light I saw in her was a mere reflection of the glory of Jesus, like the moon reflecting the rays of the sun.

And I had the sun.

God began gently removing my fingers, one by one, from my idol. My grip weakened; I released it to him. Eventually, the ache was replaced with a deep intimacy, with the felt awareness of his presence. I had let my hunger drive me toward bread that doesn't satisfy rather than the One my heart was made for.

I found myself saying, *God, if the only reason you brought her into my life was to remove my grip from that idol and help me give it to you, it was worth it.* My grumbling turned to gratitude. Although I can look back and see God's wisdom now, it was a long, painful lesson to learn.

MORE THAN ENOUGH

What does Jesus feed you with? He uses five loaves of bread for this miracle. This echoes the five books of Moses, known as the Torah, or God's Word, and conceptualized as bread in the Old Testament.[17] In the last chapter, we saw how the five colonnades of John 5 represent the Law in a negative sense, with the weight of the curse these five books brought on God's people. Now here in John 6, we see how the five loaves represent the Law in a positive sense: the nourishing sustenance of God's life-giving Word for his people.[18] Jesus wants to feed you physically *and* spiritually. He loves to feed you with his Word.

After Jesus's miracle, there are twelve baskets of bread left over. This is more than what they started with, one for each tribe of Israel (symbolically) to receive from God's life-giving Word.[19] Jesus has come to feed his people, and he has leftovers.

Jesus makes more than enough.

You serve a generous God. He wants to satiate your soul with leftovers to spare. Your heavenly Father loves to shower his best on you as his child. As James reminds us, "Every good and perfect gift is from above, coming down from the Father of the heavenly lights."[20] What good gifts—little or big—have you received lately? What daily bread can you thank him for today? Respond by living generously with others.

You don't serve a stingy savior. Don't become one of those annoying Christians who don't tip at restaurants. You know, that crew who crowds out Red Robin with Bibles open, chowing down on bottomless fries while talking loudly about Jesus— then doesn't tip the server. No, that's a sign that your savior is a scrooge.

When you experience the generosity of Jesus, it makes you want to go above and beyond to bless people like you've been blessed. This is about more than money. Some of the most generous people I know don't have a lot of dough in the bank account, but they seek to bless others with whatever bounty they've been given. And since God's Word is our daily bread, you can find nourishment for your soul in the Scriptures. You can feast in the wilderness with Jesus, then share from the leftovers.

There's plenty to go around.

COME HUNGRY

This miracle is the fifth sign of John's gospel. Don't stop at the sign; keep going to the destination: It's pointing you to Jesus himself.

"I am the living bread that came down from heaven," Jesus explains. At the sign, he's the chef; at the destination, he's the meal. "This bread is my flesh, which I will give for the life of the world."[21] This bread foreshadows his own crucifixion, where the Father will take him, bless him, break him, and give him so that we can receive life from him.[22] Jesus will give his life for the world.

"Your ancestors ate the manna in the wilderness," Jesus reminds the crowds, "yet they died. But here is the bread that comes down from heaven, which anyone may eat and not die."[23] A bread you can eat and not die? That's some true Wonder Bread. You're invited to feast on Jesus.

Jesus says, *Eat my flesh; drink my blood.*[24] That can freak us out (*Is this cannibalism?*), but he's inviting us to something powerful. Christ offers himself to us as his people. We are the great crowd in the wilderness of our world—the church journeying from our slavery under sin toward our promised land in his eternal kingdom. Like ancient Israel, we face hostility around us and hunger within us. Christ doesn't just give us a road map to get there. No, he journeys with us and feeds us with his presence along the way. He is the true manna, the bread that comes down from heaven, that doesn't spoil but brings us eternal life.

Where's your wilderness? Is it the devastating diagnosis of the cancer that afflicts your bones? Or the hostile terrain of betrayal when your spouse broke the covenant and cracked your heart into a thousand pieces? Or the insecurity when the economy tanked, your company threw you overboard, and you were left unsure how to keep a roof over your family's heads?

Before you get to the promised land, you've got to endure some wilderness. You've got to learn to depend on your Deliverer in the desert. You need some survival skills to know where to find bread.

FEAST ON JESUS

As the church, we regularly come to the bread and wine of the Lord's Table. Christ gives himself to us as his people in communion. Different traditions disagree on *how* Christ is present. Some say the bread and wine *become* the body and blood when consecrated by the priest (Catholic). Others say Christ's presence is *in, with, and under* the bread and wine (Lutheran). Others say the real presence of Christ is communicated by the Spirit when the bread and wine are received in faith (Reformed). Others say it's a mystery (Orthodox). Yet virtually every major tradition agrees that Christ is truly present.[25]

Regardless of *how* you think it happens, there is power in the mystery *that* it happens.[26] And I'm convinced that it happens. Christ is ascended and alive at the right hand of God's throne, ruling and reigning over all of heaven and earth. He has poured out his Spirit, uniting his global people. Christ is truly present when we gather in his name, offering communion with himself through this table.[27]

If you struggle with this, consider: The same Jesus who turns water to wine (transforming the *substance*) and a kid's tiny loaves into a feast for thousands (multiplying the *amount*) can offer himself abundantly through his Spirit in this bread and wine today. The dominant witness of the historic and global church agrees.

Maybe you've been feeding on others, sucking the life out of them in codependent relationships, trying to fill yourself with what you can get only from God. If that's you, Jesus says, *Come to me. My life is inexhaustible. Feed on my presence, that through me you might truly live.* When you fill yourself with Christ, you free yourself to be healthier in your relationships with others.

Don't try to do it on your own. You need life from outside

yourself to survive. Try going forty days without food and you'll feel your frailty kick in fast. This is a sign embedded in creation, pointing to a deeper truth: *You can't sustain existence on your own!* Even more than bread, you need Jesus. We're all on a trajectory toward the tomb, yet a life has been given to give you life, the Savior broken to put you back together, like a grain of wheat crushed to feed you with the heavenly bread of eternal life.

When your soul is starving, you can feast on Christ.

Jesus won't turn you away. "Whoever comes to me will never go hungry," he says. "Whoever comes to me I will never drive away."[28] You can come to Jesus in your wilderness. He wants to feed you until you're full.

Where are you turning to fill your soul craving? "Do not work for food that spoils," Jesus recommends, "but for food that endures to eternal life."[29] Don't spend all your time laboring for a moldy meal crawling with maggots, in other words, when there's a tasty feast freely available. The substitutes don't satisfy. Jesus is better bread.

Jesus tells us to work for this food, but he then explains that the work God requires is simply this: "to believe in the one he has sent."[30] That's an easy job. We feast on Christ by faith. By looking up to him, crying out to him, opening our hearts to him, receptive to his love, we open ourselves to being filled by him. It's already raining bread, in other words; just open up your basket to receive.

What if we looked to prayer not as work we do for God but a place we go to feast on God? Not a religious hoop to jump through to prove how spiritual we are but rather a way to bring our hunger to God? "Prayer is food for the soul," Saint Joseph of Optina advised. "Do not starve the soul. It is better to let the body go hungry."[31] To pray is to bring your craving to God, cultivating your appetite for him above all others, opening yourself to being permeated by the transcendence of his presence.

What if we read Scripture not to check off a rote activity from a to-do list but to feast on God's Word? "The mystery of human existence lies not in just staying alive," Dostoevsky advises, "but in finding something to live for."[32] Jesus is that greater something—the greater someone—to live for. The whole Bible points to him. You can trade mindlessly scrolling on Instagram for mindfully saturating yourself in Scripture. You can learn to live not on bread alone but on every word—especially the living Word—that proceeds from the mouth of God.[33]

There is a blessing in the wilderness. A feast prepared for you. A sacred dependence to be cultivated. Learn to depend on Christ. Contra the myth of our culture, you're not enough on your own. You were never intended to be. You were made not to *make* your existence but to *receive* it. Rather than looking inward, you were made to look outward toward the God who is ready to satiate you, toward the Bread of Life who invites you to come and feast on him.

I'LL BE YOUR EVERYTHING

On the final day of my forty-day fast, I went to the beach. By this point, I was experiencing deep intimacy with God. Staring out at the ocean, I sensed God saying, *I'll be your water of life—infinite and fully available to your soul.* I saw a lighthouse: *I'll be your light that guides you back to the safety of home.* I saw Haystack Rock, sturdy against the pounding waves: *I'll be your rock, a reliable foundation to build your life on.* The next day, I sat down to take my first bite: *I'll be your Bread of Life to satisfy the deepest hunger of your soul.*

All creation seemed to be crying out God's care for me. Through it all, I heard his voice: *I'll be your everything.*

Come hungry to Jesus. You're invited to let him be your everything.

There are always new diets out there, but let me suggest we return to an ancient regimen: the Bread of Life diet. True, many say to cut carbs—paleo, keto, Atkins—but Jesus is countercultural. Carbs are at the center of this plan. Indeed, you're invited to count your carbs—not to see how few but rather to see how many you can consume. The goal is to feast on as much heavenly bread as you can.

How much Jesus can you get into you? Feast on God's Word, the unified story that leads to Jesus. Encounter him in prayer, bringing him your deepest cravings. Try a new spiritual-formation practice, like fasting, to cultivate God-reliance over self-reliance. Come hungry to communion to feast on the presence of Jesus.

Have you ever wondered why the global church is booming while the American church is in decline? Could it be that they are hungry for God? That they want him to be their everything, while we have filled ourselves with other things?

I love Philip Yancey's theory:

My theory is this: God goes where he's wanted. That's a scary thought in a country like the United States, home to so many entertainment and electronic distractions.

Meanwhile, the greatest numerical revival in history has occurred during the past half-century in China, one of the last officially atheistic states and one of the most oppressive. Go figure.[34]

God goes where he's wanted. Where there's a *hunger* for him. There's a certain challenge to living in a land of plenty. Don't fill yourself up on other things. You can enjoy them, but don't make them your staple. Bring God your hunger. Feast on Christ as your daily bread. In whatever wilderness you might find yourself in, look up to him in faith. His presence is close enough, his power strong enough, to meet your deepest hunger. His Spirit is on your side—with you and in you. When your soul is starving, load up on the Bread of Life.

Let him be your everything.

7

BLOW THE DAM

When You're Suffering Divine Dehydration

You're going to die soon. I woke with the thought blaring in my head. It was freaky! I couldn't get it out. Whose voice was it? God's? The devil's? My own subconscious's? I wasn't sure. I was on a retreat with our leadership team. What was intended to be rest was now flooded with fear. I wanted to discern the voice but felt a major block; I couldn't make sense of it.

Where do you go when you feel blocked from the life-giving presence of God?

We drove by Hoover Dam once on a family road trip. It's massive! Nestled along the Colorado River, the dam is built smack dab in the southwestern desert, with enough concrete to pave a road from San Francisco to New York. It's impressive, using arch-gravity technology and engineering techniques never tested before the dam's construction in the 1930s. It was expensive—about a billion dollars in today's terms—involving thousands of workers and costing almost one hundred lives. We were a few of the seven million tourists who visit every year.[1]

I want you to do an imagination experiment with me . . .

Imagine you live downstream from Hoover Dam. Your once-glorious civilization was built on the Colorado River, with abundant agriculture and plenty of drinking water. There's a reason ancient civilizations were built along rivers: Water brings life. Then these Hoover engineers came and blocked up your water supply, not allowing enough to get through. Crops shriveled. Citizens were thirsty. Your civilization began crumbling.

That's a picture of our lives blocked from the presence of God. In John 7, we discover that we were made for abundant life in the glorious civilization of the kingdom of God. But sin is an obstacle—like a dam—cutting us off from the river of life.

Yet Jesus has come to blow the dam. No, I'm not saying he's an ecoterrorist (*lol!*). I'm saying he's come to remove the barrier that's blocking us from the presence of God so the river of life can rush back in again. I'll share more about what happened with that voice I was hearing, but I have good news if you're suffering from divine dehydration like I was: Jesus is a thirst quencher. He's come to bring us water in the wilderness.

BRING YOUR THIRST

"On the last and greatest day of the festival," John tells us, "Jesus stood and said in a loud voice, 'Let anyone who is thirsty come to me and drink.'"[2] Which festival? It's the Feast of Tents (or Tabernacles).[3] This was like a national camping trip, where the people spent a week living in temporary booths (like tents) they constructed. Can you imagine your whole nation going camping together? They did this to remember their years in the wilderness, when they were a civilization with no river.

When Israel left Egypt, there was no water in the desert. They wanted to enter the promised land, a land flowing with milk and honey (*and water!*). But because of their rebellion, they were cut off for thirty-eight years and couldn't enter. The walls of Jericho were like Hoover Dam, blocking them from the river of life they were made for.

So they cried out, *We're thirsty! We're going to die! We've got no water!* They cried out and God answered: "Water gushed out, and the community and their livestock drank."[4] God sustained his people on the way to their future home.

God hydrates his thirsty people.

God can give you water in the wilderness. Do you find yourself crying out, *God, I'm gonna die out here*? Maybe you're grateful he got you out of Egypt: out of the relationship that was killing you, the addiction that enslaved you, the enemy's lie that oppressed you. Yet you've still got to live in the wilderness of this fallen world, where loneliness leaves you exhausted, where chemotherapy shrivels your body, where you're not sure how you'll pay your water bill.

We're not to the promised land yet. The land of milk and honey is coming, with streets of gold and a river of life. Yet on the way there, you can cry out to God with your thirst in the desert.

Jesus says he can bring you "living water."[5] As we saw in chapter 3, that phrase was used to describe water that was moving. Rivers and streams looked *alive*, with energy and vibrancy. They brought vitality to the land, with abundant crops and fresh drinking water. Ponds and puddles, in contrast, were stagnant, collecting leaves, feces, and disease.

Still water was *dead;* moving water was *alive.*

It's powerful to see a community receive clean water. My friend Katherine is a Kenyan leader bringing clean water to her region. She says, "Water is foundational for life."[6] It's a foundation for *health:* Waterborne diseases are eradicated. For *education:* Hydrated kids can concentrate at school. For *the economy:*

Villagers who formerly walked miles to get clean water have new time to invest.

Our church partnered with a slum community called La Limonada. The church there had been crying out to God for clean water. When it arrived, the people were ecstatic: Local health skyrocketed; education improved; worship was emboldened. God answered their prayer.

Katherine was right: Water *is* foundational for life.

Jesus's water is alive. "By this [living water] he meant the Spirit."[7] Christ's Spirit isn't stagnant; the Spirit is rushing to bring vitality and abundance to your life. Not only does God have life; he also *is* life—and shares his life with you by his Spirit.

The Holy Spirit is foundational for life. Jesus wants to restore you to health, educate you in his wisdom, and make your life fruitful—by reconnecting you with the presence of the living God.

You can build the civilization of your life on the river of his Spirit. You can be like the late Chris Farley's Matt Foley (*I live in a van down by the river!*), making your home on the banks of God's presence. When you plant the tree of your life there, his love, joy, peace, patience—and other fruit of the Spirit—come bursting off your branches.[8]

Even in the wilderness, God can make you fruitful.

ALL YOU NEED IS NEED

How do you get this water? "Jesus stood up and cried out, 'If anyone thirsts, let him come to me and drink.'"[9] Jesus is echoing Isaiah 55 here, where God cried out,

Come, all you who are thirsty,
    come to the waters;

and you who have no money,
    come, buy and eat!
Come, buy wine and milk
    without money and without cost.[10]

You don't need money for this living water. You don't need to
earn it or deserve it. All you need to do is bring your thirst to
Jesus. You might think, *I'm not good enough for this water. I
haven't performed enough, worked hard enough, cleaned myself
up enough.* You don't need to! It's all about grace. The only re-
quirement is thirst.

All you need is need.

It's fascinating: Usually the thirsty cry out for water, yet here
the Living Water cries out for the thirsty. That term "cried out"
(*krazō*) comes from the sound of a raven's cry: *caw, caw!* The
association? To "cry out *loudly* with an *urgent scream* or shriek,
using . . . 'shouts that express *deep* emotion.'"[11] That's Jesus crying out gutturally for you.

You may have thought Jesus is waiting for you to cry out to
him, but he's already been crying out for you. He's on your side.
The gospel isn't about you going out to search for him; he's already come to search for you. He descended to walk our dusty
streets. He went to a cross to quench your thirst. He sprang up
from the grave like a fountain to fill you to overflowing. God
delights to give you his presence. Jesus rejoices to hydrate you.
The Spirit loves to give you life.

You can come to the One who's already come for you.

Why don't we come? Why don't we bring our need? The Isaiah 55 passage continues: "Why [do you] spend money on what
is not bread, and your labor on what does not satisfy?"[12] God
offers better stuff for free, but we're spending our time and energy chasing other things. We don't come to him, because we're
going to substitutes.

As a kid, I once ran inside thirsty. I'd been playing outside in the summer sun and was dehydrated. I flung open the fridge and saw a two-liter of Orange Crush soda. I filled up a large glass and crushed it. *Still thirsty!* I tried a glass of Pepsi. *Still thirsty!* A&W Root Beer. *Still thirsty!* My mom saw me confused and explained: Soda tastes good going down but leaves you thirstier. You need water.

Are you running to things that just make you thirstier? Running to your Instagram feed to quench your thirst for human approval? Climbing the career ladder in your search for significance? Running to that relationship thinking, *He looks like a cool drink of water!* yet he's treating you bad and leaving you thirstier? This is like trying to hydrate on soda, coffee, and Red Bull.

The substitutes taste good going down but leave you thirstier.

DON'T SETTLE FOR SUBSTITUTES

It's easy in our culture to jump from substitute to substitute. When our job doesn't give us the satisfaction we thought it would, we look for a new one. Then jump to yoga. Then try skydiving. Then a Netflix binge. Then travel. When the newness wears off, we sprint to the next thing.

We're surrounded by substitutes. We're like a place where Coke is cheaper than bottled water, where it's easier to get the thing that will rot your teeth over time. These things aren't bad in and of themselves, but when you make them replacements for God, seeking ultimate satisfaction in them, it's like guzzling various two-liter bottles of soda, wondering why you're still dehydrated.

Tom Brady testified to this truth that the substitutes won't satisfy. Back in 2005, after winning three Super Bowl rings, he confessed,

Why do I . . . still think there's something greater out there for me? I mean, maybe a lot of people would say, "Hey man, this is what it is." I reached my goal, my dream. . . . Me, I think, *God, it's got to be more than this*. I mean, this isn't—this can't be what it's all cracked up to be.[13]

He reached the pinnacle of success yet still found himself thirsty. Similarly, Billie Eilish bears witness to this thirst in her song "Everything I Wanted," in which she sings of getting all she dreamed of but, "If I'm being honest, / It might've been a nightmare." She says you can accumulate all the stuff in the world and still feel empty inside. You can be onstage at the height of fame, admired by the masses, and still not feel truly seen and known.[14]

Brady and Eilish shine light on this truth: The substitutes can't satisfy. Yet the God who is on your side will. You are seen, known, and loved—by your Creator. You were made for God, and your heart will be restless until you find your rest in him.[15] "Listen, listen to me," God concluded in Isaiah 55, "and you will delight in the richest of fare."[16] *Come to me,* Jesus says, *and I will give you living water.* The reason the substitutes won't satisfy is that you were made for something more.

You were made for the presence of God.

How do you get this water that truly satisfies? "Whoever believes in me," Jesus says, "out of his heart will flow rivers of living water."[17] That's how we access his presence. We look to Jesus in faith. When you trust in Jesus, you soak in his Spirit. Even in your driest, most dehydrated season, you can access his presence by turning your heart toward him in worship.

When Jesus says this water flows "out of his heart," is he referring to *his* heart or *ours*? Does the water flow out of Jesus's heart or out of the heart of the one who believes in him? Yes. The original language can be read either way, and as we've seen, John loves to play with double entendre.[18] Both meanings are true.

On the one hand, the Spirit flows *out of Jesus's heart.* The Spirit is not some vague, mysterious force but the Spirit of Jesus, who comes from him and connects you to him. On the other hand, when you trust in Jesus, the Spirit flows *out of your heart.*[19] "God's love has been poured out into our hearts through the Holy Spirit," Romans 5:5 says, and he fills you to overflowing.

Your heart is like a sponge. When I buy a sponge at Target, it's small, yellow, and hard as a rock. You could break something with it. But then I place it under the faucet and, beneath the flow of rushing water, it grows softer and expands until it fills to overflowing. When I squeeze the sponge, water comes pouring out.

Jesus is the faucet; your heart is the sponge.

The sign of a life soaked in Jesus is this: When you get squeezed, his Spirit flows out. When hardship presses in, praise comes out. When enemies hate on you, love comes out. When your kids are on your last nerve, patience comes out. (*Convicting!*) When there's peer pressure to compromise, courage comes out. This is the way of the kingdom: When Satan squeezes you, the Spirit flows out.

When you're experiencing divine dehydration, drink deep of Christ's Spirit. Worship him in your wilderness, placing your life under the faucet of his grace. Look up to him in trust, confident of his love for you. Soak in his Spirit, allowing his love to expand your own capacity to love, until you overflow into the desert of a thirsty world.

DRINK DEEP

How do you drink deep? How do you place yourself under the faucet to soak in Christ's Spirit? Let's get practical. Listening prayer is a practice I like to use. My wife taught me this two-step process for seeking the Holy Spirit when I'm divinely dehydrated—

feeling anxious, nervous, or afraid. First I ask, "What is the lie or the fear?" What is the lie the enemy is speaking or the fear I'm living under? I create space for the Spirit to surface anything I might need to hear—usually thirty seconds to a minute—and simply listen. The goal here is to identify any barrier between me and God's presence.

Then, with that in mind, I pray, "Jesus, what is the truth you want to speak?" What is his perspective on this thing or situation? Again, I listen for thirty seconds to a minute. The goal here is to let Jesus blow the dam, removing any barrier with his truth.

For example, when I heard that voice saying, *You're going to die soon,* I went for a walk to seek the Lord. After I prayed, "What is the lie or the fear?" I sensed the Spirit revealing something. I had just completed a major ministry project, a long time in the making. The underlying lie began to surface:

God just used you to get that done. Now that it's complete, he doesn't need you anymore. He's going to get rid of you.

Whoa! That's a pretty major block. So I prayed, "Jesus, what is the truth you want to speak?" I sensed the Spirit reaffirming the truth of the gospel:

Before I called you to use you, I called you to love you. Your worth in my eyes is not based on what you can accomplish or do for me; it's based on my heart for you and what I've done for you. I'm for you; I'm on your side.

Wow! Jesus blew the dam and brought living water to my soul.

You're invited to drink deep of the Spirit. To saturate yourself in Scripture and permeate your life with prayer. Now, two healthy guardrails for listening prayer: (1) The Holy Spirit will never contradict God's Word—so weigh anything you hear against Scripture. (2) The Holy Spirit is best discerned in Christlike community, so process anything significant or confusing with a trusted pastor or godly friend.

Listening prayer is one vehicle you can use to drink deep, but the bigger picture is to seek Jesus and soak in the truth of his gospel, to remove any obstacles and quench your thirst in his river of life.

THE CROSS AS DYNAMITE

How did Jesus restore the river of life? John says, "Up to that time the Spirit had not been given, since Jesus had not yet been glorified."[20] The cross is where Jesus blew the dam.

The cross is where Jesus was glorified. John uses this term throughout his gospel to refer to the Crucifixion, where Jesus was lifted up and exalted.[21] It may sound strange to refer to the cross as *glory*, yet this is where Jesus won the victory, atoning for the sin of the world and reconciling us to God.

This is why the Spirit "had not [yet] been given." Before Jesus could restore the river of life, he had to deal with the obstacle that was blocking us from God's presence.

The cross is foreshadowed in a powerful ceremony that took place during the festival. Every morning, the priests would fill a vessel with water in the pool of Siloam and carry it to the temple. Then one of the priests would circle the altar and pour out the water upon it, hoping God would bring life-giving water to the land. On the final day of the festival, they would walk around the altar seven times and beat the ground surrounding the altar with willow branches—reminiscent of Moses striking the rock in the wilderness.[22]

The symbolism? Jesus is the Rock who was struck so the water would flow again. The cross is the altar where he was beaten to deal with our sin. The echoes are unmistakable. Jesus cried out in the temple on "the last and greatest day of the festival,"[23] linking his climactic death with this ceremony. "That rock was Christ," Paul similarly says, which brought forth a river for Israel in the wilderness.[24] Again at the cross, Christ, the Rock of our salvation, was struck to unclog the faucet, unkink the hose, and unleash the living water again.

When Jesus died, "a sudden flow of blood and water" emerged from his pierced side.[25] This was no accident. Water and blood have sacramental associations in John's gospel: the water of his Spirit associated with baptism, and the blood of his atonement associated with the Eucharist. When the spear broke through the wall of Christ's flesh, it unleashed the river of life. John foreshadows that event here.

After Christ's resurrection, God exalted him to the highest place (the Ascension), from which he poured out the Spirit (at Pentecost) on all who would receive him.[26]

The cross is a dam-removal project. Picture Hoover Dam again, where we live downstream in a dusty and dehydrated land. There's abundant water upstream, but we're cut off from the fullness we were made for by the massive concrete obstacle of Sin—not just lowercase-s sin (of personal things we do) but capital-S Sin (of the world under the power of our rebellion). This is what blocks us from the life-giving river of God's presence.

At the cross, when Jesus was lifted up, he became sin for us—strapped to the dam like dynamite—to remove the obstacle and reconcile us to God.[27] He came onto our side, identifying with us as the guilty, experiencing our divine dehydration in his humanity when he cried out "I thirst" from the cross.[28] When he was struck on the altar and the spear pierced his side, he obliterated the blockage so the river of life could flow once more.

Jesus came to blow the dam. He gave his life to restore to you the river of life. This removal project cost him more than the billion dollars to build Hoover Dam. It cost him everything—his perfect, sinless life—but he said it was worth it for you. The extravagance of his grace is greater than the expense of our sin. The salvation he engineered at the cross is way more impressive than arch-gravity technology. It overwhelmed the weight of our sin with the heaven-to-earth gravity of his love.

Don't build new obstacles. Don't be like a beaver building little dams of twigs and stones before the mighty, rushing river of God's presence. Let go of your sin. Be washed and carried away by the streams of his mercy. Pursue holiness as your life is permeated by the Holy Spirit.

Are you clinging to anything that's blocking you from the presence of God? A habit, relationship, or pursuit that you're using as a substitute for God? A thing that's become like a dam for you? Take that thing to the cross, and blow the dam thing up.

I can hear my ten-year-old son now: *You said the D-word!* But I mean it seriously. Those things that separate us from God are quite literally *damned* things, in the dictionary sense of "to declare (something) to be bad, unfit, invalid, or illegal . . . to bring condemnation upon; ruin."[29] The things you use to rebel against God, keep him at bay, and live on your own terms are obstacles to the life he created you for.

Yet Christ became a curse for us to redeem us from the curse.[30] He descended to hell to take on the power of hell and quench it with the power of divine love. He blew the dam to reconcile you to the rushing river of God's presence. He calls to you, inviting you to drink deep.

Come to Christ, who gives you living water. Come to Christ,

who has already come to you and cries out for you. Come to Christ, knowing he's on your side—so much so that he allowed your sin to pierce his side to be with you forever.

Jesus's Spirit can bring life to your dead places. In a powerful Old Testament vision, a river would one day flow from the temple to bring life to the barren land—even the Dead Sea would be overwhelmed with life. "Where the river flows everything will live."[31]

Where are your Dead Sea places? The places where you feel emotionally spent, mentally exhausted, physically at your limit? When you're experiencing divine dehydration, come to the heart of Jesus and drink deep from his presence. Let him fill you to overflowing until life swims like salmon inside your soul again. Until the fruit of his love, joy, peace, and patience begins bursting off your branches, in season and out of season, with your roots soaking in riverside soil.

When you feel cut off from the river of life, look to Jesus to blow the dam.

You don't need to go out and find him; he's already come to you. You don't need to earn it; all you need is need. He's there, present, inviting you to look up. To bring your thirst. Before you ever cried out, the Living Water has been crying out for you. The river is here and it's free.

Drink deep.

8

RAISE THE BAR

When You're Battling Guilt and Regret

When I was around five years old, our neighbor's yard was vandalized. Lawn décor and flora had been pulled out by local hooligans and scattered around the vicinity. I saw the damage and wanted to help, so I got to work while no one else was around. As I rolled a stone paver back toward the lawn, I noticed a dead butterfly roll up on one side. It lay smashed against the stone, and I realized it had been crushed beneath the weight of my body. Bye-bye, butterfly.

I had killed a living thing. This beautiful creature's death affected me deeply. I ran inside the house, up to my room, and flung myself on my bed, weeping. Yes, it was unintentional—but I had ended its life. (I had a sensitive conscience.) One minute, it was fluttering and breathing. The next, its existence was extinguished—by me.

This is my first memory of battling guilt and regret.

A few years later, I committed my first theft. I was at the state fair, playing that game where you shoot a Ping-Pong ball from an air gun at a pyramid of bottles. My shot knocked down only two of the bottles, but the attendant was distracted retrieving something beneath the counter. She wasn't looking. At the behest of my friend Jeb, I yanked the Ping-Pong ball back to myself (via the string attached to the gun) and threw a stellar curveball to knock down that final bottle.

I had won a Spuds MacKenzie doll—the surfing dog in a Hawaiian shirt that served as Bud Light's iconic mascot, "the original party animal." I loved that stuffed animal, but I felt horrible about how I'd attained it. Afterward, I sneaked back to the carnival booth and slipped my last twenty-dollar bill quietly behind the counter—an attempt to appease my conscience. It didn't work. For months to come, I was racked by remorse and regret. (*Like I said, I was sensitive!*)

What do you do when you're battling guilt and regret? Have you ever done things you wish you could take back? Hurt people you wish you could heal? Faced shame and rejection because of your actions? I wish I could say that stopped when I grew up—it hasn't.

It can be easy to try to lower the bar. *I didn't mean to kill the butterfly . . . It's just a stupid doll . . . Other people have done much worse things . . .* When your conscience is accusing you, it's easy to lawyer up and play your own defense attorney. Yet Jesus uses the opposite method to get you off the hook.

Jesus raises the bar. In John 8, a woman is caught in adultery. Many people assume this famous story is about Jesus lowering his expectations to save her, dismissing the Old Testament law as no longer relevant. Yet as we'll see, he actually walks us *through* Old Testament adultery law, raising the bar so high that we all find ourselves under it—and in need of mercy.

Raising the bar is an expression for making things harder, increasing the competition, establishing stronger criteria for success. When a pole-vaulter sails successfully over the bar, they raise it. Similarly, your boss establishes higher benchmarks at work. The latest iPhone model sets a new standard for the industry. Your sister's boyfriend tries to impress the parents at dinner—*he's gonna have to raise the bar to win their approval!*

You might assume God being on your side means he's going to lower the bar as much as possible. (*If I put it an inch from the ground, Timmy will hop over it—no problem.*) Perhaps you're tempted to lower the bar for yourself, thinking lighter expectations will make your life easier. Yet this is an illusion—and not the Jesus way. Jesus isn't a pushover who makes things as easy as possible.

Jesus is like a pole-vault coach who raises the bar so high no one can transcend it—in order to make way for grace. Thankfully, it's a grace he's more than glad to bring. The woman caught in adultery is a picture of *us* as the church. When you're battling guilt and regret, the God who is on your side can show you how to set your conscience free.

❊ ❊ ❊

Jesus is teaching in the temple courts when the legal experts bring him a case:

> The teachers of the law and the Pharisees brought in a woman caught in adultery. They made her stand before the group and said to Jesus, "Teacher, this woman was caught in the act of adultery. In the Law Moses commanded us to stone such women. Now what do you say?" They were using this question as a trap, in order to have a basis for accusing him.[1]

This is a legal scene. The word *law* shows up multiple times. These are teachers of the law, referencing the law of Moses. They approach Jesus while he's teaching in the temple—

presumably about the true meaning of the Law, or Torah, of the Old Testament.

The trial is in session; Jesus is the judge.

It's "a trap," John says. Why? The Roman Empire didn't allow Jewish authorities to carry out the death penalty; that was reserved for Caesar's crew. So the subtext here is this: *Jesus, do you take the law seriously? If so, commanding the death penalty will put you on the wrong side of Rome. If not, you will be invalidated as a messianic contender.* Jesus is facing a choice with Moses on one side and Caesar on the other. Which route will he take? In this test, they're raising the bar to force his hand.

Can he vault it?

Jesus goes the Moses route—only not in the way they expect. He walks through three movements of Old Testament adultery law to convict the woman's accusers and set her free. He's taking the law *more* seriously, teaching us its deeper meaning. He's not lowering the bar; he's raising it—in order to set us free. Let's see how.

MOVEMENT 1: WHERE'S WALDO?

First, the dude is missing. Notice the accusation: "This woman was *caught in the act* of adultery."[2] News flash: It takes two to tango. If they were "caught in the act," where's the guy? The law of Moses requires that *both* parties be brought ("both the adulterer and the adulteress").[3] It actually emphasizes the guy: "If a man commits adultery with another man's wife . . ."[4] Jesus asks them to bring the witnesses who saw the act—and nobody steps forward.[5] A witness would have needed to identify the man as well.

Something is seriously wrong. The accusation here is not masturbation but adultery, not a solo act but something requiring a partner. Was she set up? Are they protecting their friend? We don't know, but we do know one thing: They're selectively applying the law.

Where's Waldo?

Jesus confronts the double standard. Ancient cultures like Rome gave men permission to sleep around. Adultery was seen as an offense against the husband, not against the wife.[6] Yet God's law raised the bar on the ancient world, proclaiming adultery was an offense *against God*—whether by husband or wife.[7] It called out powerful men—like Judah and King David—for their unjust violations.[8] God's law leveled the playing field before him.

Jesus taps into this radical vein of Old Testament law, which the teachers of the law standing before him conveniently ignore.

Have you ever been crushed under the weight of a double standard? Felt the sting of a one-sided accusation from others when they were unwilling to apply the same level of critique to themselves? I know I have; it hurts.

What's the accused woman feeling in this moment? I imagine a mix of emotions:

- Humiliation: the embarrassment of being dragged half naked before the crowds in front of city hall.
- Shame: *I messed up; I really did what they're accusing me of. If only I could take it back.*
- Fear: *I'm about to die before this angry mob of powerful men.*
- Anger: *Other people were a part of this situation; why am I the only one getting punished? I'm a pawn in their power play.*

Have you ever been publicly exposed? Had your stupid mistake go viral and been doxed in full view of the crowds? Felt the wild concoction of humiliation, shame, fear, and anger coursing through your veins? Stared into the eyes of an onlooking mob and wondered whether God is standing there with them?

Sometimes you don't go running to Jesus; sometimes you get dragged kicking and screaming to him. Will Jesus choose mercy or Moses, grace or truth? Jesus says, *You wanna do Moses? Let's do Moses.*

OWN YOUR JUNK

The woman's executioners are focusing on what's wrong with her and ignoring what's wrong with themselves. They're using her as a scapegoat under the power of their double standard. They're turning a blind eye to their own hypocrisy, posturing, and manipulation. They're weaponizing outrage to boost their reputation. The problem isn't that they're putting her under the bar; it's that they're excluding themselves from being under it.

Elsewhere in his teaching, Jesus confronts this hypocrisy:

> Why do you look at the speck of sawdust in your brother's eye and pay no attention to the plank in your own eye? How can you say to your brother, "Let me take the speck out of your eye," when all the time there is a plank in your own eye? You hypocrite, first take the plank out of your own eye, and then you will see clearly to remove the speck from your brother's eye.[9]

We find faults in others more readily than we find them in ourselves. We put a microscope to our enemies' flaws but refuse to put a mirror to our own. Don't believe me? Spend ten minutes on cable news, pundit podcasts, or the dumpster fire that is X (formerly known as Twitter). Our side of the aisle can do no wrong, but we hold the other tribe to a higher standard. Yet people who live in glass houses should be wary of throwing stones.

Something powerful happens when we own our junk before pointing at someone else's. Marriage has been my mentor in this. Even when I'm only 10 percent at fault and my wife 90 percent (*okay, honestly, it's usually the other way around*), something powerful happens when I start by owning my 10 percent. The atmosphere changes. Defenses come down. We move *toward* each other. Reconciliation is possible.

The Jesus way works.

Own your junk first. Start with your plank. The best way to enter a confrontation is to take responsibility for your contribution to the mess. This doesn't mean you ignore their side. Jesus doesn't say, *Don't help your brother remove the speck from his eye.* He just says, *Deal with your log first so that you can see clearly to address the problem on his side.*

Why does your posture shift when you raise the bar? Because people who need mercy are much quicker to give mercy. When you recognize you've been forgiven much, you forgive much. So turn the pointing finger of accusation toward the bull's-eye on your own chest. Trade the microscope for a mirror.

MOVEMENT 2: THE FIRST STONE

Jesus says, "Let anyone of you who is without sin be the first to throw a stone at her."[10] This brings us to the second movement of Old Testament law: You needed at least two eyewitnesses who saw the act. In Deuteronomy 17, the two eyewitnesses were to be the first to throw a stone.[11] In rabbinic law, the spouse couldn't be included as one of those witnesses (to prevent false accusations from other motives).[12] If the witnesses were found to have lied or entrapped the accused (as appears likely here in John 8), they were liable to the same punishment.[13]

Why this first-stone policy? It deterred a mob mentality. Think about it: You had to put your money where your mouth was—with your own life on the line. And the hardest stone to throw is the first. You had to look into the eyes of the accused, see their helpless fear, with their fate in your hands. It's easy to join the avalanche once there's momentum.

Mobs are easy to join but hard to start.

When Jesus says, "any one of you who is without sin," he's referring first and foremost to this particular scenario. He's not necessarily saying they need to be perfect in order to carry out the law. He's saying, *Whoever of you has no sin—no fault, no liability—in the accusation of this woman, make the first move.* He's confronting their double standard, calling out the entrapment, spotlighting their own liability under the law.[14]

Jesus doesn't go *around* the law; he goes *through* it. He doesn't lower the bar so the woman can jump over it; he raises the bar so her accusers find themselves under it. He doesn't *excuse* the woman's sin; he *exposes* her accusers' sin. Bob Dylan echoes Jesus: "Everybody must get stoned."[15]

God raises the bar to make way for grace. As Romans 11:32 puts it, "God has consigned *all* to disobedience, that he may have mercy on all."[16] God doesn't say, *You don't deserve punishment.* He says, *You all deserve punishment—and the reason I've raised the bar is so that my mercy will not be based on your behavior but rather be freely given to all who will receive it.*

We often lower the bar so everyone can hop over it. Our culture lowers the standard to make sure everyone's a winner. (*Everyone gets a trophy.*) Yet Jesus raises the bar—and raises it so high that everyone comes underneath it.

Take sexual ethics, for example. That's the subject here in John 8, and we still face this tension today: Mercy or law? Grace or truth? On one side, some Christians hold a high bar, but it can make them judgmental. They rightly say, *Save sex for marriage,* but wrongly look down on the sexually broken in our culture. They rightly uphold sexual integrity but wrongly become prudish in their approach. They wisely say divorce cracks the beautiful image of Christ and the church but become naïve to the circumstances that permit a battered or cheated-on spouse to separate.[17] They rightly say adultery is a horror that God hates yet miss out on the redemptive vision of our gracious God, who pursues *us* as an adulterous spouse.

On the other side, some Christians lower the bar and become lax in faithfulness to Jesus. They say porn is no big deal and miss how it powerfully manipulates the plasticity of their brain, lowers their view of the opposite sex, and can lead them into all kinds of relational dysfunction and distance from God.[18] They hop on Tinder for a one-night stand and sin against their own body while misusing another person.[19] They redefine marriage from the one-flesh union of one man and one woman in lifelong covenant before God and miss how this distorts God's divine design to reflect the marriage of heaven and earth, the mystery of Christ and the church, the coming wedding feast of the Lamb, and the life-giving loyal love of God.[20]

Lighten up, some say. *The law's not a big deal!* Yet it's awkward to say yes to what God says no to. You can drift from God, finding yourself in the distance, on a dangerous path that leads to destruction. You can wind up with guilt and regret, easily hopping over the bar while knowing in your gut that the victory feels cheap.

Jesus's advice? Raise the bar high enough to find yourself under it. You thought porn was wrong. Jesus says if you even look at a woman lustfully, you're guilty.[21] You thought same-sex sexual activity was wrong. Jesus says *American sexuality* is wrong—how we approach it, the idol we've made it.[22] You thought adultery was wrong. Jesus says we *all* have cheated on God with other lovers—making other things ultimate in our lives instead of God.[23]

The solution isn't to *minimize* the faults of others; it's to *maxi-*

mize your own faults. The best way to avoid becoming judgmental is not to *excuse* the sin of others but to *expose* your own sin—under the magnifying glass of God's magnificent grace. Conviction leads to celebration under his merciful gaze. When you raise the bar high enough to find yourself under it, you become willing to extend the mercy you yourself need.

MOVEMENT 3: THE TRIAL OF JEALOUSY

I love what Jesus does next: He "bent down and started to write on the ground with his finger."[24] *Check out that non-anxious presence!* This is a matter of life or death, but Jesus simply stoops down to draw in the dirt. That's how Jesus rolls: asleep in the boat while the disciples are freaking out in the storm; silent before Pilate while threatened with execution; quiet before the crowds as they cry, "Crucify him!"

Jesus is calm before the mob.

Your savior is not stirred by popular opinion, not swayed by the masses. He's stable in whatever storm you're in. You can cling to him when you're surrounded. His confidence is rooted in his Father, who is with him, who is for him, who is on his side. His confidence is rooted in his identity as a beloved son—as *the* beloved Son. When the world is swirling around you, you can find stability in your savior. Hold on to him in the face of hostility.

What does Jesus draw in the dirt? Some speculate he's writing the names of the woman's accusers. Or what they did last night so they'd shudder at the thought of it coming to light. Personally, I think it's a stick-figure drawing to show off his creative prowess. Just kidding . . .

Jesus is actually writing something much more significant to the message of this passage. I'd suggest he's turning to the third and final movement of adultery law. As theologian Alastair Roberts observes,

> Jesus does more than show the inapplicability of the regular adultery law to the woman's case [since there are no qualified witnesses]. He follows the law that does apply to the case of a woman suspected of adultery without qualified witnesses: the Numbers 5 ritual of jealousy.[25]

In the Old Testament, the trial of jealousy was for assessing a spouse suspected of adultery when no two witnesses were present to provide hard evidence. Check out these parallels with the John 8 passage:

- The suspect was brought before the priest at the temple (similar to how this woman is brought before Jesus—who is presented like a priest in the surrounding passage—"in the temple courts").[26]
- The priest swept dirt from the ground into an earthen cup filled with holy water and wrote down the curses of the Law against the suspect (similar to how Jesus here writes in the dirt, presumably—against this Old Testament backdrop—regarding the accusation against the woman).[27]
- The curses were then mixed into the holy water in the earthen vessel (similar to how Jesus has just been depicted as the earthen vessel containing Living Water from the true temple).[28]
- Next, a grain offering of barley was burnt on the altar (similar to how Jesus has just been depicted, through a miracle with barley bread, as the Bread of Life who offers himself sacrificially for his wayward and needy people).[29]
- Finally, the accused would drink the bitter water, and it

would surface their guilt or innocence. If they were guilty, their belly would "swell" and thigh "fall away" in "bitter pain." If innocent, they would go free to be fruitful. (Jesus *does* surface the woman's guilt—telling her to "go and sin no more"—yet doesn't condemn her. More on that in a moment. Interestingly, Jesus's test *also* brings hidden guilt to light—the guilt of her accusers—as he walks through the law of Moses to expose them before its elevated bar.)[30]

Whoa, that ancient ritual is crazy! Am I alone in thinking this? It sounds archaic to modern ears. Let me offer a few observations, however, that I find helpful to put it in its ancient context: First, the ritual seems more likely to render an innocent verdict than a guilty one. If you drank some water with dirt mixed in (*like my messy kids often do on camping trips*), I imagine it wouldn't taste great. Yet I wouldn't naturally expect the crazy symptoms, like your belly expanding and thigh falling off, outside divine intervention. The point seems to be rendering innocence unless Yahweh intervened to convict.

Second, the elements in this ritual seem symbolic: water for purity, dirt for bitterness, grain for thanksgiving. Indeed, biblical scholars note how this ritual is based on the golden calf incident of Exodus 32, when Israel first cheated on God (idolatry is understood as adultery in the Bible). Moses smashed the stone tablets of the Ten Commandments—which God had just written with his divine finger[31]—that condemned both idolatry and adultery. Moses then ground the bovine idol into dust, mixing the dirt with water and forcing the wayward people to drink the bitter water. (*I love that image: Later that afternoon the nation was peeing the golden calf all over the desert.*)

Moses held trial. God's bride was found guilty, yet he would find a way to set her free.

Third and finally, a jealous spouse is dangerous. If a husband suspected his wife of adultery, he could mistreat, abuse, or even kill her. (The tragic reality of domestic violence shows how common such behavior still is today—especially when jealousy is present.) Putting discernment into God's hands, rather than those of a jealous husband, could clear a suspected spouse in the eyes of the community and put pressure on the husband not to take vengeance into his own hands.

Back to John 8: Jesus is presented as the Great High Priest, who the adulterous woman is brought before. Jesus is Yahweh in the flesh, who writes with his finger on the earth like those stone tablets of old.[32] Jesus is the Living Water, who stirs the dirt of accusation to discern her guilt or innocence. Jesus is the Bread of Life, who will offer himself at the cross for her. Jesus is the true temple, in whose courts her judgment is determined.

Jesus will drink the bitter cup to set her free.

The woman is us. She is not only a historic individual but also—like all of John's key characters—a representative of a greater reality. She is like a stained glass window into the bride of Christ, the people of God. When you were dragged into court and thrown down by your accusers—led by your arch accuser, the devil—they threatened to condemn you to death. Yet as you lifted your eyes to the Judge, you surprisingly found yourself in the presence of the Lover of your soul. The only One who *could* condemn you bore your condemnation to set you free.

He brings conviction without condemnation.

CONVICTION VERSUS CONDEMNATION

After Jesus walks through all three movements of adultery law, what is the result?

Jesus was left alone with the woman standing before him. Jesus stood up and said to her, "Woman, where are they? Has no one condemned you?" She said, "No one, Lord." And Jesus said, "Neither do I condemn you; go, and from now on sin no more."[33]

Jesus convicts her ("sin no more") but doesn't condemn her ("Neither do I condemn"). He exposes her guilt—in order to flood it with grace.

Jesus takes your sin seriously. Don't misunderstand: God being on your side doesn't mean he's lax toward your disobedience. Christ knows how your sin alienates you from God and hurts those around you. He pulls your misdeed into the light in order to set you free from it. He calls you to repent in order to restore you.

Have you been minimizing disobedience in your life? Jesus loves you too much to downplay your rebellion. He loves you too much to endorse your wayward ways. He's jealous for you, desiring all your affection.

What does the woman see in Christ's eyes? As she looks into his face, what emotions does she encounter? What disposition does she discover? As she sees him seeing her, she sees love in its purest form. As she stares into his holy gaze, she encounters the Artist who made her, receiving his divine affection that floods the world. I imagine she catches her breath and cries for joy.

She encounters the God who is on her side.

Jesus doesn't beat you up over your past; instead, he fights for your future. "God did not send his Son into the world to condemn the world, but to save the world through him."[34] Christ is out not to tear you down but to build you up in himself. He's out to forgive your willful unfaithfulness, to make you wonderfully fruitful again. And he's the right one to do it.

There's one thing the woman *doesn't* see in Christ's eyes: sin. Out of the whole crowd there that day, he's the one person who *could have* thrown the first stone. Yet he doesn't. His perfect humanity gives him a legitimate right to judge. Yet he delights to save.

The seriousness of your sin points to the splendor of your savior. As the late pastor Tim Keller liked to say, "The gospel is this: We are more sinful and flawed in ourselves than we ever dared believe, yet at the very same time we are more loved and accepted in Jesus Christ than we ever dared hope."[35] When you feel the immense weight of your guilt displaced by the immanent gravity of his grace, it lets down your guard and leads you to worship. Do you wonder where this judgment and mercy meet?

Look to the cross.

TAKING OUR PLACE

Jesus can set you free because he took your place. In John 8, the religious leaders place the woman "in the midst" of the crowd.[36] When they depart, she's left "in the midst" with Jesus.[37] The religious leaders then try to stone *Jesus* after his ensuing teaching, and he departs "through the midst of them."[38] That term *midst* is rare in John's gospel and ties this sequence together: Jesus has narratively taken the place of the woman, surrounded by her accusers, who now seek to stone him.[39]

She won't be killed by them—but he will.

The cross is where this term next appears, as Jesus is crucified "in the midst" of two condemned criminals.[40] This intertextual link loads John 8 with atonement overtones. The accusers' attempt to stone Jesus foreshadows the cross, where Jesus will take the place of the adulterous woman and, by extension, the community she represents: us, as the church. Jesus is our substitute who bears our condemnation.

Jesus takes our place.

One other instance of foreshadowing: John 8 opens with Jesus going up to the Mount of Olives at night, then into the temple courts at dawn.[41] This mirrors the eve of his crucifixion, when Jesus will again go up to the Mount of Olives to pray in its Garden of Gethsemane as he prepares to drink the bitter cup of condemnation. He'll then be arrested, dragged before the high priest, and placed in the midst of his accusers. The woman won't be crushed by her accusers.

But he will.

Like olives crushed by stones, he'll be crushed under the weight of our accusation—and the healing oil of his Spirit will flow. We are the woman caught in the wrong. We've cheated on God, and the accuser condemns us, but Jesus takes our place. This means "there is now no condemnation for those who are in Christ Jesus."[42] Jesus broke the power of the law not by lowering its demands but by raising them and fulfilling them himself.

Like a butterfly, Jesus is the beautiful creature crushed under the weight of the stone we rolled over his grave. We vandalized his body and stole his life; ironically, in so doing, he broke our curse of condemnation. "Christ redeemed us from the curse of the law by becoming a curse for us—for it is written, 'Cursed is everyone who is hanged on a tree.'"[43] Jesus was cursed, mocked, and flogged as he bore our condemnation.

So when you're humiliated and rejected, you can look up into the eyes of the One who was dragged naked before the mob, who was surrounded, humiliated, and rejected. You can look up into the eyes of Love and see him seeing you.

When you're battling guilt and regret, you can look up to the One who was hung "in the midst" of the condemned—to take your place. He won the battle. "It is finished."[44] He did it to set you free.

You can be set free because Jesus didn't lower the bar; he

raised it—then won the victory for you. The One who *could* jump it, who *did* meet all the requirements of the law, bore its punishment on your behalf.

Jesus drank your bitter cup of guilt and regret to set you free and make you fruitful. He did it because he's jealous for you. He wants to bring us—his once-wayward bride—home with him, to wash us clean and dwell with us forever. He loves you that much. He's that radically on your side.

9

OPEN YOUR EYES

When You Can't See Meaning or Purpose

Earlier, I shared about my eyesight struggles. I now want to share with you the story of Ursula Mercz, the first recorded patient with Anton's syndrome. When this nineteenth-century seamstress went to visit the doctor, as Adam Grant recounts in his book *Think Again,*

> she complained of headaches, back pain, and dizziness severe enough that she could no longer work. Over the following month her condition deteriorated. She struggled to locate the glass of water she put next to her bed. She couldn't find the door to her room. She walked directly into her bed frame.[1]

Here's the crazy part: She claimed she could see just fine. Dr. Gabriel Anton was confused by this mysterious case. Ursula insisted she saw the objects in front of her, but she was unable to describe them. She couldn't distinguish light from dark. Even when her eyesight faded completely, she remained in denial. Dr. Anton observed,

It was now extremely astonishing that the patient did not notice her massive and later complete loss of her ability to see. . . . She was mentally blind to her blindness.[2]

More cases emerged in the century to come. In what is now known as Anton's syndrome, patients are blind but claim to be able to see. They bump into things and don't recognize faces but may explain it away, saying, "It seems dark in here"—unaware of the gravity of their condition.

While this is a rare physical condition, it has a common spiritual counterpart. In John 9, Jesus confronts those who are spiritually blind yet claim to be able to see. It's possible to stand before the Light of the World yet remain in the dark. It's possible to bump into God's redemptive work and see it as an obstacle, missing out on what he's doing right in front of you. Fortunately, however, Jesus is a better physician than Dr. Anton.

He can open your eyes.

LOOKING FORWARD

Jesus and his disciples come across a man blind from birth. His disciples ask, "Rabbi, who sinned, this man or his parents, that he was born blind?"[3] The disciples are looking *backward* to try to explain why this tragic thing happened. Pop culture at the time thought a baby could sin in the womb (*kicking Mom's belly too hard?*). Maybe Dad cheated on his taxes or Mom was the local gossip girl. This is common: When bad things happen, we look for someone to blame.

Yet Jesus looks forward. He responds, "Neither this man nor his parents sinned . . . but this happened so that the works of God might be displayed in him."[4] Jesus calls them to look *ahead* to see what God's going to do through it. The Messiah doesn't play the blame game ("Neither this man nor his parents sinned"); rather, he plays God's fame game ("that the works of God might be displayed in him"). When you can't see meaning in the midst of your suffering, Jesus gently turns your face to look toward the future.

The purpose of your pain is the glory of God.

I found myself looking backward recently. When my eyesight began deteriorating, I wanted to know *why* I was losing my vision. Was it the fault of genetics? Was it because I stared at the sun as a kid, read in the dark growing up, or didn't clean my contacts regularly enough? Was it due to the Covid I caught a month before the symptoms started? Or the delayed impact of an eye injury earlier that year? Was it a fluke? Or an eventuality that was unavoidable?

I wanted a reason.

Are you stuck looking backward, trying to place blame for the suffering you're in? *Was it their fault or mine? Was I wrong, or was I wronged? Did the relationship end because I let it go too far too fast or because they became a jerk? Is my chronic pain due to my poor diet or that distracted driver that hit me? Are my adult kids no longer talking to me because I pushed them too hard growing up or because they're in a rebellious phase?* It's easy to get stuck in the blame game.

Jesus wants to change your questions. On a foundation of trust, you can begin to ask, *God, what do you want to do through this? What kind of intimacy do you want to cultivate with me? What kind of glory do you want to display through me?*

Will you accept this invitation? Looking back can breed bitterness, confusion, and despair, while looking forward can cultivate trust, hope, and love. You can pray, *Jesus, I want to see you in this. Open my eyes to see your glory, my ears to hear your voice, and my heart to know your presence. Restore my vision.*

RESTORING THE IMAGE

Jesus uses an interesting method to open the man's eyes:

> He spit on the ground, made some mud with the saliva, and put it on the man's eyes. "Go," he told him, "wash in the Pool of Siloam" (this word means "Sent"). So the man went and washed, and came home seeing.[5]

What's up with the saliva? I love how the word "spit" (*ptuō*) is, in the original language, like the sound you actually make—*phtooey*—when you hock a loogie. Jesus *does* give living water (we saw this earlier in John 7), so this liquid from his lips restores the man's eyes. But there's something more going on here: an echo of a foundational Old Testament story.

In Genesis 2, God created Adam from the clay. A mist watered the face of the dry ground, and the Maker plunged his hands into the resulting mud—a mixture of mist and dust—to form the first human, exhaled breath into his lungs, and brought him to life. The Spirit is associated with the *mist* of this Old Testament passage (as well as the *breath* Yahweh breathed into Adam's lungs).[6] Fast-forward to John 9: Jesus is Yahweh in the flesh, who mixes the mist from his mouth with the dry ground to make mud and restore this child of Adam.

The blind man is a picture of Adam broken and remade. This is all of us: cracked under the weight of a fallen world, walking in darkness, yet able to be restored by the hands of a loving savior.

Adam was made to be something more: an image of God. Follow me for a minute. In the ancient world, craftsmen made idols in their workshops. The image was still considered lifeless, however, until a series of rites was performed on a riverbank, in a garden, and finally in a temple. The image was then considered alive, indwelt by the presence of the god.[7]

Now, this was a pagan practice—not a biblical one. God condemned such idolatry of the surrounding nations. Yet biblical scholars observe how Yahweh's creation of Adam in Genesis 2 mirrors this pattern: the river, garden, and temple imagery are all at play in Eden.[8] There are differences: Adam was made of flesh and bone, not wood and stone. Yet there are similarities: Adam was crafted by the hands of God and indwelt with his breath. God is the master craftsman, who placed humanity in his temple-garden to be a divine representative.[9]

Adam was an image of God.

The point? You were made to be an image of God. He doesn't want us to *make* divine images, because we *are* divine images. That's the problem with idols (the Hebrew word for "image," *selem,* can also be translated "idol"[10]). You were made by Yahweh, not puny human hands. You were made of flesh and bone, not wood and stone. You were made to represent the Creator, not false gods. God has placed you, like a living statue, in the garden of his world to display his glory in creation.

The ritual that was used to turn an image into a living statue (in the eyes of the ancient nations surrounding Israel) was considered a kind of cleansing ceremony. As they washed the image, one scholar observes, they believed this rite "activated the image's senses and caused the human senses (smell, taste, seeing and hearing) to become enlivened so that the image became both human-like and a representation of the divine."[11]

Again, this was a pagan practice, not a biblical one. Yet God used a similar pattern in Scripture when he cleansed Isaiah's lips to make the prophet his spokesman and representative.[12] Arguably, Jesus is riffing on this theme here: cleansing the image to open his senses. This doesn't mean the blind man is previously not in the image of God. (*By no means! All humanity is made in the divine image.*) But it means, symbolically, Jesus is out to activate us as his representatives and restore us as his image-bearers.[13]

The blind man is a picture of us all. We are like sightless statues: We have eyes but can't see. On a spiritual level, we're blind to the glory of God. Yet Jesus has come to turn the lights on. "The people walking in darkness have seen a great light," the prophet Isaiah foresaw.[14] "The true light that gives light to everyone was coming into the world," John celebrates, and "we have *seen* his glory."[15] Jesus has come to open your eyes—so you can look into the gaze of the Artist and see him seeing you.

Behold the glory of God.

WASHED AND SENT

Jesus tells the blind man to "wash in the Pool of Siloam," located by the King's Garden in Jerusalem.[16] Like that ancient image-making ceremony, its water will wash the mud from his eyes—to establish him as an image in the garden of the King. The pool of Siloam is also associated with the future river of life, the Holy Spirit.[17] Like that ancient image-making ceremony, Jesus will wash this man through the power of his Spirit to establish him in the temple of God.

The pool of Siloam is a picture of our baptism. We're told its name means "Sent."[18] As the Father sent the Son, and the Son sent the Spirit, so the triune God sends the church as his representatives. We're baptized in the triune name of God—"in the name of the Father and of the Son and of the Holy Spirit"—to bear his name in the world.[19] We rise from the waters of baptism, our eyes opened to behold his glory. We're sent as children of the Father, united as the bride of the Son and born from above by the Spirit, to carry his family name into the world.

We're sent to bear the image.

You're an ambassador. Christ washes you not just to cleanse you from your past but to prepare you for your future. To forge you in the fullness of the image—*his* image—for he himself is "the image of the invisible God."[20] As you're molded into his character, you become not a reflection of some abstract, distant deity but a bearer of the all-encompassing, all-out-pursuing, all-in, life-giving love of God. He sends you as a citizen of his kingdom, a representative of his grace.

This is your highest calling. You were made in the image of God with a destiny to reflect your maker in the world. Our fallen world didn't destroy that calling, but it distorted and damaged it in a variety of ways.

Jesus heals this blind man to give you a sign of what he's come to do for you. None of us experience the full flourishing we were made for. You were born in a dark and fallen world, bumping into things that bruised you and unable to see the radiance of God.

God has entered onto your side, in Christ, to raise the shades and let in the light. Jesus has come to flood the interior of your life with his glory.

NOW I SEE

The religious leaders interrogate the blind man. They try to tear down his testimony and get him to discredit Jesus. They threaten to kick anyone out of the synagogue—the center of their community—who says Jesus is the Messiah. They're in the dark.

This healed man has no apologetics training. He's never read *Mere Christianity* or *The Skeletons in God's Closet* (wink, wink).[21] He can't read. Yet with beautiful simplicity, he tells his story:

He put mud on my eyes . . . and I washed, and now I see. . . .
One thing I do know. I was blind but now I see! . . . Nobody

has ever heard of opening the eyes of a man born blind. If this man were not from God, he could do nothing.[22]

I love how straightforward he is: *I once was blind; now I see.* This man is a model for when you face opposition to your faith: Just fall back on your story. You may not feel like you've read the Bible enough, and you may not have all the answers to all the questions, but you don't need to. You have a story. You have a testimony of your encounter with Jesus. You don't need to get defensive. Simply celebrate what God's done in your life.

Your story is powerful. Elsewhere, John says the saints overcome "by the blood of the Lamb and by the word of their testimony."[23] He doesn't say "by the strength of their muscles and by the brilliance of their arguments." No, when you face opposition, you have these same two dynamic ingredients: the power of what Jesus has done ("the blood of the Lamb") and the power of your own story ("the word of their testimony"). People can nitpick your explanation, but they can't deny your experience. They can't deny the transformation Jesus has accomplished in your life.

Wield your testimony with humility and courage.

The neighborhood is shocked by the man's before and after. "Isn't this the same man?" some ask. "No, he only looks like him," many insist.[24] They can't believe it's the same guy.

How's your before and after? Do people see a difference in your life? The impact Jesus has made? Enough to question, *Can this be the same person?* The man has to insist he's the same guy and points to Jesus to explain the difference. *How is this possible?* "The man they call Jesus."[25]

Who's the hero of your story? Do you highlight your own striving? Your New Year's resolutions and taking responsibility for yourself? Your diet and exercise and long hours at the office? Or is Jesus the hero of your story? Who he is and what he's done?

How he blessed your mess and took responsibility for you when your life was falling apart?

Here's something crazy to me: The healed man still hasn't seen Jesus yet. Think about it. Jesus puts mud on his eyes (*still can't see at this point*) and tells him to go wash in the pool of Siloam (*still needs to walk there*). So, when his eyes are opened, he hasn't yet beheld his healer. He's heard Jesus's voice but hasn't yet seen his face.

How do you testify about someone you haven't seen? You and I have been washed in baptism by Jesus, have heard his voice through his Word, but we haven't yet seen his face. We're still waiting to behold the beatific vision in the kingdom. We've encountered his presence through his Spirit but are still waiting to see him face-to-face. We know now in part but shall then know fully, even as we are fully known.[26]

You can testify to his work in your life. *I haven't yet seen him, but I've experienced him. I've heard his voice. Encountered his Spirit. He's opened my eyes.*

Ironically, the Pharisees *have* seen Jesus but reject him. It's a mistake to think if you only saw Jesus in person, all your doubts would melt away. Jesus is looking for faith, "the assurance of things hoped for, the conviction of things not seen."[27] There's a blessing when you trust him, even though you can't yet see him. As Jesus tells Thomas, later in John,

> Have you believed because you have seen me? Blessed are those who have not seen and yet have believed.[28]

You can trust Jesus, even when it's hard to see what he's doing. You can be like Moses, who endured adversity because "he kept his eyes on the one [true King] who is invisible."[29] You can trust when you're in the valley of the shadow and can't yet see the sunny pastures on the other side. It's powerful when you say,

Jesus, even here I trust you. I know you have me. I may be in the
shadow, but I know sunrise is on its way.

When the collision breaks your body and the doctors say it'll
never be the same . . . When your leaders pressure you to go
against your conscience or be cast out of your community . . .
When your spouse breaks your heart and you're unsure you'll
ever be able to trust again . . . When your future seems uncertain
and you can't see what God is doing . . .

You can trust your savior in the struggle.

HEALING AS JUDGMENT

The religious leaders "cast out" the man, the same term used for
driving out demons.[30] They see him as an enemy, an infection, a
wicked threat to be driven from their synagogue and community. When Jesus fixes one part of your life, don't be surprised if
other parts get harder—like they do for this guy. On the heels of
blessing, there is often a cross to bear. The enemy hates God's
good work in your life and will do anything to spoil it.

Why do the elite cast him out? They look down on him as one
"born in utter sin."[31] How could he have anything to teach them?

The irony is, we were *all* born in utter sin. These cultural
leaders can't see that they also need healing and forgiveness.
They have spiritual Anton's syndrome. They claim to be able to
see, yet they're blind to the Light of the World, who's standing
right in front of them.

As the Great Physician, Jesus calls out their condition:

If you were blind, you would not be guilty of sin; but now that
you claim you can see, your guilt remains.[32]

Jesus declares the healing he just performed is also a judgment on them: "For judgment I have come into this world, so

that the blind will see and those who see will become blind."[33] Jesus's glory is strange: It not only opens the eyes of the blind but also shuts the eyes of the self-righteous. They take offense and ask, "What? Are we blind too?"[34] Jesus responds, *Yep!* Their problem is they think they don't have a problem.

They're in denial of their blindness.

Early researchers of Anton's syndrome were shocked by the ability of patients to make excuses for their condition. Read this description—it sounds a lot like the spiritual condition of Jesus's critics:

> One of the most striking features in the behavior of our patients was their inability to learn from their experiences. As they were not aware of their blindness when they walked about, they bumped into the furniture and walls but did not change their behavior. When confronted with their blindness in a rather pointed fashion, they would either deny any visual difficulty or remark: "It is so dark in the room; why don't they turn the light on?"; "I forgot my glasses," or "My vision is not too good, but I can see all right." The patients would not accept any demonstration or assurance which would prove their blindness.[35]

Are you repeatedly bumping into obstacles in life that you didn't see coming? Do you still make excuses for the bruises of your own making? Are you still pretending the problem is "out there" rather than "in here"?

Don't make excuses for your darkness. Christ wants to shine his light on you. As Helen Keller said, "The only thing worse than being blind is having sight but no vision."[36] The greatest hindrance to your healing is pretending you don't have a problem.

My friend Zach used to think everyone else was the problem. In every story he told, he was the victim. At work, in his family, with the law, in his friendships, with his church. There was always an excuse, always a reason, for his side of the story. Then God's Spirit began gently nudging him to take a closer look within. "I began to realize," he said, "the common denominator in all these stories was me." He grew convicted of his poor character in the collisions he regularly encountered. He had been blind to his own condition.

Yet Jesus opened his eyes.

Stop thinking you can do things on your own. Ask the Great Physician to make you his patient. Jesus loves to heal. Let God touch your eyes through his Word, wash you in baptism through his Spirit, and make you new. When your eyes are opened to Jesus, you behold his brilliance. Jesus is majestic; he's beautiful; he's everything! Let him uncloud your vision so you can gaze on his glory.

Why can't some people see him for who he is? John tells us earlier in his gospel:

> This is the judgment: the light has come into the world, and people loved the darkness rather than the light because their works were evil. For everyone who does wicked things hates the light and does not come to the light, lest his works should be exposed.[37]

Our problem is when we love darkness. When we don't want to be exposed. This is the root of spiritual Anton's syndrome: We don't want to be found out!

Hiding is the biggest enemy to your spiritual life. It causes you to run for cover from the light. The desire, often subconscious, to self-protect will cause you to miss the glory of Jesus staring you in the face. John says this problem runs deeper than what you think in your brain; it's what you love in your heart ("people loved the darkness"). That's the subterranean bunker where the desire for darkness can hide.

The heart of the problem is the problem of the heart.

Don't close the curtains of your heart to block out the Light of the World. Step out of the shadows. Come out of the cave; the sun is shining out here. It's brilliant. Are there secrets you're hiding? Areas you're afraid to have discovered? Join the club! We've all had skeletons buried in the backyard, wickedness we didn't want uncovered. Don't self-protect; turn to Jesus.

The solution is confession. Drag that desire out of the darkness and into the light. Bring your whole self before your savior. Mold festers in the closet but shrivels in the sun. Sunshine is the best disinfectant—and Jesus is the Light of the World. He's come not to lecture you for the darkness that lurks within but to draw you into the light of day with him.

When you know he's on your side, you no longer need to hide. When you realize he's for you, you can bring your darkest secrets before him. You can emerge from self-preservation and embrace vulnerability, transparency, and divine protection in the arms of grace. You can exit the claustrophobic darkness of your underground tunnels and breathe deep before the glory of the Son.

LIGHT OF THE WORLD

The healing of the blind man is the sixth sign of John's gospel. How does this event point to Jesus's death and resurrection? At the cross, the Savior's eyelids fell like a curtain. The Light of the World stepped down into our darkness as the sun went out and the pitch black took hold. His vicarious humanity went blind to the shining face of God.[38] This was not because of his sin, however, but that the glory of God might be revealed.

While the darkness overpowered his humanity, his divinity shone the light of the Father's love within the cavernous shadows of our grave. "The light shines in the darkness, and the darkness has not overcome it."[39] He harrowed hell as he slept in the somber realm of Sheol. The ray of eternal love shone on us, united with us in death to raise us up in life.

Then, on the third day, Christ opened his eyes. He awoke from his slumber and emerged from the twilight of the tomb in blazing glory. The new creation has dawned with the rising of the Son. In his countenance, we now behold the radiance of God.

The opening of the blind man's eyes is a living parable of resurrection.

You want to know my favorite part of this passage? Jesus sees the blind man before the blind man ever sees Jesus. This strikes me as so, so beautiful. "Passing by," John 9 opens, "[Jesus] saw a man blind from birth."[40] I skipped over this important detail earlier, but the Hebrew equivalent of that phrase "passing by" is famously used for the glory of Yahweh passing by Moses ("I will cause all my goodness to *pass by* you") and for the Lord's presence passing by other figures, like the suffering Job, in the biblical story.[41] Here again, the glory of God—Yahweh in the flesh—*passes by* this blind man. And stops to see him.

Before mud is placed on this man's eyes . . . Before he hears Jesus's voice . . . Before he washes in the pool . . . Before the light breaks through his darkness . . . Jesus moves toward him with compassion.

Jesus sees him.

Jesus sees you. This is the beauty of the gospel: God sees you, even when you can't see him. The Light of the World is still shining, even when you find yourself on the far side of the moon.[42] Jesus has compassion on you and moves toward you, even when you feel in the dark.

You might be asking, *Do you see me, God? Do you notice me here in the shadows? Do you hear my cries at night? Have you abandoned me, or are you truly for me? Are you on my side?*

Jesus's sixth sign answers "Yes." He sees you. Even when it doesn't look like there's meaning or purpose to the suffering you're in, he sees you. Even in your confusion, stuckness, and frustration, his gaze is set on you. Your heart might feel cold, but his is warm with affection and compassion toward you. You might feel distant from Christ, but his presence is moving toward you.

The Great I Am sees you where you are.

The time is coming when you will see him too. It may be in the mundane, when his Spirit opens the eyes of your heart to encounter him afresh in your situation. It may be in the miraculous, when his Spirit moves with resurrection power to bring emotional or physical healing. It will definitely be in his eternal kingdom, when at last you gaze into his glorious eyes.

And find him gazing back at you.

"You have now seen him," Jesus tells the (formerly) blind man when he finally encounters Jesus face-to-face in the finale of John 9. "In fact, he is the one speaking with you."[43] This moment foreshadows the beatific vision, your eschatological destiny, when you—astounded and agape—behold the glory of God in the face of Christ.

Your eyes will be opened.

How does the man respond? "He worshiped him."[44] This is it. This is how you respond when you see Jesus as he truly is. You fall to your knees in worship. You rejoice in awestruck wonder. You magnify the Light of the World, who opened your eyes. You no longer say simply, "I once was blind; now I see," but you all the more declare, "Now I have seen *him*."

The day is coming when you shall open your eyes to the dawn

of the new creation and exuberantly declare that you once saw through a glass darkly, you once walked through a valley of shadows, you once endured hostility and storms, you once were interrogated and cast out of community, you once held "the assurance of things hoped for, the conviction of things not seen" . . . but at last those days are over. The radiant city has come:

> The city does not need the sun or the moon to shine on it, for the glory of God gives it light, and the Lamb is its lamp. The nations will walk by its light, and the kings of the earth will bring their splendor into it. On no day will its gates ever be shut, for there will be no night there.[45]

The Light of the World shall overcome the darkness. "I once was blind," we shall sing, "but now I see."[46]

10

DISCOVER YOUR DEFENDER

When They Should Have Protected You but Didn't

David asked to meet for coffee. He wanted to process some events from his childhood. Growing up, David's family trusted Marty. He was their pastor and a close family friend. Marty talked eloquently about God and had a good reputation. He lived in the neighborhood and their kids loved to play together, so David spent many days playing in their front yard, eating snacks in their kitchen, and sleeping over at their house. Especially given the trust David's family put in Marty, it came as a shock when they discovered he had been molesting David for years.

As David faced this reality from his past, he experienced deep sadness and loss. *I wonder what role my abuse plays in my struggle with clinical depression.* He wrestled with trust. *I tend to isolate myself and struggle with vulnerability and intimacy in relationships.* He wrestled with anger. *How could Marty do that? Does Jesus's call to forgive mean I need to just forget and pretend it never happened?* He wrestled with God. *Where were you when I was mistreated? God, do you see me? Do you care about the pain I've endured?*

My heart breaks for my friend. What he went through was horrific, unjust, and evil in the eyes of God. It has impacted his life for decades. I feel sad and angry on his behalf. There is a particular kind of pain that comes when church leaders, who are supposed to represent Christ to us, instead betray our trust.

Where do you go when someone you look up to misuses their power against you? When a father, whose hands are designed to guide and guard you, instead leaves bruises and scars on your body? When a pastor, who is called to shepherd you, harms you? When a friend, who is supposed to have your back, turns and walks away? Where do you go when they *should* protect you but don't? These experiences leave craters in your soul.

It can be hard to trust again. Easy to feel like you're all alone. Natural to put up walls and not let anyone get too close. David wrestled with all these things, yet didn't want to stay there. How do we avoid retreating into cynicism, suspicion, and isolation? Is there a way back to an abundant life?

In John 10, Jesus describes himself as the Good Shepherd. Let's see how he can meet you in your vulnerability, help you name the evil done to you, define the marks of good leadership, guide you through your valley of the shadow, and teach you to trust again. Whatever you've been through, he can bring you to greener pastures on the other side.

THE SHEPHERD-KING

What comes to mind when you hear the word *shepherd*? I have to confess, I imagine a carefree wanderer, whistling through the fields. Ragged and rugged, with relatively few responsibilities. (*Sheep can't be that difficult, right?*) So when Jesus calls himself the Good Shepherd, it might surprise you to know this was, back in the day, a leadership image.

Kings and other leaders are referred to as shepherds in the

Bible. God installed King David, saying, "You shall be shepherd of my people Israel."[1] His royal legacy was later celebrated: "With upright heart he shepherded [Israel]."[2] Ezekiel confronted the leaders of Israel as *bad shepherds,* and held out hope for the coming rule of God's *good shepherd.*[3] Good leadership reflected God, who "led out his people [from Egypt] like sheep and guided them in the wilderness like a flock."[4] Leadership was a chance to image God's good character. In other words, it was a high calling with a lot of responsibility.

Leadership isn't for the faint of heart.

In the ancient Near East, the shepherd's staff was a symbol of royalty. It symbolized the *purpose* of leadership: to serve, guide, care for, and protect their people. Bad leaders were in it to serve and enrich themselves; good shepherds were in it to care for their people. If the title "king" speaks to the *authority* of a ruler, "shepherd" speaks to their ideal *heart.*

God's ways work. Simon Sinek, the popular leadership guru, wanted to know why some organizations thrive with trust and teamwork, while others fight, fragment, and fall apart. Why will Marines, for example, famously entrust their lives to one another with thick bonds of camaraderie? Here's how one Marine Corps general answered: "Officers eat last."

During meals, junior marines eat first while senior officers head to the back of the line. "What's symbolic in the chow hall is deadly serious on the battlefield," Sinek observes. "Great leaders sacrifice their own comfort—even their own survival—for the good of those in their care."[5] Sinek explores how servant leadership creates healthy teams and thriving organizations, a philosophy summarized in his three-word catchphrase.

"Leaders eat last."

That sounds like a good leader I know, who "did not come to be served, but to serve, and to give his life as a ransom for many."[6]

Let me suggest Sinek's leadership principle is rooted in something deeper than statistics or the chemical reactions in our brains. Keep digging; there's gold down there. Servant leadership is rooted in the character of the greatest leader the world has ever known: Jesus is the Shepherd-King.

The King of the universe comes not to take from you but that you "may have life, and have it to the full."[7] He doesn't run from the battle but "lays down his life for the sheep."[8] He's out not to use you but to serve you. He's in it not to flatter his ego but to fend off your enemies. His leadership is marked by sacrifice, protection, and care. That's why servant leadership works; it echoes the heart of the world's true King.

Jesus confronts bad shepherds. He calls out rulers who love to "lord it over" others, saying, "It shall not be so among you."[9] Jesus's followers are not to jockey for position: "Instead, whoever wants to become great among you must be your servant."[10] *Stop fighting to be at the front of the line*, the Good Shepherd is saying. *Get behind the counter and serve.*

Now, positions come with real responsibilities. I'm not saying the mayor should spend all day scrubbing toilets—that wouldn't serve the city well. Yet a good heart check for leaders is, *Am I in it for me or for them?* Shepherd-kings aim to serve.

THIEVES, ROBBERS, AND HIRED HANDS

Jesus confronts three types of bad leaders in John 10. First, he calls out "thieves and robbers" who climb into the sheep pen "to kill and steal and destroy." Thieves (*kleptai*) were known for stealth: using deceit, treachery, and secrecy to take what they wanted.[11] (Later in John's gospel, this same word is used for Judas, who steals from the kitty and sells out Jesus for thirty pieces of silver.[12]) Robbers (*lēstai*), on the other hand, were violent: brigands who would assault you on the open road, using weapons, force, and intimidation to get their way.[13]

Maybe you've faced thieves in your life, who operated in stealth. The boss who went behind your back. The mentor who deceived you to take what they wanted. The gossip who leveraged people's trust and manipulated their network to tarnish your reputation.

Or maybe you've had robbers overpower you. The stepdad who used force to get his way. The uncle who used threats to intimidate you. The abuser who scared you into silence, saying, "If you ever tell anyone, I'll . . ."

Jesus says such actions are evil. He doesn't sugarcoat it or beat around the bush. They are pawns of Satan—the Thief with a capital *T*—who is out to steal, kill, and destroy.

Jesus also confronts a third type of bad leader: "the hired hand," who sees a wolf coming and "abandons the sheep and runs away."[14] This is the father who walked away. The mother too consumed with her own trauma to see you in your pain. The fairweather friend who bailed when the pressure hit. The mentor who left you hanging. This is the loss from abandonment.

They were supposed to protect you. But they didn't, so now what?

You can go to Jesus. He knows firsthand what you've experienced. He was abused and abandoned. He was beaten and betrayed. He was stabbed in the back and pierced in the side. He was left hanging, then ditched all alone in the grave. There's an intimacy to be found with him in your suffering.

Jesus names what was done to you as evil. This is the first step toward healing. You have to be able to name what was done to you as wrong—even if only to yourself. In my own life, this was one of the hardest things. Growing up, I assumed the problem was always me. By the time I was an adult, I had spent a lifetime learning how to walk on eggshells, avoid the bullies, and duck aside when I felt in the way. It was easy to assume the problem was me. I didn't want to upset the applecart or be an inconvenience. Old habits die hard.

Yet Jesus addresses bad leadership. He names thieves, robbers, and hired hands. It helps when others name as wrong what was done to you. When the father who failed you calls to repent. When the mentor who hurt you owns it. When the church leaders who mishandled your situation reach out to apologize.

Yet even if those who have hurt you never identify their wrongs as wrong, Jesus does. There are leaders in my life who I anticipate never will. Ironically, it's often those who've inflicted the deepest wounds. But I've found you can bring Jesus your sorrow. He welcomes your sadness and your anger at the injustice you've endured. He can handle it. There's a solace to be found in your communion with him.

In the care of your good shepherd, the stark contrast with the thieves, robbers, and hired hands will never be clearer. His presence throws their bad leadership into dramatic relief. Sometimes it's not until you experience the good that you realize how awful the bad really was. Sometimes it's when the lamb is in the embrace of the shepherd that its nervous system calms down and the threat is most vividly seen. Sometimes it's in the presence of King Jesus that you can see more clearly, and name more directly, what was done to you.

That's not the final step; it's a vital first step on the journey back to green pastures.

ON CHURCH HURT

Sometimes the deepest hurt can come from church. The word *pastor* means "shepherd." So a pastor is supposed to represent

Christ, the Good Shepherd. Wounds from church leaders sting so badly because of the gravity of who they're meant to represent. It's one thing to get mugged by a criminal; it's another by an agent for Jesus. It's one thing to get hit by a boxer; it's another by a priest who does it in God's name.

I've heard it said the only thing worse than wolves disguised as sheep are those disguised as shepherds.[15] My friend Jeremiah was molested throughout his childhood by a priest.[16] Sure, God calls out the Harvey Weinsteins of Hollywood, but does he hire a PR firm when it comes to his own people? Or does he confront the corruption?

There's an important Old Testament backdrop to our good shepherd passage. In Ezekiel 34, God confronted Israel's leaders as bad shepherds "who only take care of yourselves" and don't "take care of the flock."[17] Check out God's indictment of these bad pastors:

> You have not strengthened the weak or healed the sick or bound up the injured. You have not brought back the strays or searched for the lost. You have ruled them harshly and brutally. So they were scattered because there was no shepherd, and when they were scattered they became food for all the wild animals.[18]

These were the leaders of God's people. What was their crime? They were harsh dictators rather than healing caretakers. They were too busy scrolling their mentions to notice when the little ones got lost. They ate first and didn't care if anything was left for their hungry people. They were in it for themselves, not for the sheep. In God's eyes, their title had been taken away.

They were "no shepherd."

As a pastor, I feel the weight of Ezekiel's critique. Do I see my office as a position to be exploited to my own advantage or a privilege to lay down my life and serve? Do I strengthen the weak, search for the strays, and protect from the predators? Or do I take the path of least resistance and pursue comfort while the people of God are scattered and devoured? Have I turned a holy vocation to represent the Good Shepherd into the job of a hired hand to earn a paycheck?

Now, some nuance. It's common to beat up on pastors today. To cry foul whenever they make a decision you don't like. God's not calling pastors to be people pleasers who try to accommodate everyone. Leaders have to make difficult decisions. They don't need to carry the weight of unrealistic expectations. But they *are* called to carry the weight of godly character. There's a way to carry conviction with care rather than cruelty.

Also, sheep hurt shepherds too. The reality is, some sheep have a gnarly bite: unfair criticism, unrealistic expectations, unjust treatment. While there's been a lot of (important) talk recently about how abusive pastors have hurt their churches, we should also probably talk about how abusive churches have hurt their pastors. Many, many leaders are discouraged, beaten up, and ready to throw in the towel.[19]

Yet our focus here is on shepherds. If you've been hurt by bad leaders, Ezekiel 34 also offers hope. In a prophetic foreshadowing of Jesus, God promised he's on his way:

> I myself will search for my sheep and look after them. As a shepherd looks after his scattered flock when he is with them, so will I look after my sheep. . . . I myself will tend my sheep and have them lie down, declares the Sovereign LORD. I will search for the lost and bring back the strays. I will bind up the injured and strengthen the weak. . . . I will shepherd the flock with justice.[20]

That's Jesus! Jesus is God himself come to shepherd his people. That word "LORD" in Hebrew is *Yahweh:* the covenant name for God. Jesus is Yahweh in the flesh come to rescue his flock. When Jesus calls himself the Good Shepherd, it's much more than a declaration that he's nice. Jesus is saying he is the God of Israel come to confront the wicked leaders (bad shepherds) of his people, to search for and rescue his scattered people ("my sheep"), to gather, guide, and care for them as their mighty shepherd-king.

Wait a sec. Is Jesus really identifying himself with God? In case there's any doubt, later in John 10 Jesus says, "I and the Father are one"—and the bad shepherds pick up boulders to stone him for blasphemy.[21]

My friend Rick wants to make a picture of Christ hanging on the cross, with the caption "I was hurt by the church." The point? Jesus knows the particularity of this pain. Sometimes we want to use church hurt to distance ourselves from Christ. But properly understood, it should draw us closer to him. Especially when we realize that we—both shepherds and sheep—are the ones who crucified him. Our savior was hurt by us; that's the central event of salvation.

Jesus was hurt by the church.

If you've been wounded by the church, there's power when you bring your hurt to the cross. Not only does Jesus name what was done to you; he also meets you in your ache. "He was led like a lamb to the slaughter"; the Shepherd became a sheep. "By his wounds we are healed"; there's power for you in his pain. "He took up our pain and bore our suffering"; the Good Shepherd was cast out to gather you in, injured to bind you up, mistreated to meet you in your woundedness and tend to you with his care.[22]

This power is not only for those who've been wounded but also for those of us who've inflicted wounds on his church. "He bore the sin of many"; our mistakes were on his back as he carried that cross to Calvary. "He was crushed for our iniquities"; his body was broken to atone for our breaking of others. He "made intercession for the transgressors"; forgiveness flowed from his lips for you and me as he exhaled his final breaths: "Father, forgive them."[23]

This forgiveness is for shepherds and sheep alike. "We all, like sheep, have gone astray, each of us has turned to our own way"; we have all wandered at times from our good shepherd. "The punishment that brought us peace was on him"; our mutual recovery is found in his cross. "He will be raised and lifted up and highly exalted"; this Suffering Servant brings healing in his outstretched wings.[24]

There's healing for the world in the Shepherd-King.

THE SHEPHERD'S VOICE

I spent six months herding sheep on the Navajo reservation. It was an amazing experience. My favorite phrase was *diigis dibé* (Navajo for "crazy sheep"). If you were up on the mesas, you could probably hear me shouting it. Sheep can be crazy and wander off. They need guidance.

Jesus guides his sheep. John 10 says, "He goes on ahead of them, and his sheep follow him because they know his voice."[25] This is different from Navajo shepherding. In the Western hemisphere, shepherds *drive* their sheep from behind. In the Middle East, they *guide* them from the front. For *diigis dibé*, both ways work. But when it comes to our spiritual life, the difference is significant.

Jesus goes before us. He leads from the front; he's the first into the battle. He doesn't call you to go somewhere he hasn't already gone himself. Jesus may be last to eat, but he's first to encounter the thieves, robbers, and bears. When the Crucified One calls you to pick up your cross and follow, you're stepping onto a trail he's already blazed.[26]

How do you keep from wandering off? You have to know his voice. Jesus continues:

> His sheep follow him because they know his voice. But they will never follow a stranger; in fact, they will run away from him because they do not recognize a stranger's voice.[27]

A shepherd has a distinctive voice. Back in World War I, Turkish soldiers stole a flock of sheep on a hillside outside Jerusalem. They used stealth like thieves, weapons like robbers, and the apparent indifference of a hired hand for the flock's welfare. The shepherd looked like no match for them. What was his staff against their guns? His solitary effort against their collective strength?

Yet the shepherd had a secret weapon. He put his hand to his mouth and gave the familiar call he used every day to gather the flock. At the sound of his voice, the sheep turned from the enemy and ran back to their shepherd.[28]

Get to know the voice of your savior. The villains may seem strong and scary, but you can find comfort and security in Jesus's voice. When strangers approach to lure you away, you can learn to distinguish their call from Christ's. They may intimidate you in the moment, but his kingdom is stronger, and his victory will endure. The day will come when "the kingdom of the world has become the kingdom of our Lord and of his Christ."[29] Turn from your enemy and follow the voice of Jesus.

How do you learn to recognize his voice? Listen for him in the story of Scripture, which sings his name. Seek him in prayer, where he invites you into loving communion. Learn from him in a healthy church with leaders who feed his sheep faithfully.

Grow in community with other disciples who are following him together.[30]

As you grow, you'll find it easier to distinguish his voice from the voices of strangers. His sound will become more familiar. The volume of the voices in your head that tear you down will diminish as his voice builds you up. The playlist of memories you used to hear on repeat will grow fainter as his future grows stronger before you. The siren call of culture will increasingly sound like screeching nails on a chalkboard. The once-tantalizing allure of temptation will begin to grate on you. When your enemy puts his lips to that megaphone, you'll boldly turn and run to your shepherd's feet. And he will embrace you in his arms, dress your wounds, and carry you home.

OPEN THE GATE

The early church put the image of the Good Shepherd on their tombs.[31] Why? Because it was a sign of their trust in Christ, their shepherd, to guide them through "the valley of the shadow of death" to "green pastures" and "still waters" on the other side.

Even on this darkest journey, they didn't have to fear any evil, because Christ was with them. His rod and staff comforted them. His mighty hand dispelled the demonic powers. He prepared a table before them, even in the presence of these mysterious enemies. As his lamb, you, too, can be confident, not because the predators aren't powerful but because your Shepherd is stronger.

Even in this darkest hour, God is on your side. His "goodness and mercy" will follow you, pursue you, go chasing after you "all the days of [your] life"—and even beyond life through the grave—until you arrive to "dwell in the house of the LORD forever."[32]

The early church knew this; they were right.

In the very next chapter of John, Jesus raises Lazarus from the dead. This sequence is no coincidence. The resurrection of Lazarus—the seventh and final sign of John's gospel—is Jesus's exclamation point on his identity as the Good Shepherd. It brings to life (pun intended) everything he just talked about. The Savior arrives at the tomb of Lazarus and finds his little lamb trapped inside:

> Jesus called in a loud voice, "Lazarus, come out!" The dead man came out, his hands and feet bound with linen strips, and his face wrapped with a cloth. Jesus said to them, "Unbind him, and let him go."[33]

Okay, check out these parallels between the Good Shepherd speech (John 10) and the raising of Lazarus (John 11). Jesus "calls his own sheep by name"; he calls Lazarus by name. "The gatekeeper opens the gate for [the Shepherd]"; at Jesus's command the tombstone is rolled away. The sheep "follow [the Shepherd] because they know his voice"; Lazarus knows Jesus's voice and obeys, walking out to him from the grave. Jesus is "the gate for the sheep"; he is the Resurrection and the Life, through whom Lazarus exits the grave.[34]

There's more. "The thief comes only to steal and kill and destroy"; the devil has brought death to Lazarus, as to our world. The Shepherd has come "that they may have life, and have it to the full"; he brings life to Lazarus as he will to us. The Shepherd will "lay down [his] life for the sheep"; Jesus raises Lazarus, knowing his enemies will kill him for it, and lays down his life for us too.[35] "I give [my sheep] eternal life," the Shepherd says, "and they shall never perish; no one will snatch them out of my hand"; Jesus raises Lazarus as a sign of this gift of life to us.[36] You can place your trust in him.

You're safe in the Shepherd's hand.

The raising of Lazarus is not only a sign, a *living parable*, of Jesus's own coming resurrection. It's a picture of what he's come to do for you.

Jesus came to set you free. Not only from bad shepherds but also from the bondage of bitterness and pain. He knows you by name; he calls you his own. When the Good Shepherd tells the gatekeeper to roll away the stone, he's saying, *Open the sheep gate—let out my lamb!* He wants to free you from claustrophobic captivity and lead you into green pastures of abundant life. Jesus invites you into freedom. Follow his voice.

In my own life, some deep wounds from church leaders were followed by a long, dark night of the soul. It felt like a tomb. I told my wife, "I feel like I'm in the grave, waiting to be raised." The bonds of anger and enmity were cuffed around my hands and feet. Graveclothes like bandages were wrapped around a wound I didn't know how to heal. I didn't have the power to climb out of that grave myself. I needed to hear the voice of my shepherd.

Gradually, I began to hear his voice. He was calling me to forgive. How could I, though, when my own resources were so depleted? Yet his voice drew my eyes up, off myself, toward him.

I saw my shepherd lay down his life for me, his sheep. I realized that even when I had wounded him and made myself his enemy, he came to find me, embrace me, and carry me home. I heard his voice praying for me: *Father, forgive him.* Jesus was leading me from the front, calling me to something he had already done himself. By his wounds I had been healed, with a balm I was now called to extend to others.

Those who have been forgiven much, love much.[37]

When you can't find the strength within yourself to forgive, you can find that strength by looking at how much you've been forgiven. By looking up to the Shepherd hanging on that cross, offering you his body and blood.

Jesus loves you so much he prepares a table for you in the presence of your enemies. Even when you've made *yourself* his enemy, he invites you to the front of the line and serves you himself so you can eat first—even if it means he goes last.

You can feast on his love in your famished state and in his nourishment find the strength to forgive.[38] This doesn't mean you need to befriend those who wounded you. Boundaries are important. Bad shepherds don't always repent. Forgiveness is a posture of the heart; reconciliation is the restoration of relationship. Especially when there is a pattern of abuse, or the offense is significant in other ways, reconciliation can require their repentance, the respecting of boundaries, and the rebuilding of trust.[39] In our broken world, reconciliation isn't always possible.

Even so, when it comes to your heart, forgiveness sets you free. Holding on to bitterness, it's been said, is like drinking poison and waiting for the other person to die. Unforgiveness hurts you. It's staying in the enemy's muddy sheep pen while Jesus is calling you out into green pastures. My friend David, whose story opened this chapter, said he's discovered this to be true. Forgiveness releases the restraints of resentment. It lets you follow your good shepherd to the green pastures of abundance and quiet waters of peace. He knows how to lead you there.

When you discover your defender in Christ the Shepherd-King, you can forgive and still desire justice. You can still want the wrongs put right. You can still long for the day when thieves, robbers, and hired hands can no longer hurt or destroy. For he will shepherd with justice. The day is coming when he will call us out of our graves like Lazarus and fulfill this prophetic hope:

He shall stand and shepherd his flock in the strength
    of the LORD,
  in the majesty of the name of the LORD his God.
And they shall dwell secure, for now he shall be great
    to the ends of the earth.[40]

11

WALK FREE

When Your Mind Is a Prison

I can be my own worst critic. At times, I'm weighed down by regret for mistakes. I feel guilt over things I wish I'd done differently. I walk the labyrinthian maze of past choices, wondering, *If I'd turned right instead of left, would life have turned out differently?* I can obsessively replay the scenes of the past that brought me here and despondently worry about the future that hangs before me.

I'm my own harshest judge, jury, and executioner.

On July 2, 1830, George Wilson was scheduled to be executed by hanging. He had been found guilty of robbing a United States mail carrier and "putting the life of the driver in jeopardy." But influential friends pleaded with President Andrew Jackson on his behalf, and the president issued a pardon.

Shockingly, however, Wilson refused the pardon. As the court record puts it, he chose to "waive and decline any advantage or protection which might be supposed to arise from the pardon." Why? He declared that he "had nothing to say and . . . did not wish in any manner to avail himself, in order to avoid the sentence." The Supreme Court was asked to weigh in on the case and ruled that if a prisoner doesn't accept a pardon, it isn't in effect.[1]

In the end, Wilson judged himself more harshly than those around him. He was tormented by guilt, unable to accept grace.

Can you relate? Where do you go when you feel trapped in the prison of your own mind? When you assume God is the warden just waiting to send you to the gallows? If you had a pardon, why would you refuse it? What would it look like to walk free?

Jesus *has* given you a pardon. In John 18, Barabbas is a criminal on death row who's set free. Like George Wilson, he's given a pardon. Yet unlike Wilson, he gladly accepts it. When you're trapped in the prison of your own mind, Barabbas shows you how to walk free.

THE GREAT EXCHANGE

The Jewish leaders hand Jesus over to Pilate, the Roman governor, to be executed. Pilate interrogates Jesus yet finds nothing wrong with him. So he goes outside his palace walls and says to the crowd,

> "I find no basis for a charge against him. But it is your custom for me to release to you one prisoner at the time of the Passover. Do you want me to release 'the king of the Jews'?"
>
> They shouted back, "No, not him! Give us Barabbas!" Now Barabbas had taken part in an uprising.[2]

Okay, three observations. First, Jesus is innocent, while Barabbas is guilty. Pilate defends Jesus's innocence three times to the crowd and tries to get him released: "I find no guilt in him."[3] It's a sham trial on trumped-up charges. The Roman leader executes the world's true King not to satisfy the demands of justice but to satiate a bloodthirsty mob. He's more interested in appeasing the masses than exalting the truth.

Barabbas, on the other hand, is guilty, and everyone knows it. The crowd knows what he's done; Barabbas doesn't even voice his disagreement. He's a convicted criminal. As Peter later confronts the Jewish crowds in Acts 3:14, "You disowned the Holy and Righteous One and asked that a murderer be released to you." A violent felon is traded for the only truly righteous person in history.

Jesus is the innocent exchanged for the guilty.

Second, Jesus is the King exchanged for a rebel. "Barabbas had taken part in an uprising." He's a revolutionary, an insurrectionist. Some translations call him a "robber," but this doesn't do justice to the violence associated with the term: one *"who also plunders and pillages*—an unscrupulous marauder . . . exploiting the vulnerable without hesitating to use violence."[4] Crucifixion was designated for political revolutionaries. It was a bloody billboard to send a public warning: *Don't mess with the empire.* Barabbas isn't a shoplifter or pickpocket; he's a terrorist, a freedom fighter, a cutthroat ideologue using violence and inciting fear to accomplish his revolutionary ends.

He's not just a robber; he's a rebel.

Jesus, on the other hand, is "the king of the Jews." Pilate places a crown of thorns on his head, a robe on his bloody back, and a sign on the torturous cross as a testament to this title. Pilate's interrogation reveals Jesus's kingdom is "not *of* this world"; otherwise, his followers "would fight to prevent [his] arrest."[5] Yet Jesus's kingdom is *for* this world. Its method is subversive: Like a seed cracked open to bring forth life. Like yeast working its way gradually through dough.

The life-giving King is exchanged for a death-dealing rebel.

Finally, the beloved Son is exchanged for an estranged son. Barabbas's name means, literally, "son of the father"—from *bar* ("son") and *abba* ("father").[6] That's interesting. What is Jesus's primary identity in John's gospel? The Son of the Father. Jesus is the "only begotten Son," whom the Father has loved from "before the creation of the world." Jesus is "in the Father," and "the Father is in [him]." Jesus is so identified with his *Abba* that he can proclaim, as his *Bar,* "I and the Father are one."[7]

Jesus is the true *Bar-Abbas.*

TO SET YOU FREE

Barabbas is a picture of Israel. The nation was a *son of the Father:* As God's "firstborn son," they were called to live and reign with him among the nations of the world.[8] Yet they were also a *rebel:* They had engaged in the harlotry of worshipping idols and wreaked the havoc of injustice. Israel took the path of violent revolution. At least, many did. The temple had become "a den of robbers," a hideout of revolutionaries—like Barabbas—plotting ways to "fight for God."[9]

They were *guilty:* The rebel nation lived under a death sentence. Rome hovered over them as executioner, an angel of death threatening to bring down the sword on God's firstborn son. Yet there was hope for a new Passover. A new Lamb to be slain so "the son of the Father" could be released. Did you catch when Barabbas is pardoned? "It is your custom for me to release to you one prisoner at *the time of the Passover.*"[10] A new Passover Lamb is about to be slain; a new exodus is afoot.

The beloved Son must die so the condemned son can go free.

Not only is Barabbas a picture of Israel; he is also a picture of you and me. When you were guilty, Jesus, the innocent one, came onto your side and took your place. When you were condemned, he bore the punishment of the law on your behalf. When a death sentence hung over your head, he took the weight of your guillotine on Golgotha. The empire was set to crush you; he stepped into your stead.

Jesus is the King who gave his life for you. When you were a rebel, he went to the cross to bring you back into his kingdom and make you a citizen again. When you sought to live on your own terms rather than his, he exchanged his obedience for your insurgency. His arms are stretched out wide on the cross to welcome you into his redemptive kingdom of love.

Jesus trades your insurrection for his resurrection.

He does it to make you a son or daughter of the Father. To restore you as a child of the King. To wrap you in a royal robe, put the family ring on your finger, slaughter the fattened calf, and throw the biggest party the town has ever seen. He does it to bring you home.[11]

So when you're trapped in the prison of your own mind, listen for the liberating voice of your King. When your own conscience convicts you, let his Spirit release you. When the voice in your head blasts like a megaphone—*You're not worthy!*—his great exchange proclaims your great worth to him. Listen for his Spirit, who bears the good news of his gospel, to unlock your cage.

Step out into the sunlight; walk free.

IN OUR PLACE

Many people struggle with *substitution,* the idea that Christ was substituted for us. *Can you really substitute an innocent person for the guilty?* It seems unfair. If you had two kids and one got in trouble, would it really be fair to give the consequences to your other kid who did nothing wrong? (*No way!* I can hear my kids screaming.) Also, Jesus could look at first glance like a hapless victim caught in the wheels of fate. The *mob* asks for him to be substituted for Barabbas. How much control does Jesus have? But look closer.

Jesus is an active agent, not a passive victim. He valiantly declares, "No one takes [my life] from me, but I lay it down of my own accord."[12] Indeed, he says the very reason he came was "to serve, and to give his life as a ransom for many."[13] Some mock the cross as "divine child abuse," but Jesus is a fully grown man, not a five-year-old. He's "a jaguar out to devour death," as I put it elsewhere, who "run[s] toward the cross as a man on a mission . . . like a pro wrestler who tackles the cross to body slam it":

He is not coerced or manipulated to the cross against his will. . . . Jesus goes of his own volition to accomplish *his* purposes. He is taking down the destructive power of sin, death, and hell.

Jesus is a lion; the cross is his prey.

Jesus "set his face [toward] Jerusalem" long before his execution and, like an arrow streaming toward its target, made his way toward Zion to atone for the sin of the world. Jesus is constantly saying things like, "the Son of Man must suffer, be rejected, and be killed," while the disciples, confused and blind, rebuke him, saying, "May it never be!" While we see the cross as a detour, Jesus sees it as a destination.

Jesus sets sail into the storm to bring us home.[14]

Jesus boldly tells Pilate, "You would have no authority over me at all unless it had been given you from above."[15] In other words, *You're not as in charge here as you think you are.* Jesus isn't an accidental bystander, caught off guard before Pilate. No, Jesus is "the Lamb who was slain from the creation of the world."[16] The Father, Son, and Spirit were planning their triune redemption of the world in love before their creation of the world in love. They saw the train wreck coming and planned to love us through it anyway.

"The cross is not happening to Jesus; Jesus is happening to the cross."[17]

I VOLUNTEER AS TRIBUTE

Active substitution isn't as strange as it seems. Or perhaps it *is* strange—yet in a way our hearts long for. Self-sacrifice in a self-protective world. Indeed, this is the stuff of epic drama. (*Spoiler alert:* Movie montage coming.)

- This is Katniss Everdeen saying "I volunteer as tribute" so her sister can go free.
- This is John Krasinski's character screaming at the top of his lungs in *A Quiet Place,* bringing the wrath of the monster down on himself so his children can escape.
- This is Iron Man snapping his fingers to take down Thanos, knowing he'll go down with him.
- This is Aslan laying down his life on the Stone Table to set a traitor free.
- This is Bruce Willis's character sacrificing himself to detonate a nuclear bomb in an asteroid and save the world.
- This is Leonardo DiCaprio's character staying in the icy waters so his beloved's heart can go on.
- This is Harry Potter surrendering himself willingly to Voldemort so his friends can live.

Why do these blockbuster images captivate our hearts? What is it that leaves us spellbound before this dramatic narrative arc? Could it be that such epic moments top the Hollywood charts because they echo the crucial—cross-shaped (literally, from the Latin word *crux*, or "cross")—center of history?

Such images echo the true story of the world. They are shadows cast on earth by the heavenly shape of Jesus, the one who actively goes to the cross to lay down his life for you. The gospel is, as Tolkien observes, a fairy tale come true.[18] Or as his friend Lewis describes it, the grand reality to which myths point.[19] Other stories work their way from earth up to heaven, but the gospel moves in the other direction: from heaven down to earth, revealing the heart of God for you. The God who makes his way to you, gives himself in Christ for you, and takes your place so you can go free.

Jesus trades places with Barabbas—and with all of us—as the ultimate act of love. Jesus is like Kate Bush in that epic chorus, who wants to make a deal with God: "I'd get him to swap our places."[20] Only, Jesus is able to do it! Watch him "running up that hill" of Calvary to swap himself for you. "God made him who had no sin to be sin for us," the gospel proclaims, "so that in him we might become the righteousness of God."[21] Behold this great exchange, and let your affections be captivated by the Son of God, who loves you and gave himself up for you.[22]

Jesus loves Barabbas—and he loves *you*.

The cross is, from this angle, not a tragedy but a victory. The place where our sin is atoned for and we're reconciled to God. This is why the Christian tradition calls this day Good Friday. *How could an unjust execution be good?* Because this is the place where you discover the profound truth of your pardon. Where you encounter God's extravagant love in your most desperate estate. Where you find that even when you face the firing squad, with the executioners on one end of the chasm and yourself isolated on the other . . . God is on your side.

What could be better than that?

FINAL MEAL

I wonder what Barabbas's last night on death row was like. As he ate his final meal, did he savor every bite or was he too nervous to hold it down? Did he say goodbye in his mind to the family he'd never see again, or did he figure they were better off without him? As the sun went down, did he face nightmares in the dark or was he unable to fall asleep? Like Jacob, his ancient ancestor, did he wrestle with God through the night?

The Father had abandoned him as a son. He was a *bar* without his *Abba*. Left to die. Forsaken. Or so it seemed. Pilate and the pagan powers were now his only apparent authority. Did he question whether, on the other side, he would meet God or the cold black *nihilo* of nonexistence? Did he wonder whether he would be rewarded for his bravery or punished for the harm he'd inflicted? Did he harbor any guilt or remorse for the people he'd killed? Did their faces flash before his eyes? Mothers holding their dead sons? Did he second-guess the ideology he'd given his life to? And wonder whether it was worth giving his life for?

Imagine you're Barabbas, anticipating the public mockery. The scourging of your back. The nails piercing your flesh. Hanging naked and ashamed. Dehydrated and suffocating. Guilty and alone. Listen to the footsteps approach your cell to drag you to this fate.

"You're free to go."

What?

"The governor has issued your pardon."

Why?

"Another has taken your place."

How beautiful are the feet who bore that good news. They carried a different message than you expected. Can you hear the clink of the key in the lock as your cage opens and your shackles drop from your feet? Can you smell the fresh air of the blue sky as you exit your dungeon and enter Jerusalem, the city of the king? Can you see the light glisten on the crowds, hustling and bustling, oblivious to the sweet gift of life you now savor? Can you feel the wonder: *Why me? Why was I given this second chance? This fresh start?*

Who is this stranger who took my place?

Jesus. The Son of the Father. In the great exchange, Christ swaps your sin for his salvation, takes on your wickedness for his righteousness, barters your poverty for his riches, receives your brokenness for his healing.

This is unfair, I guess—though not in the way critics suggest. While it may not be a fair trade, it is just, for it is where justice and mercy meet. It is beautiful and good, for the cross is where love and holiness kiss—or, better yet, where the holy love of God kisses us in our spellbound slumber under the shadow of sin to wake us and welcome us into his life-giving kingdom, where we will reign forever with him.

Jesus died to set you free.

Why would you reject the pardon?

CONFRONTING TWO LIES

When the Supreme Court was called in to rule on George Wilson's case, Chief Justice John Marshall wrote,

> A pardon is an act of grace, proceeding from the power entrusted with the execution of the laws. . . .
>
> [But] delivery is not complete without acceptance. It may then be rejected by the person to whom it is tendered.[23]

Why did Wilson reject the pardon? We don't know; he wouldn't say.

Barabbas may have a lot of things going against him, but at least he has common sense. Just imagine him telling the jailer who opens his cell, *No thanks. I'll just stay in here. I'm good.*

Here's the thing, however: Some of us reject the *much greater* pardon Christ offers us. This pardon is from a higher authority than the president of the United States; it's from the King of the universe—a *much higher* office. This clemency isn't just for robbery or tax evasion; it's for rebellion against God—carrying a *much greater* consequence. This pardon comes not because a friend put in a good word with the president but because God's Word became flesh and willingly took the punishment on himself—a *more powerful* deed. Your pardon is secured not by a signature on a document but by nails pierced through hands, the Savior hung, a last breath exhaled, a covenant ratified in blood—a *more unbreakable* bond. It doesn't just get you out of jail; it reinstates you as a citizen with full rights and inheritance in the kingdom of God—a *more glorious* kingdom.

Why would anyone turn down this pardon? I suspect there are two main lies that can keep us captive. Let's explore both.

Lie 1: I'm Not That Bad

First, it's tempting to think, *I'm not that bad!* We can tell ourselves, *I've lived a pretty good life. Gotten good grades. I'm respected in the community. Sure, Jesus's blood was shed for the drug addicts and murderers, but I'm doing okay. Yeah, I might have said a few choice words here or there, but only on the occasional bad day.* It's easy to believe our own hype.

The problem? We are Barabbas.

You and I are criminals on death row, under the weight of the curse, with a one-way ticket to the grave. While the law of God exposes the gravity of our behavior, the gospel goes even deeper and lays bare the corruption in our hearts. As Aleksandr Solzhenitsyn famously observes, "The line separating good and evil passes not through states, nor between classes, nor between political parties either—but right through every human heart."[24] You and I are in line for the gallows, and before the bar of justice, we deserve it.

It's easy to point to the bad guys "out there" to distract from the ugly "in here." To minimize our own malady. Yet getting honest that there's a cancer inside you is the first step to receiving treatment. In the Gospels, it's the "good guys"—the polished perfectionists, the upright and uptight with great track records— who assume their sin isn't that bad. In reality, they're the worst opponents of grace.

You won't experience the depths of God's love until you expose the depths of your sin. When you have the courage to gaze into your own abyss—the heart of darkness within your chest cavity—you discover the deepest dungeon is your life without God. This is where God's great love encounters you in your solitary confinement and calls you out of yourself into communion with him.

You don't need to be the hero of the story; Jesus is. This good news is where freedom is found. You're free to forgive when you realize how massively you've been forgiven. You're free to love when you realize how deeply you're seen and fully you're known—warts and all—and yes, even there, fully loved.

If you have a hard time loving God or loving others the way God calls you to, don't focus on trying harder. Instead, look higher. Look up to God's great love for you, the divine love displayed in the extravagant exchange of the cross, where Christ took your place to set you free. When we encounter how high and wide and deep and long is this unshakable love, our hearts are set free to love in return.

Lie 2: I'm Too Bad

Some of us have the opposite problem. The second lie that leads us to reject God's pardon is "I'm too bad." You might tell yourself, *I'm too far gone. There's no way God could ever love me. If you only knew what I've done. The people I've hurt. The habit I can't break. The addiction I'm trapped in. My kids hate me. My friends don't respect me. I've jacked up my life beyond repair.* Your shackles of shame might seem unbreakable.

But your savior is stronger.

Jesus's blood is powerful enough to break every chain. His sacrifice is strong enough to remove any stain. When you say your sin is too bad, what you're really saying is that Jesus is not enough. That his life is not righteous enough, his blood not strong enough, his sacrifice not sufficient to save you from that grave. Stop banking on your résumé, and start relying on his.

Again, don't try harder; look higher.

Look up to Jesus in trust; he has the strength to set you free. Don't listen to the voice of your accuser; listen to the voice of your savior! Don't diminish the power of his sacrifice; trust in the only truly holy one, who shed his priceless blood for you. There's no prison door too heavy for his Spirit to swing open, no grave too deep for his resurrection to raise you from.

When you realize God is on your side—*so much* on your side that he's taken your place, the Innocent for the guilty—you can step out in confidence. You can step onto his side, a citizen in the land of the free.

❖ ❖ ❖

True freedom isn't freedom *from* God; it's freedom *for* God. Christ freed us from *our own way* (that leads to bondage and death) to be united with God *in his way* (that leads to freedom and life). Christ offers you this freedom by freely offering you himself. This is where true freedom is found. He gives you all that he is and invites you to bring all that you are. His Spirit draws you out of the self-serving ways of sin to graft you into the self-giving love of the triune God. Communion. Joy. Peace.

What are we free *for*? Quite simply, *God*. His Spirit can take your hand and lead you out of that dungeon. Into the fresh air of his kingdom. Into the light glistening off crowds of brothers and sisters in your newfound family of God. Into the embrace of your heavenly Father, who welcomes you home as his child. A daughter or son.

Free at last.

12

ANTICIPATE SURPRISE

When It Hurts to Hope

Growing up, when I was going through difficult times, my grandfather loved to say, "It's always darkest before the dawn." It sounded a bit cliché as I faced the latest out-of-state move, drama with a girl, or fight with my father. *C'mon, Grandpa.* As I grew older, however, I learned why this statement was so significant to him. It wasn't advice from the cheap seats; he had lived it.

My grandfather survived three tours in Vietnam. He led his company deep into the jungles, from which a third of his men didn't return. He was haunted by memories: The fear, loss, and weight of responsibility were crushing. He had seen the darkest of times. Yet he had also encountered the dawn.

God got ahold of his life in a powerful way. The trenches of war were where he met God. He learned to process his pain with a counselor, other veterans, and trusted confidants. He experienced healing with family and community. He was able to share what he had experienced with us in helpful ways. Gradually, the light of the risen Christ dawned on the dark graveyard of his memories, cultivating a new garden filled with life.

When I encounter my own dark times today, I still remember his truism. When I wake at three in the morning with debilitating thoughts, my mind racing and memories replaying, my grandfather's voice reminds me that this, too, shall pass. To look forward to the future. To anticipate surprise.

Where do you go when it hurts to hope? When God's gone missing and you're left to fend for yourself? When the enemy tempts you to believe it would be better for everyone if you just went away? That's a horrid lie, by the way, straight from the pit of hell. It's the voice of the enemy, not the voice of God. Where do you go when the rug gets pulled out from under you and you feel like you have no future? It may sound counterintuitive, but the gospel invites you to the hard place. The place of the wound.

Go to the tomb.

YOUR DARKEST HOUR

"Early on the first day of the week," John tells us, "while it was still dark, Mary Magdalene went to the tomb [of Jesus]."[1] Imagine the scene: It's early, it's dark, and Jesus—so far as Mary knows—is still dead. This is the biggest loss, the deepest wound, in her life. God's left the building; all hope is gone. Yet Mary doesn't suck it up and move on. She doesn't distract herself by doomscrolling. No, she picks up her courage and, in the bleakest darkness, makes her way to the tomb.

It's the first day of the week, which is a little clue about the story that follows: We're about to see some new creation. Jesus's final week is patterned on the seven days of creation. He enters Jerusalem on the first day of the week. He is crucified on the sixth day, completing his work as he says, "It is finished"[2] (like God completed his work in Genesis 1). Then, on the seventh day, Christ rests in the grave (entering his Sabbath, like God did in Genesis 2). Now, on the first day of a new week, a new day has dawned. He is risen.

Jesus has launched a new creation.

Other new creation clues abound. This scene takes place in a garden, and Mary mistakes Jesus at first for the gardener.[3] Jesus and Mary are like a new Adam and a new Eve in the garden of the new creation. The serpent's head has been crushed; Christ's heel has been wounded, but he has risen victorious. The Seed of the woman has vanquished the enemy.[4]

The new Adam has risen victorious.

Jesus can turn your "graves into gardens." He can take your darkest memories, your deepest losses, and make them locations for new creation. What looks like an end can become a gateway to a new beginning. So when you feel like hope is gone, hold on—it's always darkest before the dawn.

I need more than a cliché, you might say. And that's true. You need the power of the risen Christ. Yet in the light of Jesus, the darkness is defeated. Resurrection is coming. He's gone into the trenches and led the way through to the other side. All shall be raised. "As in Adam all die, so in Christ all will be made alive."[5] Death no longer has the last word on your story; Christ does—he is the Resurrection and the Life. Darkness no longer has the last word; light does—he is the Light of the World. Destruction no longer has the last word; love does—he is the lover of your soul. This means you can hold on when hope is gone. A new day has dawned.

Even when you can't see it yet.

A SIGN OF LOVE

Mary doesn't yet know that Jesus is alive. She arrives at the tomb and "saw that the stone had been removed from the entrance."[6]

Mary stood outside the tomb crying. As she wept, she bent over to look into the tomb and saw two angels in white, seated where Jesus' body had been, one at the head and the other at the foot.

They asked her, "Woman, why are you crying?"

"They have taken my Lord away," she said, "and I don't know where they have put him."[7]

Mary thinks someone has robbed the grave. And in a sense, she's right. Jesus is a grave robber who's cheated death and emptied the tomb. He's the victor, not a victim, but Mary doesn't know that yet.

Mary's tears are a sign of her love. When Jesus wept at the tomb of his friend Lazarus, the people responded, "See how he loved him!"[8] They were right.

Tears are a sign of love.

I once cried every day for three months straight. We were preparing to move from our hometown in Oregon to Arizona. We were leaving our family, our friends, and a church we loved. At one level, we didn't want to go. It felt like a death. But at another level, we strongly sensed God's calling. (That's a story for another time.) The leaders and mentors in our life confirmed it. Still, I wondered, *Are my tears a sign that we're making the wrong decision? Would it really be this hard if we were making the right move?*

My lead pastor, Rick, with his typical fatherly wisdom, counseled me: "Tears are a sign that love is there." I've known plenty of people who don't find it hard to leave their church or community. They're angry or wounded—and *stoked* to be gone. While tears can be a sign of hurt or betrayal, my tears were the opposite: a sign that I loved what I was leaving.

When God calls you to do something hard, weeping doesn't

mean you're making the wrong decision. It might mean you're willing to sacrifice something real for the sake of obedience. When you stand at the grave of a loved one and the tears fall, it means you love the one you lost. Your tears are a sign that love is there.

Our culture is bad at grief. We want to ignore it, sugarcoat it, or distract ourselves from it. Yet Jesus invites us *into* it. Mary goes to the place of the wound, the place of loss, of absence. Why? She loves him. She doesn't run from the pain; she courageously enters into it.

It takes guts to gaze into the tomb. It takes courage to go to counseling. To explore your deepest wounds. To face the loss with trusted friends. To bring the pain before God in prayer. It's interesting to me that Mary is alone in this scene. Solitude and silence can play an important role in the journey. Sometimes you have to be willing to sit in the grief rather than ignore it, to honor who or what you've lost rather than rush to move on. When you do, I believe you'll discover—even if it takes some time—the same thing Mary does.

Christ meets you there.

A HARD PLACE, A HOLY PLACE

When Mary looks into the tomb, she is shocked to discover two angels. They're sitting on the slab where the Savior was just sleeping, "one at the head and the other at the foot."[9] This echoes the ark of the covenant in the Old Testament, which had an angel sitting atop each end of the ark. Beneath the angels lay the stone tablets of the covenant within the ark, like the new covenant Christ just sealed with his blood to bring us into union with him.[10] On the Day of Atonement, blood was sprinkled on the ark, like Christ's blood was sprinkled on the slab on which he lay. In other words, atonement has been made.

The new covenant is here.

The old ark rested within the Most Holy Place, the hot spot of God's presence in the temple. The space between the two angels was empty—with no idol or image for the invisible God—where the divine glory would reside. Now Jesus's empty tomb is depicted as the new hot spot from which God's glorious presence goes forth into all the earth. Jesus's empty grave is the crater site where the resurrecting power of new creation first breaks through. Mary looks into the pain point, expecting desolation; she instead finds resurrection.

The hard place has become a holy place.

Earlier in this book, I shared about a time I was tempted with suicidal thoughts. I went to see my counselor. Rather than avoiding the painful place, I wanted to prayerfully process it before God and a close circle of trusted friends. God began revealing deeper layers of my story: rejection and other wounds from my childhood, when I was beaten and mocked, and how I learned to belong by being the "smart" kid and the "nice" kid. It was my formula for acceptance and affirmation, and later in ministry, the pattern continued.

The hard season had essentially sent this message: *You're not smart; your ideas are stupid. You're not nice; you're a hateful jerk.* Those messages weren't true, but they worked to unravel layers of belonging (reputation, network, job, stability, community, future, calling). Like Mary, I eventually couldn't see God in the storm. Everything went dark.

Yet God began ministering to me there. Slowly, I began hearing his voice:

What was meant for evil, I'm using for good. I've allowed all these layers to be unraveled to get to your heart. I want to instill a deeper layer of belonging that nothing can take away. I want to make my home in you, through Christ and by the

Spirit, with a deeper layer of belonging than you've ever known. Before I called you to use you, I called you to love you.

My hard place became a holy place. I experienced some of the deepest transformation of my life. His presence salved my wounds, like medicine reaching the root of an infection that ran deeper than I knew. It was gradual over the course of many months, with many ups and downs, but I began to heal. What felt like a grave eventually became a garden, with Christ the good gardener cultivating new life in me.

I was transformed at the tomb.

Your hardest places can become your holiest encounters with Christ. Your deepest wounds can be salved with the warmth of his presence. The painful terrain in your story can become the geography of redemption. That can sound cliché, but like my grandfather taught me, sometimes the truisms are true for a reason. It takes courage to go to the place of the tomb. It's brave to face the cataclysm within. Like Mary, you can look into the heart of darkness and encounter the surprising power of resurrection. This is not a Band-Aid on your deepest wound but an invitation to gently pull off the bandage and get honest about the pain before the Great Physician.

When God seems absent, sometimes that's when you discover he's right beside you. It may not happen in a moment, but Jesus is more committed to you than you are to him. Even the hardest place in all of history (the tomb) has become a holy place that will eventually transform all our graves into gardens. Keep pressing in: He can transform your hardest place too.

While you're waiting, remember it's always morning somewhere. When it's midnight in New York, it's sunrise in Paris. Similarly, even when you face your darkest hour, the dawn is on its way. Christ is still shining radiantly, even when your vision is shrouded in shadow. The entrance to Jerusalem's temple faced east, toward the rising of the sun. Even in the darkness, the people could look toward the horizon and anticipate the breaking of dawn. You can too.

WHO IS IT YOU SEEK?

Mary turns toward Jesus but doesn't realize it's him. He asks her, "Who is it you seek?"[11] Interesting. When the band of soldiers, officers, chief priests, and Pharisees come a few days earlier to arrest him, Jesus asks them this same question. They're hostile, carrying lanterns, torches, and weapons—like a mob with pitchforks. That scene is also in a garden, we're told.[12]

Two gardens. Same question.

The Crucifixion and Resurrection are bookended by this question in a garden: "Who is it you seek?" The questioners are all looking for Jesus but have different motives. The soldiers want to arrest him; Mary wants to honor him. The religious leaders are out to kill him; Mary is out to worship him.

We are faced with the same question: *Who is it* you *seek?* Do you see Jesus as an obstacle, a threat to your own agenda? Or do you see him as a hero, your rescuer, the one who can save you from yourself and a world that's run you ragged? Do you seek to put Jesus "in his place" and remain under cover of darkness? Or to gaze on his glory and reflect the radiance of his character in your life? Do you come to make war on him or to worship him?

Why does Mary love Jesus? She has an interesting backstory: Jesus drove seven demons out of her.[13] Before she met him, her life had been like that dark tomb: haunted by the powers of death. She was tyrannized, driven mad, and dominated by the demonic. (Remember, seven is the number of completion in the Bible, so "seven demons" carries a sense of complete domination.) I imagine a young girl living scared of the darkness within her own body.

Yet Jesus came to clean house. He drove out the ones who were driving her mad. He not only drove out the bad but also filled in the good. She became one of his disciples, walking with him and following in his footsteps. He can do the same for you— replacing your gloom with glory. He's come not only to drive out your demons but also to fill you with the presence of God.[14]

Mary Magdalene is the first person to encounter the risen Jesus. Not only the first person in John's gospel but also the first person *in history.* Think about that—it's crazy. What is it like to be witness to something no one has ever seen before? Yet she is also something more: She represents all of us as the church.

Jesus asks her, "Woman, why are you crying?"[15] As we saw in chapter 1, when Jesus calls someone "Woman," that may sound condescending in English, but in the original language it's like calling her "Madam." This is the fifth scene where John has used this term; there are important echoes here. Check out these four crucial earlier scenes, and see if you can find what links them:

- "Woman . . . my hour has not yet come," Jesus says to his mother, Mary, when the wine has run out at the wedding.[16]
- "Woman . . . a time is coming and has now come when the true worshipers will worship the Father in the Spirit and in truth," Jesus tells the woman at the well as she seeks the living water.[17]
- "Woman, where are they? Has no one condemned you?" Jesus tells the woman caught in adultery when her accusers depart.[18]
- "Woman, behold, your son!" Jesus tells his mother from the cross as he entrusts her to the care of his beloved disciple.[19]

Did you catch the theme that ties these passages together? All four highlight what Christ accomplishes at the cross for us. In the first scene, the wedding at Cana, the hour has not yet come for Christ to turn water into wine. But now the hour has come: Jesus pours out the wine of his blood on the cross to inaugurate the new covenant and wash us spotless as his bride. Friend, you are invited to a resurrection wedding. You are invited to enter into union with the Spirit of the living God, who lifts the veil from your eyes to behold Christ the Son, who calls you his beloved and brings you into the home of his Father forever.

You are invited to become the bride.

In the second scene, the woman at the well confronts Jesus with the conflict that's keeping their people apart: *You Jews worship on that mountain; we Samaritans worship on this mountain.* It's a temple conflict, but now the hour has come: The temple of Christ's body is torn down on the cross and rebuilt in three days. All are now invited—Jew, Samaritan, and Gentile—to come to him and worship in Spirit and truth.

Christ, the living temple, calls you to himself. He wants to give you the water of his Spirit to quench your deepest thirst. He wants to make you a living stone in his new temple, built on himself as our chief cornerstone, our firm foundation. He wants to build you up to be a dwelling place in which God lives by his Spirit, to fill the earth with his glory.[20]

He invites you to become his living temple.

In the third scene, Jesus defends the woman caught in adultery from her accusers. He raises the bar so that all find themselves under it—and in need of grace. At the cross, Christ defended us from our accuser. Jesus drank the cup of jealousy and bore the curse of the law to set us free. He brought the grace we needed. We are the bride of Christ, and the enemy no longer has any authority in our lives. His accusations no longer stick. There is now no condemnation for those who are in Christ Jesus. Nothing will be able to separate us from his love.[21]

We belong to Christ, and he to us.

In the fourth scene, at the cross, the mother who loved Jesus from the womb is joined with the disciple whom Jesus loved and brought forth from his side.[22] They aren't called by their names, Mary and John. Rather, they are referred to as "Woman" and "the disciple whom he loved," more expansive terms, to represent the church in her collective identity as mother and in our personal identity as disciples, the children of God.[23]

Child, you are part of a new family. The church is our mother, called to nurture and raise us up as children of God. We are beloved disciples, called to honor and care for the church as our mother. You aren't alone anymore. You are born from above as a daughter or son, born of water and Spirit, born into the church, born of the love of the Father and power of the Son.

You are welcomed into communion with the family of God.

At the Resurrection, when Jesus calls Mary Magdalene "Woman," she gathers all these realities into herself as a sign of the church, the new Eve with our new Adam. You are invited to become his bride, to be built up as his temple, and to belong in his family—as a foretaste of new creation. This is what it means to be the church.

HOLD ON

I've gotten ahead of myself. Mary thinks Jesus is the gardener, so she says,

> "Sir, if you have carried him away, tell me where you have put him, and I will get him."
> Jesus said to her, "Mary."

She turned toward him and cried out in Aramaic, "Rabboni!" (which means "Teacher").[24]

I love that Mary doesn't recognize Jesus until she hears his voice. I imagine her with head down, looking at this gardener's feet, when she suddenly hears him say her name. She lifts her gaze at the sound of the familiar voice, and their eyes lock. She sees him seeing her. She is the first person to look into the face of resurrection, to hear his risen voice speaking a new world into existence.

Have you heard the voice of the risen Jesus calling your name? Earlier, I asked whether you've *seen* him seeing you. Here we witness the power when you *hear* him calling your name. The One who knows your story in all its intimate detail knows the losses you've experienced, knows the demons that once haunted you, knows your fear that you've been left on your own.

All that changes when you hear his voice.

Jesus's voice brings healing, comfort, and authority. Mary "*turned* toward him," a word used for conversion,[25] and calls him "Rabboni!"—an emphatic term stronger than *rabbi*—designating "the *top religious leader in Judaism* . . . who functioned as *the* religious leader of the nation."[26] The Savior has come and his messianic age is here.

She tries to cling to him, and surprisingly, he says,

> Do not hold on to me, for I have not yet ascended to the Father. Go instead to my brothers and tell them, "I am ascending to my Father and your Father, to my God and your God."[27]

Jesus commissions Mary as the first evangelist, to proclaim the good news that the Crucified One has risen. She represents the missionary calling of the church, to take the gospel to the world.

When Jesus says, "Do not hold on to me," that can sound cold. If I saw a lost loved one back from the dead, I would hug them with all my might. Yet there's something more going on here. That term "hold on to" (or "touch," "cling to," "hold fast") has covenantal associations with marriage in the biblical story.[28] If John is painting this picture of their encounter with typological associations—as we've seen frequently in his gospel—then it represents the reality that as the church we still await the wedding feast, when we shall be "the wife of the Lamb."[29]

Consider how a groom and bride often choose to keep their distance leading up to the wedding ceremony. This is not because they don't want to see each other but precisely because they *can't wait* to see each other at the ceremony. Even those who choose to do a first look on the big day typically spend ten minutes max with each other. Why? Because it's fitting to wait to embrace until the actual wedding. The distance is a temporary reality, meant to make the moment of union even more special.

This is not to imply anything literally romantic between Jesus and Mary Magdalene but rather to see how she is a representative of the church—as the "Woman," a new Eve—destined for union with Christ. Indeed, Christ says the reason not to hold on to him is that the time has *not yet* come (not that it's inherently bad to *want to*). The time is coming, however, when we will be united with Christ as his bride, when heaven and earth will become one, when we shall *hold on* to our groom in this eternal divine embrace.

Until then, the Spirit and the bride say, "Come, Lord Jesus."[30]

Even now, however, Jesus says *his Father* has become *our Father* and we are *his sisters and brothers*. Through his death and resurrection, we've been born from above as children of God. His victory has become our victory. He has ascended and sent forth the Spirit, bringing us into the family of God.

❊ ❊ ❊

Mary is the first to encounter the risen Lord, but she won't be the last. Over the centuries, hundreds of millions—nay, billions—have met the resurrected Christ. We have heard him call our name and experienced his presence through the power of his Spirit. We have worshipped him as Lord and gone to proclaim the good news of his victory to the world. We are all represented in the "Woman" who is the church.

Like a new Eve with our new Adam.

You can take courage to go to the tomb—to face those areas where God seems absent, to honor the Christ you love even when he doesn't seem present, to confront your deepest fears when your future's been shattered. Jesus wants to bring life to the areas of your deepest disappointment, disillusionment, and disorientation. He has inaugurated new creation and invites you to encounter him afresh and reign with him forever. When it hurts to hope, be like Mary and push through the dark to the place where you buried what you love. And as you investigate that crater . . .

Anticipate surprise.

13

CHANGE THE WORLD

When Your Past Seems Bigger than Your Future

Do you have memories that haunt you? I remember the day the grenade went off that blew my world apart. Attacked by a mob. Betrayed by a friend. Cast out from a community. The shrapnel in my wife and children. In me. The course of our future seemed altered forever. The memories were haunting, awakening me at three in the morning for a year. *Was the grenade set off by mistakes I made or by the brokenness and immaturity of others? Where is Jesus in the midst of it all?*

My past seemed bigger than my future. Like the good old days were behind me. Like Jesus had moved on, my calling had gotten canceled, and I was now in survival mode on my own.

What's your grenade? We all have one. Or if you don't yet, you will. The day the diagnosis comes back, the divorce papers arrive, the company implodes, or your child ends up behind bars. In those moments, regret floods your mind. *Maybe if I'd eaten healthier, shown more affection, become a better leader, or been more present at home . . .*

You can wrestle with God. *Am I being punished or perse-*

cuted? Facing the consequences of wrong I've done or enduring the wickedness of others? Jesus, have you left the building? Where are you in the midst of it all? Do you see me? If so, how do you see me?

Where do you go when your past seems bigger than your future?

In John 21, Jesus walks Peter through some painful memories. They're memories of mistakes Peter made: a best friend he abandoned, a threat he fled from, a calling he botched. The grenade's gone off—Peter knows he pulled the pin. His past hangs like a dark cloud over his future. He's filled with remorse, not nostalgia. The good old days are behind him. His mistakes have left an unerasable mark on his life.

Or so he thinks.

Jesus can tenderly walk you back through your memories, like he does for Peter—not to shame you but to restore you. Let's see how your encounter with Jesus can transform your regret and call you into a better future.

GATHER THE NATIONS

The scene opens with a fishing expedition:

"I'm going out to fish," Simon Peter told [the disciples], and they said, "We'll go with you." So they went out and got into the boat, but that night they caught nothing.[1]

Jesus is alive, but Peter has gone back to what he knows: fishing. Peter abandoned him at the cross. At the most crucial moment, when Jesus needed him the most, Peter turned his back on his best friend and blew his shot. In the aftermath, Peter goes into survival mode and slips back into the life he knows.

Yet Peter's still a leader. He's listed first here among the disciples.[2] He says, "I'm going out to fish," and everyone joins in. He's the natural-born connector who rallies the crew. He's that friend who says, "Let's go to the movies!" and everyone jumps on board. Peter can't get away from his calling. It's in him; it's who he is.

The disciples work all night on the lake and catch nothing. Then the risen Jesus appears:

> Early in the morning, Jesus stood on the shore. . . .
> He called out to them, "Friends, haven't you any fish?"
> "No," they answered.
> He said, "Throw your net on the right side of the boat and you will find some." When they did, they were unable to haul the net in because of the large number of fish.[3]

Jesus restores Peter's calling here: to gather the nations. *Wait,* you might be saying. *I don't see any nations here. Just fish.* Let me explain.

Jesus walks Peter back into the memory of his initial calling. When they first met, he told Peter to let down his nets for a catch. Peter had worked all night and caught nothing, but he obeyed, and "they caught such a large number of fish that their nets began to break." Peter fell down at Jesus's feet, amazed.

As Luke's gospel recounts, Jesus then called him: "From now on you will fish for people."[4]

Jesus re-creates that scene here. He tenderly welcomes his despondent disciple back into the wistfulness of when they first met: the sight of the great catch, the smell of the fish, the thrill of the net overflowing. All his senses activated. The hope of his calling to fish for people.

Peter's calling is to gather the nations. *Fish* represent people in this calling. The *sea* is an Old Testament image for the Gentile nations—chaotic and stormy, raging and wild.[5] So this miraculous catch is a sign of Jesus restoring Peter's calling. You can read about this calling fulfilled in Acts: Peter will go on to lead the disciples in proclaiming the gospel to the ends of the earth, gathering in people from every nation, tribe, and tongue.

It will be a miraculous catch.

I recently visited my childhood home. I wanted to show my kids where I grew up on Cynthia Street. There it was: the front porch and trees in all their glory. The family now living there happened to be in the front yard and kindly invited us in. We walked within the wood and windows I was raised in.

Memories came flooding back. *This was our dining room.* I could almost smell Mom's famous spaghetti. I pointed out the back window. *That was our tree fort.* I recounted adventures we used to have. *Whoa, this was my bedroom!* I showed them my secret exit to meet up with friends in the neighborhood and TP buddies' yards. The sentimental flashbacks were pouring in.

Jesus is doing something similar with Peter here. He's walking Peter back into his foundational memories, like that family giving us a tour of my childhood home, to restore the hope and wonder of when he first met Jesus.

Maybe you fear you've blown it, like your best days are behind you. Maybe you've gone "back to fishing," to the familiarity of what you know. Maybe you've settled into survival mode: *I just have to get by.* Yet Jesus wants to take you back to the innocence and joy of earlier days, back to before the grenade went off, back to the grace of when you first met him.

Before your fall was your creation. Before you and I were sinners, we were all made in the image of God. Before the drama of Genesis 3 was our home in Genesis 1. Jesus wants to give you a guided tour back through the home you were made for with him.

Maybe you worry you've strayed too far, let Jesus down more

than he could ever forgive. Yet his grace runs deeper than you can fathom. He's faithful when you've been unfaithful, more on your side than you could dream. And as theologian Herman Bavinck put it, "Christ gives more than sin stole."[6] Jesus still has a future for you, a mission for you.

Jesus recalls your past to set you up for your future.

Two interesting details. First, the disciples count 153 large fish. There is only one other place in Scripture where the number 153 shows up: During the glory days of Israel's kingdom, Solomon counted the foreigners in the land and discovered 153 thousand of them.[7] In other words, these were the Gentile nations residing in Israel's kingdom. The miraculous catch evokes this number to point to the future: Jesus is bringing back the glory days, gathering the nations into a restored kingdom.[8]

The best days are ahead.

Another Old Testament echo: Ezekiel said one day the river of life would flow from the temple again. It would bring abundance everywhere it went, even to the salty dead waters:

> Swarms of living creatures will live wherever the river flows. There will be large numbers of fish, because this water flows there and makes the salt water fresh; so where the river flows everything will live. Fishermen will stand along the shore; from En Gedi to En Eglaim there will be places for spreading nets. The fish will be of many kinds.[9]

Did you catch that? Fishermen. Abundance of fish. And guess which Hebrew number is associated with "En Gedi" and "En Eglaim"? Yes, it's 153.[10] Jesus popped up out of that grave—a new and living temple—to bring a river of life to our world, to pour Holy Spirit power into your life, like he's about to restore abundance to the parched places in Peter.

A second interesting detail: We're told that "even with so many [fish] the net was not torn."[11] Why include that tidbit? Well, when Jesus first called Peter, they caught so many fish that "their nets began to break." So they called their friends in a second boat and "filled both boats so full that they began to sink."[12] They couldn't hold the catch. Their nets were tearing; their boats were sinking. Before Jesus's death and resurrection, the disciples weren't ready for the ingathering of the nations.

Now, however, things have changed. After spending three years with Jesus, they're ready for the move of God that's coming. They're ready to launch an international movement that will change the world. The church will go global, proclaiming the gospel with evangelistic power and welcoming people of every stripe and background. Even under the weight of such a great catch, the boat won't sink. The church won't go under. The gates of hell won't overcome it.[13]

Our nets will hold.

A MIRACULOUS CATCH

Years ago, my wife, Holly, had a vision of renewal in our city. People lining up down the block outside our church for prayer. The Holy Spirit breaking through in churches across our city. The broken bound up and the wounded healed. Rebels on the run caught by the pursuing King. The afflicted and addicted released from bondage. The wicked turning to the Way who leads to life. Orphans welcomed into the family of the Father. The hungry feasting on the Bread of Life. The divinely dehydrated quenching their thirst in the River of Life. The lost found, the dead raised, and the ragamuffins rejoicing in their redeemer.

It would be a miraculous catch.

We sensed, in prayer, that this future was years away. *What*

would it look like, we wondered, *to prepare for that vision today?
To grow in maturity, character, and depth of life with Jesus? To
grow in dependency on and intimacy with his Spirit? To let him
tenderly walk us into our own painful memories and restore us
so that when renewal comes, our nets can hold?*

The risen Jesus restores you to gather the nations. To help
people encounter the power and presence of the risen King.
What if you let Jesus redeem your past to restore your mission?

What Jesus does *in* you, he wants to do *through* you. He has
good works he's prepared in advance for you to do.[14] Hurting
people he wants to use your hands to heal. People trapped in
regret and despair he wants to use your story to touch. People
whose eyes need to be lifted to a future that's bigger than their
past.

The world needs your healing so that you can help heal the
world. You don't have to go to the other side of the globe to do
this. My home in Oregon *is* "the ends of the earth" from the Sea
of Galilee, where Peter and Jesus had this conversation. We *are*
the nations. You can go fishing right there in your neighborhood.

I know *evangelism* can be a dirty word in some circles today,
so here are two encouragements. First, you don't need to bait
and switch. You don't need to put shiny bait on the line, wrap-
ping prizes and false promises around the gospel to lure people
in and hook them. No, the gospel is good news all on its own. For
it is, most simply, the good news of who Jesus is and what he's
done. As we saw earlier, you can simply share how you've experienced his goodness in your own story. "They overcame . . . by
the blood of the Lamb and by the word of their testimony."[15] His
work and your story. That's the magic combo.

The second encouragement: You don't need a better strategy.
You simply need the presence of the risen Jesus. Before he appears, the disciples are fishing all night long with nothing to

show for it. Evangelism in your own strength is fruitless. The power is not in your fishing ability but in the magnetic power of God's presence.

It's when Jesus appears, in the morning light, that the great catch comes in. The power for evangelism is found when we press into intimacy with Jesus, devotion to the Father, holiness in the Spirit. Fish in the light with Jesus, not in the dark on your own.

When I first came to faith, my friend's father, Mike, was constantly sharing inspiring stories of people he'd led to Jesus. I was confused and intimidated: *How do you do it? Isn't it awkward or embarrassing?* "No," he said, then shared his secret: "Every week I pray, asking God to bring that one right person onto my path." He prayed that the conversation would arise naturally, that God would give him wisdom and words of life. He asked the risen Jesus for the opportunity to share in a way that was not forced but life-giving for all involved. He wasn't fishing in the dark on his own.

He was fishing in the light with Jesus.

You can too. But first we need to experience the healing power of Jesus in our own lives. That's not to say we need to be perfect, but we need to taste the medicine we're offering. We need to experience his tender care in our painful memories, the challenging parts of our story. That's where he takes Peter next.

BREAKFAST ON THE BEACH

Jesus cooks breakfast on the beach. I love it! *Just conquered the grave. What's next on my to-do list?* I'd be on a world tour, making the disciples cook breakfast for me. (*You guys can be my roadies!*) Yet Jesus is still a servant, showing hospitality to his closest friends. He wants to make them brunch.

Jesus cooks this breakfast over "a charcoal fire" (*anthrakia*).[16] Does that sound familiar? The word appears only one other place in the New Testament: When Peter denied Jesus, in John 18, he was standing before a charcoal fire. Peter was warming himself in the cold of the night, next to the servants and officials, when they asked him whether he was a disciple of Jesus.[17] Three times he was asked; three times he denied. While Jesus was being interrogated inside, Peter was being questioned outside. While Jesus testified to the truth, Peter denied the truth.

Three times he blew it.

So now Jesus asks three times, "Do you love me?"[18] Once for each denial. He asks not whether Peter *knows* him (like the servants did on that horrible night) but whether he *loves* him. Peter responds positively each time. By the third time, however, he gets the point: "Peter was hurt because Jesus asked him the third time."[19] He knows he blew it.

Memory is an interesting thing. A smell can conjure it; a song can evoke it; your senses can take you back. Recently at a haircut, one whiff from a complimentary can of orange-vanilla sparkling water took me all the way back to grade school—those orange-vanilla Creamsicle cups with the wooden spoons we all loved. *Mmm, waves of nostalgia.*

Jesus is doing something similar here with the charcoal fire. He intentionally walks Peter back into the painful memory, recreating the sight, sound, and smell of the scene. Yet the warmth of the flames and waft of the charcoal evoke not elation but regret. Jesus's purpose is not to torment Peter, however, but to heal him. He tenderly walks Peter down memory lane not to shame him but to restore him.

I love my counselor. He asks great questions. He pokes and prods, but he does so tenderly. When he inquires, I know it's because he cares for me. He doesn't let me get away with cheap answers or sugarcoated platitudes, because he knows you can't bring healing to a wound you pretend isn't there. Similarly, Jesus is the Wonderful Counselor who gently lifts your self-protective bandages to reveal the painful places because that's where the medicine is needed.[20]

Peter thinks he's blown his calling. *I ran away at the cross. I talked a big game, but I abandoned Jesus in his darkest hour. Some leader I am. John stayed; I fled. Jesus will move on with someone better than me.*

Peter doesn't yet realize that not only did Jesus die for the world; he also died for Peter. The Savior went to the cross to deal with Peter's own shortcomings, failure, and shame. Even when Peter was rejecting Jesus, Jesus was loving him.

Jesus died for you. Maybe you have an easier time accepting that Jesus loves the world—an abstract geographical sphere, the nations as a conceptual generality, or other people with all their mess and brokenness—but have a harder time accepting that Jesus loves *you.* The real you. With all your flaws and failures. That he died for *your* mistakes, wounds, and scars. That he cares about *your* memories. Yet it's true.

Jesus loves you.

The risen Jesus wants to make you breakfast, so to speak. To sit and converse with you. The Savior can speak into the scars from your story. Maybe like Peter, you've got a charcoal fire of things you've done. Maybe like me, you've got a grenade that's gone off in your life. Maybe your past feels bigger than your future.

Jesus gently beckons from the beach. He prepares a table before you in the presence of your memories, with holy hospitality. *Sit and join me.* When you join him, you discover he is on your side, with you to strengthen you.

What you did doesn't define you anymore. My forgiveness covers you; my blood purifies you; my death pays your debt; my Spirit washes you clean. I've met you in your mess; I've covered your mistakes.

What they did to you doesn't define you anymore. I've met you in your shame. I was mocked, rejected, and cast out; I did it to welcome you back in. I'm here; I'm for you.

Jesus calls you into a future that's bigger than your past.

STINKY CLOTHES

"Feed my sheep," Jesus tells Peter.[21] When the disciple declares his love for Jesus three times, the Good Shepherd responds three times: asking Peter to feed and care for his sheep. As if to say, *This is how you can show your love for me. Care for my people.*

Not only is Peter a fisherman called to gather the nations; he's also a shepherd called to care for Christ's people.[22] As we saw in chapter 10, *pastor* means "shepherd." The job of a pastor is to care for God's people, like a shepherd caring for sheep. Jesus gives two commands here: to *feed* and *care for* his sheep. Pastors are to feed Jesus's flock with God's Word and sacrament and to care for them with pastoral wisdom and love.

A good pastor is defined not by the size of their platform but by the faithfulness of their presence. By the integrity of their teaching and the quality of their care. As an Italian saying goes, "If you can't smell the stink of the sheep on their clothing, they're not really a pastor."[23] A willingness to get into people's mess reveals your love for Jesus and them. The stink on your clothes bears witness to your care for his people.

This passage is about more than just pastors, however. Whatever your vocation, a sign of Jesus's healing in your life is an expanded capacity to love. To care for his people. As grace takes root in your life, you're gradually less fixated on your own trials or failures. Instead, you're increasingly able to look outward toward others, to see their hunger and wounds, to share what you've received from Christ. To feed with truth and care with compassion.

You might wonder, *What would I have to offer?* But in Christ, you've received so much. As with Peter, Jesus first feeds you breakfast on the beach before calling you to turn around and feed others. He first cares for your painful memories before sending you to care for his people. The Christian life starts with receiving; this is the way of grace. Jesus fills you up so you can share from the abundance of that overflow. This is what changes the world.

Yet as with Christ, changing the world comes at a cost.

GIVE YOUR LIFE

Jesus foreshadows the future of his fisherman Peter:

> "When you were younger you dressed yourself and went where you wanted; but when you are old you will stretch out your hands, and someone else will dress you and lead you where you do not want to go." Jesus said this to indicate the kind of death by which Peter would glorify God. Then he said to him, "Follow me!"[24]

Jesus tells Peter "the kind of death" he's going to die—a death like Jesus's. When he's old, someone else will dress him (in martyr's clothes), he'll stretch out his hands (to be cuffed and chained), and he'll be led somewhere he doesn't want to go (a cross). Peter was martyred for his faith. Tradition tells us Peter requested to be crucified upside down, during the reign of Nero, because he didn't feel worthy to be crucified in the same manner as his Lord.

I wonder what memories were sparked for Peter as he went

to the cross. At the smell of the cruciform wood, did his imagination flood with memories of the tree on which his savior died? As his arms were stretched out on the beams, did it evoke his Lord's arms stretched wide to embrace him in his denial—and a world in its rejection and rebellion? As he felt the nails pounded through his palms, could he feel with new depth the love of his Lord, pierced to atone for his sin and reconcile him to God?

Peter's worst memory—the cross—had changed. It was transformed to a place of intimacy with his savior. The very tool of execution he once ran from at Jesus's death, he could now embrace as his own. This fisherman's most frightening future had now become an opportunity to more faithfully know his Lord. He no longer feared the death he once cowered before. As Peter hung on that cross, as he exhaled his final breath and gave up his spirit, his vision upon closing his eyes was the horizon of eternity set before him, which Jesus had secured. Even in the gravity of his death, his glorious destiny yet loomed larger.

His future was now bigger than his past.

With Jesus, even your starkest moments can become an opportunity for intimacy. Even a grueling death can unite you with the Crucified One, whose body was demolished to rebuild you in risen life and glory. You can rise with boldness and courage, unafraid in the midst of danger and storm, with your face set like flint toward a future that expansively unfolds before you.

You can give your life for the One who gave his life for you.

WATER TO WINE

Jesus wants to continue turning water to wine through you today. He tells his disciples, "I am the vine; you are the branches."[25] A vine is God's vehicle for turning water to wine. It soaks in the water that rains down from heaven above, carrying it to its branches to produce grapes. Similarly, Jesus the Vine imparts the living water of his heavenly Spirit to us as the branches as we remain connected to him. "If you remain in me and I in you, you will bear much fruit; apart from me you can do nothing."[26] Jesus wants to grow the fruit of his Spirit on the branch of your life.[27]

Like grapes must be crushed, however, it costs us to bring the wine of his sacrificial love to the world. This love is a "greater love," which "lay[s] down one's life for one's friends." "Remain in my love," Jesus commands us as his branches so that we might "love each other as I have loved you."[28] As we take up our cross, like Peter is called to here at the end of John's gospel, it's our crushing that bears Christ's redemptive power to the world. This cruciform love "fill[s] up in [our] flesh what is still lacking in regard to Christ's afflictions, for the sake of his [wounded] body, which is the church."[29] Be his branch; bear his fruit.

Let Christ turn water to wine through you.

Jesus doesn't lead you somewhere he hasn't first gone himself. Jesus fishes for Peter at the Sea of Galilee, catching him in the net of his mercy, before he calls him to fish for others. Jesus feeds Peter, the lost lamb he's brought back home, breakfast on the beach before he calls him to feed his sheep. Jesus gives his life for Peter, in sacrificial love for his friend, before he sends Peter to give his life for God.

Jesus practices what he preaches. Like washing his disciples' feet, then sending them to do likewise, Jesus first catches, feeds, and loves us before sending us to do the same.

It starts with receiving. Receive Jesus gathering you into his arms, caring for your wounds, and feeding your soul with his words. Receive Jesus pouring out his life for you, in blood and water from his side, to cleanse and revive you. Receive Jesus tenderly walking you into your painful memories to heal you and make you whole. Our self-giving overflows from the abundance of grace we've received. Our fidelity follows in the footsteps of his faithfulness to us. What do we have that we haven't first received?[30]

All is gift; all is grace.

Yes, Jesus has come to restore the world; he starts with restoring you. He empowers you with his presence, unleashing you into a future that is bigger than your past. You might question your meaning and purpose, but Christ calls you to join him in the greatest mission the world has ever known: the restoration of all creation.

There are people swimming in the swirling and chaotic sea of our culture, surrounded by danger and storm, who need to be gathered into the unfathomable, oceanic love of God. The Fisher of men catches you to gather the nations into his glorious, reconciling kingdom.

There are starving and bloodied lambs in the flock of God, confused and straying, who need the truth of his Word to nourish them, the sound of his voice to guide them, and his tender care to nurse them back to health. The Good Shepherd calls you to extend what you've received.

There are people dying for meaning, giving themselves to all sorts of things that only increase the ache, who need to *experientially encounter* the life-giving Spirit of the One who laid down his life to rescue them. You can give your life boldly for the One who gave his life for you.

Do you hear the God who is on your side beckoning, as his voice called to Peter on that beach so long ago? "Follow me!"[31] There is a great restoration afoot. Let's pick up our cross and follow. Even if it means we get crushed along the way, there's resurrection on the other side. Besides, that's how the good wine gets made.

Join the risen Jesus; change the world.

CONCLUSION

Be the Beloved

"What do you want on your tombstone?" my friend Jason asked.

"That's morbid," I replied.

We were in college, and my grave was—hopefully—a long way away. Yet what he meant was, *How do you want to be remembered? If you started with the end in mind and could encapsulate what was most important to you, what would those few words be?*

Some people go humorous. Mel Blanc—the voice of Bugs Bunny, Daffy Duck, and other *Looney Tunes* characters—put his famous sign-off line on his tombstone: "That's all, folks." TV host Merv Griffin—the creator of *Wheel of Fortune* and *Jeopardy!*—riffed on a well-known refrain: "I will not be right back after this message."

What do you want on your tombstone? What do you want your legacy to be? Perhaps an accomplishment or trophy? A passion or hobby?

The apostle John concludes his gospel by identifying himself as "the disciple whom Jesus loved."[1] That's how he wants to be remembered. That's the legacy he puts on his tombstone. John doesn't even use his own name in his gospel. Instead, five times he refers to himself as "the disciple whom Jesus loved."[2] That's his way of saying there's no greater identity, no deeper calling he desires, than to be the beloved of God.

As we put a bow on this book, how do we live in response to the God who is on our side? How do you worship the God who is in it with you, fighting for you, and working for your good?

You be the beloved.

A BELOVED DISCIPLE

When John calls himself a beloved disciple, he's not saying Jesus loved him more than the other disciples. No, Jesus loved those who were his own to the end.[3] He commanded that they "love one another as I have loved you."[4] John's not saying he had a special relationship with Jesus the others didn't have; he's rather saying how special his relationship with Jesus is to him—and that *you* can have that relationship too.[5]

Beloved means to be the object or recipient of love and affection. John's emphasis is not on *how much he loves Jesus* but on the inverse: *how much Jesus loves him.* That's striking. It cuts against a "super-spiritual" culture, where everyone tries to compete with one another to show who has the greatest devotion to God. Where those who experience the greatest miracles or divine power must be the closest to Jesus. Where spirituality is a performance for divine approval. No, the exclamation point in being the beloved is not on your great love for God but on God's great love for you.

Beloved is a theme in Scripture. The name David means "beloved," so every time Israel spoke of their great King David, they

heard "King Beloved." Every time they mentioned the messianic Son of David, they heard "Son of the Beloved." In Song of
Songs, Israel sang of their relationship with God: "I am my beloved's and my beloved is mine."[6] At Jesus's baptism, the voice of
the Father publicly proclaimed over him, "This is my beloved
Son."[7] This was before Jesus started his ministry, before he'd
done anything to earn it or prove it. Jesus worked not *for* his
identity as beloved but *from* his identity as beloved.

David. Israel. Jesus. All saw themselves this way. My point?
The apostle John joins a mighty chorus in declaring his core
identity: God's beloved.

This can be your deepest identity too. The God who is on your
side invites you to find yourself in his love, to make this your
name—who you are, how you identify yourself, the deepest
thing about you—to the point you write it on your tombstone.

The *New York Times* opinion columnist David Brooks contrasts
résumé virtues with *eulogy virtues*. Résumé virtues—a student's
high test scores or an adult's professional accomplishments—are
valued in the contemporary marketplace, rewarded with bigger
paychecks and public applause. In contrast, eulogy virtues—
character traits like humility, kindness, and bravery—are what
are talked about at your funeral, what are praised when you
aren't around to hear it.[8]

Eulogy virtues are more relational. They have to do with how
you are in relationships with others. It takes effort to cultivate
eulogy virtues in a résumé-virtue society obsessed with image,
success, and performance. But it's worth it.

Being beloved is a eulogy virtue. It's relational, having to do
with your most foundational relationship: your relationship with
God. It shapes your character, giving you confidence and security because you have an unshakable foundation to build the rest
of your life on.

Jesus doesn't love you based on your résumé. He loved you before the foundation of the world—before you did anything to deserve it. He loved you when you weren't virtuous. When you were a rebel and made yourself his enemy. He loved you enough to give his life for you. He'll love you in the future—whether you get it right or make mistakes. He'll love you forever; he's faithful like that.

Jesus calls you a beloved disciple. So stop relying on your résumé and start relying on his. You can rely on his reputation of unflinching goodness. His record of perfect humanity. His perfect test score of faithfulness accomplished in a complete victory on the cross. His relation toward you of unbending divine desire and unbreakable loyal love.

INTIMACY WITH JESUS

In closing his gospel, the beloved disciple describes himself as "the one who had leaned back against Jesus at the supper."[9] He's referring to the Last Supper. On the eve of Jesus's crucifixion, "one of his disciples, whom Jesus loved, was reclining at table *in the bosom of Jesus*."[10] That's a strange phrase: *in the bosom of Jesus*. In that culture, the bosom was a place of security and vulnerability. In other words, it was "the position synonymous with *intimacy* (union)."[11]

This intimacy echoes the Son's eternal relationship with the Father. John opens his gospel saying that while no one has ever seen God, "the only begotten Son, who is *in the bosom of the Father*," has made him known.[12] Did you catch that? The Son is in the bosom of the Father; John is in the bosom of Jesus.

Jesus's relation to the Father has now become John's relation to Jesus. Jesus came forth from the bosom of the Father to make him known. John comes forth from the bosom of Jesus—born from above, through his cross and resurrection—to make him known. The Father loved the Son before the creation of the world; the Son loved John before the creation of the world.

Jesus is the beloved of God; John is the beloved of Jesus.

John wants you to know yourself as the beloved of Jesus: born from above, through blood and water; born of the Father, through Word and Spirit; born of Christ's power, through cross and resurrection. You were made for security and vulnerability with God. This intimacy isn't dependent on what you've done or haven't done, how good you've been or haven't been. It's dependent, rather, on how good he is toward you and what he's done for you.

Jesus teaches you to receive your identity as beloved. There's a difference between *creating* an identity and *receiving* an identity. Our culture is captivated by trying to create an identity. Online influencers offer a dizzying menu of options from which to craft a persona. At first, this can seem freeing (*I can be whoever I want to be!*), but it soon becomes exhausting (*I have to keep up the performance*). This pressure to construct an impression that impresses arguably plays a major role in the mental health crisis of our age.[13]

The God who is on your side brings real freedom, however. You don't have to create a core identity; you can receive your core identity from him. Jesus calls you beloved. This means you don't have to define who you are by your tastes (liking the right music, clothing, or brands). Or your friend group (searching for approval, so you tell people what they want to hear). Or your cultural tribe (fearing isolation, so you conform to the patterns around you). Or your romantic success (thinking you're not complete in yourself, so you have to unite with someone or anyone else). Or your political party (throwing all your hope into a sinking ship). Or your addiction (covering unaddressed wounds with a coping device). These can exhaust you, make your life miserable, and lead you to an early grave.

There's freedom in being God's beloved.

When you know you're loved, you don't have to prove yourself. You're secure and can put others in the spotlight. You can follow and lift up others, knowing you're a part of something bigger. You can make Jesus the star of the show. Your language shifts from "Look what I've done for God" to "Look what God's done for me!"

When you know you're loved, you can trust Jesus with your destiny. When tragedy hits and your next step is unclear, you can be confident that the One in charge of your future is the One who is for you with an affection that nothing—not disease, disaster, demons, or even death—could ever separate you from. Even when you're scared about what the future holds, you can rest in knowing God holds your future.

ON YOUR SIDE

Your deepest calling is to be the beloved. John wrote his gospel so that you would know this call—and Christ as the One who calls you. John could've written about many other things that Jesus did, he says:

> But these are written that you may believe that Jesus is the Messiah, the Son of God, and that by believing you may have life in his name.[14]

That's the goal of John's gospel. It's why he wrote his book (and why I've written this one). He wants you to experience what he experienced, to encounter the One he encountered, to know the God who is on your side and experience life in his name.

He wants you to know yourself as the beloved.

How do you receive the love of God? God communicates his love to us through his Word and Spirit. The Word and Spirit are more than *things;* they're *persons*—the second and third persons of the Trinity. This frames why we do Christian practices—I don't want to invent new things for you to do here so much as to explain the things we beloved disciples do that are designed to make us new.

We gather weekly as God's people in church services to receive from God's Word and Spirit. We read Scripture to encounter the living Word through the written words that point to him. We pray to encounter the Spirit of the living God, who communes with us. We receive the sacrament to encounter the presence of God through his means of grace. We worship and serve to respond to the God who has first loved us.

Traditional Christian practices of spiritual formation are not rituals for *performing* but rather postures for *receiving.* They're vehicles for knowing ourselves as God's beloved.

Starting with God's love for you keeps you from two dangers. First, it keeps you from the danger of legalism: trying to earn God's affection. Second, it keeps you from lawlessness: trying to find such love elsewhere. We counter these by centering our lives on the fount of the Father's love, received through his Word and Spirit.

God's love for you isn't fluffy or trite. Our culture has some diminished definitions of love, but God's love is holy. He disciplines those he loves with an affection that cares enough about you to confront the sin in your life. His goal is your wholeness— that you would become like Christ, conformed to his character.

Toward the end of his life, the famous theologian Karl Barth was asked to sum up all his theological work in a sentence. His answer was shockingly simple: "Jesus loves me. This I know, for the Bible tells me so."[15]

Barth is widely considered the most significant theologian of the twentieth century. Pope Pius XII called him "the greatest theologian since Thomas Aquinas," even though he was Protestant.[16] Barth wrote so many books he's said to have joked, "Not even I have read everything I've written."[17] Yet when asked about the central truth of his theology, he joined the apostle John.

Being God's beloved.

As we prepare to part, that's what I want you to know. What I want you to experience. What I want to leave you with. John didn't write his gospel to leave you with a history lesson, like Indiana Jones digging up interesting archaeology on some ancient figure. Or to leave you with trivia facts so you can impress strangers with your depth of knowledge in party conversation.

No, he wrote it "that you may believe" that God is for you in Christ, even when everything else seems against you. "That by believing you may have life in his name," encountering in Christ the God who is on your side.

So let's go back to the question we opened this conclusion with: What do you want on your tombstone? I'll share my answer; you're free to steal it if you want:

Beloved of God.

This is, I believe, my deepest identity. My greatest calling. I long to see myself as a disciple whom Jesus loves. And I want the same for you.

You are loved by the One who has no tombstone. The stone has been rolled away. He slept with you in death to raise you with him in life. His tomb is now empty. Because of his cross and resurrection, the words engraved on your tombstone won't be the last words of your story either.

The day is coming when Christ will call you out of your grave: "Arise, my beloved!" He will take your hand to raise you up with him, into the wedding feast at the consummation of history. We won't be spectators on the sidelines, looking at him from a distance. We will be his bride, standing face-to-face with our future before us, transfixed by his gaze. We will see him seeing us. We will be united with God: indwelt by the Spirit, beholding the Son, in the home of the Father, forever.

God is more for you than you ever dared imagine. Even when everything seems against you, he is for you. He is the Word become flesh, who is in it with you. He is the Lamb once slain, who fights for you. He is the Resurrection and the Life, who brings heaven to earth in you and works through you for your good. You can know yourself as his beloved.

For he is the God on your side.

APPENDIX

An Elegant Design

John's gospel has a beautiful literary structure that helps reinforce its meaning. I didn't want to bog down the main text with too much of this detail, but it's worth highlighting here to show how John's structure supports the overall themes we've explored. John famously orders his events *theologically* instead of chronologically. He's arranged the events of his gospel in a particular order, for a specific purpose. Let's check it out.

FROM CANA TO CANA

After the introduction, John 2–4 forms the first section of the gospel. This section is bookended by *third day at Cana* scenes. In John 2:1 (the front bookend), we read, "On the third day a wedding took place at Cana in Galilee." In John 4:43–46 (the back bookend), that first scene is echoed: "After the two days [that is, on the *third* day] he left for Galilee. . . . Once more he visited Cana in Galilee, where he had turned the water into wine."[1] John thus sets up a literary *inclusio* with the third-day wedding at Cana (where Jesus performs "the first of the signs") and the raising of the official's son ("the second sign" he performs from Cana).[2]

The journey from Cana to Cana is a chiasmus—a popular Jewish literary structure—with two sides that mirror each other and work their way in toward the middle. Within this structure, there is a correspondence between Jesus's wedding miracle and his conversation with the Samaritan woman, on the one hand, and Jesus's temple actions and his conversation with Nicodemus, on the other hand.

Passover

Temple (John 2b)　　Nicodemus (John 3)

Wedding (John 2a)　　Samaritan Woman (John 4)

The significance? This literary structure reinforces the befuddled Nicodemus as a representative for the Jerusalem leadership: They are in the dark, confused by Jesus, and will ultimately tear down the temple of his body. Yet he will rebuild it in three days, and they must be born from above, of water and Spirit, if they are to enter his kingdom.

This literary structure also reinforces the Samaritan woman as a representative for the church as the bride of Christ. We saw in chapter 3 how the well—where Christ meets the Samaritan woman—held typological significance as the place where a groom met his bride. The chiastic connection of this scene to the wedding at Cana further supports this marital motif. The church as bride will receive the living water of Christ's Spirit, be purified by the wine of his atoning blood, worship in Spirit and truth as the new living temple, and rejoice in a wedding celebration where the best has been saved for last.

This wedding brings new life to the world, as seen in the sign that follows: the raising of the official's son from the brink of death.

One more note: There is an interesting segue between Nicodemus and the Samaritan woman that further highlights this theme. John the Baptist declares he is not the groom but rather "the friend of the bridegroom,"[3] who rejoices when he hears the bridegroom's voice, for "the bride belongs to the bridegroom."[4] It's as if he's saying, *Cue the music; here comes the bride!* And in walks the Samaritan woman in the story that follows.

The context for John the Baptist's remarks is a dispute about baptism and ceremonial washing, which has ties to the wedding at Cana (the water jars "used by the Jews for ceremonial washing"[5]), the conversation with Nicodemus (one must be born of water and Spirit—that is, the baptism Jesus brings from above), and the conversation with the Samaritan woman (regarding living water). John is thus passing the baton, so to speak, from his ministry as the greatest prophet under the old order of things, who prepares the way for the Messiah, to Jesus, who inaugurates the new order of things in the kingdom.[6]

The middle of a chiasmus is its climax, or main point. At the center of this chiasmus is Passover, which occurs between Jesus's actions in the temple and his conversation with Nicodemus.[7] As we've seen, Passover points forward to the crucifixion of Christ. So, Jesus's death is the center that moves us from the old order to the new order, from the temple in Jerusalem to the church as a living temple indwelt by the Spirit, from a disappointing party that ran out of steam to a wedding celebration running with new wine.

Jesus's victory will flow down from Mount Zion to the sea. There is a downward geographical movement from Jesus's conversation with Nicodemus (in Jerusalem), to John the Baptist's pronouncement (in Judea), to Jesus's encounter with the woman at the well (in Samaria), to his healing of the royal official's son (in Galilee, known as "Galilee of the nations" because of its Gentile majority[8]). In other words, the blood and water that flow from Jesus's side in John 19:34 will flow down from Jerusalem, to Judea, to Samaria, and to the ends of the earth.[9]

John's elegant design points to the victory of the gospel.

THE SHEEP GATE

John 5–11, the second section of John's gospel, is marked by two references to "the sheep gate." At the first bookend, Jesus encounters a paralytic by the Sheep Gate in the Jerusalem wall.[10] At the second bookend, Jesus says, "I am the gate for the sheep,"[11] and launches into a discourse on his identity as the Good Shepherd. As we saw in chapter 10, this discourse is connected with his raising of Lazarus in John 11. Jesus opens the sheep gate, so to speak, and calls out his lamb by name.

This section is set against the backdrop of Israel's wilderness wandering. Jesus raises the man paralyzed for thirty-eight years: a sign that he has come to raise God's people up from under the curse of the law and bring them by grace into the promised land. Jesus feeds the five thousand: a sign that he is the heavenly bread that sustains us on our wilderness journey toward our eternal home in his kingdom. Jesus invites all who thirst to come to him and drink: a promise that we can receive the life-giving river of his Spirit, like water from a rock, to quench our divine dehydration in the wilderness of our world.

The Good Shepherd guides us through the wilderness to our eternal home with God.

Following this, the third section (John 12–19) is structured around a Passover theme, and the fourth section (John 20–21) around a new-creation theme. I'll discuss both of these below.

PLAY IT IN REVERSE

Have you ever rewound a movie and watched the scenes flying by in reverse? You catch the settings and characters, though it's going too fast to capture all the details. You're left with the big-picture flow of the story but in reverse.

I'd suggest John does something similar. His gospel moves backward—rewinding, so to speak—through major scenes from the Old Testament. You catch Christ moving through and redeeming the big-picture flow of the biblical story in reverse. Let me explain.

In John 2–4, we start with the wedding motif: a picture of the eschatological wedding where Yahweh will be united with his bride and abundant wine will flow, foreseen by the prophets of old like Isaiah, Hosea, Joel, and Amos. We then move to the temple motif: an image from Israel's glory days in the land—an era racked by sin and corruption. Next comes the reunion with Samaria: a scene hearkening to the split of the northern and southern kingdoms, a dark moment in Israel's history. Finally, we have the motif of blessing: Christ moves down from Jerusalem, to Judea, to Samaria, and, figuratively, to the ends of the earth.

In other words, we've moved from the prophets' hope, to the corruption of the kings, to worship in the temple, to blessing in the land. Christ is walking through the flow of the biblical story in reverse order, moving backward through Israel's history in the promised land.

Next, in John 5–11, we move to the wilderness section. There are echoes of Israel paralyzed in the wilderness for thirty-eight years, unable to rise up and enter the land (John 5), of grumbling and manna in the wilderness (John 6), of grumbling and water in the wilderness (John 7), of Israel's adultery in the golden calf incident (John 8), of a pillar of fire and cloud as a guide in the wilderness (John 8–9).

In other words, Christ is walking backward through the wilderness years of his people's history. He does so as the Good Shepherd (John 10), like Yahweh did when he "led out his people like sheep and guided them in the wilderness like a flock."[12]

This brings us to the Exodus motif (John 11): Lazarus is bound in the grave like Israel was in Egypt, yet Jesus says "Unbind him" like God declared "Let my people go."[13] There is a tyrant greater than Pharaoh, the cosmic thief who comes to kill, steal, and destroy, yet Jesus will defeat this enemy and defend his sheep. As we saw in chapter 10, the sheep gate becomes—through John's use of allusion—an image for the exit from the grave. The Good Shepherd will open the gate and deliver his sheep from bondage.

So, we can think of John 5–11 as the wilderness section, which—again, in reverse order from the Old Testament—starts at the gates of the promised land and ends with an exodus from bondage.

This brings us to Passover: John 12–19 takes place during Passover week. References to Passover bookend this section.[14] The word "Passover" (*pascha*) is used seven times, highlighting its thematic significance.[15] The pace of these chapters slows down as we approach the climax of John's gospel, the crucifixion of Christ. This is where Christ, the Passover Lamb, is slain to take away the sin of the world, inaugurating a new and greater cosmic exodus and setting God's people free.[16]

The seven signs of John's gospel all point to the significance of Christ's crucifixion and resurrection, powerfully helping us interpret what is happening. The signs that most dramatically prefigure his crucifixion (as opposed to his resurrection) are explicitly said to occur near Passover.[17] When it comes to rewinding the Old Testament, we are here at the foundational event of Israel's history: her deliverance from slavery into union with God. Jesus walks back into this part of the story to set us free.

Finally, John 20–21 takes us back to creation. Christ, the new Adam, encounters Mary, a representative for the new Eve, the church, in a garden (John 20). She mistakes him for the gardener—but she's more right than she knows. It's the first day, we're told, of a new week—a reference to new creation.[18] In an echo of the seven days of creation, Christ died on the sixth day, rested on the seventh day, and rose on a new first day to inaugurate the new creation as the firstfruits of resurrection.

Then, like God speaking over the dark waters of Genesis 1, Christ calls out to his disciples over the sea (John 21). They have been fishing all night, hovering over the dark waters in their boat, and have caught nothing. Yet Christ appears "early in the morning" and speaks a sovereign word,[19] like the God who spoke light into darkness and brought forth the abundance of creation. The miraculous catch that follows is a foreshadowing, as we saw in chapter 13, of God gathering the Gentile nations out of the chaotic waters of a turbulent world and into the peace of his kingdom through the church.

So, John's gospel ends at the beginning. This final section echoes Genesis 1–2. Jesus has walked all the way through the Old Testament in reverse. Why? Is there a theological meaning to this literary structure?

Yes. I would suggest John depicts Christ walking backward through the story of Israel—and of all humanity—to redeem it. This is similar to *recapitulation,* a theological theme where Christ relives the story of Israel—and of all humanity—succeeding where we failed, in order to redeem us as our new Head.[20] We might call John's theme, however, *reverse-capitulation:* Christ is reliving the biblical story in reverse to redeem our history and reestablish our destiny.

Similar to how *reverse* can mean "to undo something," so Christ walks back through our story to undo our waywardness and set us on the right trajectory again. John's gospel has an elegant design that points to the jaw-dropping reality of Christ's redemptive work and his unswerving commitment to being on our side.

GRATEFUL

Every book is a team project, and I want to give a shout-out to some of the amazing crew who had a crater-size impact on this one.

First, Jenni Burke is the most amazing literary agent in the world. That may sound like hyperbole, but I'm serious. Jenni, you've brought wisdom and depth to every stage of the project. Over the years, you've been a friend in the fire with courage, integrity, and counsel more valuable than gold. There's no team I'd rather be writing with than Illuminate Literary.

To the whole team at Multnomah: Laura Barker, Tina Constable, Bev Rykerd, and Tina Richey Swanson, thank you for believing in me, for the time together in Dallas, for your wisdom and friendship in the storm—thank you for being a tangible expression of the God who is on our side. Will Anderson, your vision as an editor helped take this project to a whole other level. Laura Wright, your attention to detail and humor have made it a true joy to work together on the last few projects. Kayla Fenstermaker, wow, you truly have eyes like a hawk—they made this book so much stronger! Brett Benson and Douglas Mann, it's such a treasure getting to make this resource available with you both.

To the Willamette family of churches: Thank you for embracing our family and welcoming us into a new season of life and ministry in the kingdom together. While I love you all, a special shout-out is due to these three: Chris Yarco, you're one of the wisest servant-hearted leaders I know. John Rosensteel, love being in it together, friend. Just free up some space for me on those bookshelves! Alex Lessler, diving in together has been a highlight of this season. Let's keep the meme thread going.

A crew of friends has particularly ministered to me in this last season of life: Ben Thomas, Jesse Lusko, Ashish Mathew, Tony Scarcello, Brenna Blain, Gerry Breshears, Bre Golden, Preston Sprinkle, Patrick Miller, Christopher West, Rick McKinley, Luke Hendrix, Chris Nye, Naseem Khalili, Father Ignacio Llorente, Eric and Hilary Shreves, Andrew Murch, John Heintzman, Ben Wachsmuth, Paul Ramey, Brian Cox, Jon Collins, A. J. Swoboda, Nijay Gupta, Sebastian and Catherine Rogers, and Maurice and Leslie Cowley. I'm beyond grateful for you all.

Thank you to Michaela Miller, A. J. Swoboda, and Brad Sarian for feedback on early drafts of the book. Also to John and Teri Sramek and to Jeremy and Brenda Jones for writing retreats at your Mount Hood cabin (and thanks to Mike, Merv, and Barbara for helping me get unstuck from the snow!).

This book would not have been possible without my family. To Aiden, for endless games of Rummikub and Nerts when I needed a break; to James, for making constant cups of coffee to keep me caffeinated; to Jake, for nightly reading on the couch together, bringing comfort to the research. To Holly, for being for me when everything seemed against us. Christ continues to encounter me through you.

Father, Son, and Holy Spirit, you are my everything. Thank you for a divine affection and holy belonging more extravagant than I ever could have dreamed. *Soli Deo gloria.*

NOTES

INTRODUCTION: ON YOUR SIDE

1. Brenna Blain, *Can I Say That?: How Unsafe Questions Lead Us to the Real God* (W Publishing, 2024), 199.
2. John 1:14.
3. Genesis 1; Psalm 33:6; Hebrews 11:3; 2 Peter 3:5.
4. John 1:29, 36.
5. John 1:29.
6. John 1:51. This image is based on the story of Jacob's ladder in Genesis 28.
7. Jesus tells Nathanael he'll *see* "greater things" (John 1:50), and he later tells his disciples they'll *do* "greater things" (14:12). United to Christ, the global church will accomplish a far wider scope of work through the power of his Spirit than Jesus did solo in his ministry on earth. We are the agents through which Christ does his greater things in the world.
8. Brandon Lake, "God Is Not Against Me," track 7 on *Coat of Many Colors*, Provident, 2023.
9. Joshua 5:13–14.
10. John 1:14.
11. In the dialectical theology of Barth's *Church Dogmatics*, God's "Yes" is his affirmation of creation and his revelation in Christ, while his "No" is his rejection of human attempts to define or limit him. Barth reflects on the development of this theme in Karl Barth, "A Thank-You and a Bow—Kierkegaard's Reveille," in *Fragments Grave and Gay*, ed. Martin Rumscheidt (William Collins & Sons, 1971), 102–4.
12. Jason Edward Kaufman, "Abramovic Takes Over MoMA with the Artist Is Present and a Selection of Past Works," *The Art Newspaper*, May 31, 2009,

www.theartnewspaper.com/2009/06/01/abramovic-takes-over-moma-with
-the-artist-is-present-and-a-selection-of-past-works.

13. The Museum of Modern Art, "Marina Abramović: The Artist Is Present—
Portraits," Flickr, accessed December 18, 2024, www.flickr.com/photos/
themuseumofmodernart/albums/72157623741486824.

14. John 1:45–51. When Jesus sees Nathanael "under the fig tree," this
echoes a prominent prophetic picture of the righteous sitting "under
their own fig tree" when the Messiah comes, inheriting the promises of
God (Micah 4:3–4; Zechariah 3:10; cf. Psalm 1). So Jesus is describing
Nathanael here as a righteous remnant of the people of God, destined to
inherit his promises. Similarly, when Jesus calls Nathanael one "in whom
there is no deceit," this echoes Jacob, forefather to the people of God,
whose name meant "deceiver" until God named him Israel. Nathanael is
a true Israelite, in other words, reinforced by this Old Testament imagery.

15. Ephesians 2:8–10, NLT.

1: SET THE GPS

1. John 2:1.
2. As biblical scholars observe, John's order of events is more *theological* than
chronological. For example, Jesus's actions in the temple occur early in
John's gospel (chapter 2) but toward the end of Jesus's ministry in the Synoptic Gospels (shortly before his crucifixion).
3. John 2:3.
4. John 2:3–5.
5. John 2:4.
6. This helps explain why Jesus doesn't make a big show out of the miracle.
Nobody at the wedding knows what he's done except the servants (a picture of his disciples). If the point of turning water to wine had been to
bring the fireworks in a jaw-dropping display of his power, then Jesus
would have made sure everyone attending knew. But he's giving his mother,
his disciples, and the servants a behind-the-scenes sign of his coming hour.
It works: "His disciples believed in him" (John 2:11).

    Additionally, drawing attention to himself would have detracted from
the couple's wedding day. Maybe Christ is just so humble that he can take
on flesh, come to your party, save your day, and keep the attention on you.
Maybe the Spirit is just so selfless that he can show up when you've run out
and fill you up with something better when you've got nothing left to give.
Maybe God is just so great that he can prevent your embarrassment, purify
your stains, and party with you as you bask in the joy of your special day.
God *is* just that great because God is on your side.

7. Romans 8:18.

8. John 2:6–7.
9. Isaiah 25:6–9; cf. Matthew 22:1–14.
10. Amos 9:13–14, ESV.
11. Joel 3:18, ESV.
12. John 2:6, ESV.
13. Ritual purity went beyond just sin or hygiene in the Old Testament, involving things that were associated with decay and death—and thus distance from God's life-giving presence. See Michael Morales, *Who Shall Ascend the Mountain of the Lord?* (Intervarsity, 2015), 153–67, in which he summarizes: "The contrast between life and death is at the heart of the clean/unclean laws," 157.
14. Matthew 26:28.
15. 1 John 1:7.
16. Revelation 7:14.
17. John 19:34.
18. William Cowper, "Praise for the Fountain Opened," 1772, Hymnary.org, accessed December 18, 2024, https://hymnary.org/text/there_is_a_fountain_filled_with_blood_dr.
19. John 2:9–10.
20. C. S. Lewis, *The Last Battle,* The Chronicles of Narnia (HarperCollins, 2015), 157.
21. Hebrews 9:26; 10:14.
22. Isaiah 25:6–8.
23. John 2:11.

2: BRING DOWN THE HOUSE

1. *American Heritage Dictionary of Idioms,* 2nd ed. (2013), under "bring down the house."
2. John 2:13.
3. John 2:14–15.
4. Deuteronomy 14:24–26, ESV.
5. The merchants may have been charging exploitative prices; Jesus does critique them for turning his Father's house into a market (John 2:16). Yet there is still something deeper going on, if we accept that Jesus's dramatic actions are intended as a prophetic sign with symbolic significance.
6. Ezekiel 4.
7. Isaiah 20.
8. Jeremiah 19.
9. N. T. Wright, *Jesus and the Victory of God* (Fortress, 1996), 334–35.
10. Wright, *Jesus and the Victory of God,* 423–25. In the Synoptic Gospels, Jesus's actions in the temple are the catalyst for his crucifixion. In John, it is the raising of Lazarus from the dead that is highlighted.

11. Jesus's actions in the temple have three layers of meaning:

    1. *The Immediate:* a confrontation with the temple leadership of his day.
    2. *The Cross:* a foreshadowing of his own coming crucifixion.
    3. *The Temple:* a prophetic sign of imminent judgment on the temple (in A.D. 70).

    The immediate confrontation (layer 1) is a warning of the approaching judgment (layer 3), and the cross (layer 2) provides a way of escape from that judgment. God's people are invited to turn from their path toward destruction (led by the corrupt temple leadership) to follow Christ (who will bear the judgment on their behalf), yet their rejection of Christ and refusal to turn will lead, within a generation, to the destruction of the temple.

12. John refers to "the Jews" (*hoi Ioudaioi*), but this term is a reference not to Jewish people in general—Jesus, his disciples, and nearly everyone else in John's gospel is Jewish—but to Israel's leadership. This is important to recognize, particularly given the horrific history of anti-Semitism and the ways this phrase has at times been improperly used in this awful history.

13. Jesus is also softer on the doves (John 2:16), which were an alternative for those who couldn't afford the larger animal sacrifices. On Jesus's inspection of the temple the day before, compare the account in Mark 11:11–17.

14. Jason Isbell, "24 Frames," track 2 on *Something More Than Free*, Southeastern, 2015.

15. See my previous book *The Party Crasher: How Jesus Disrupts Politics as Usual and Redeems Our Partisan Divide* (Multnomah, 2024).

16. John 2:18, NKJV.

17. The question translates, literally, "What sign show you to us that these things you do?" This question can be accurately interpreted with both meanings. Most translations render it with the second meaning, an interpretation that distances Jesus's temple actions from being recognized as a sign. Yet if the first meaning is also recognized, this is the second sign and Jesus's response explains what the sign points to (his death and resurrection). If John's literary genius in his use of double entendre is recognized, this first meaning need not discount the narrative force of the second meaning.

    It is somewhat akin to Caiaphas's unintentional prophecy in John 11:50, where John brings out the double entendre in the temple leader's statement with force. The proper interpretive focus is not simply on the temple leader's *intention* with the statement but also on John's *literary* use of the statement, as the author of his gospel, with a double meaning higher than the high priest intends. I would suggest here in John 2:18, similarly, the religious leaders *intend* the second meaning on a historical level (cf. the parallel in Matthew 21:23), yet John intentionally phrases their interrogation in a way that adds a second *literary* layer of meaning, framing Jesus's temple actions as the second "sign" of his gospel: a sign of Christ's death and resurrection.

On double entendre in John's gospel, David Ford observes that John frequently makes "use of ambiguity and double meanings" in his gospel in a way that "serves to deepen the theology" and "where either [reading] makes appropriate sense and both together may well be intended, one effect of which is to stimulate rereading and further thinking." *The Gospel of John: A Theological Commentary* (Baker Academic, 2021), 1, 104, 340; cf. 350.

18. John 2:19.
19. John 2:20.
20. John 2:21.
21. Jesus is also the place where atonement happens, with a sacrifice that will take away the sin of the world. He is the place where mediation happens, with prayer for the healing of the nations. He is the center of cosmic order, where the Creator sustains creation through the power of his Word and Spirit. Jesus is the house of God. John unveils this identity of Jesus in the introduction to his gospel: "The Word became flesh and templed [*eskenosen*] among us. We have seen his glory" (1:14; my translation). God "moved into the neighborhood," in Eugene Peterson's memorable paraphrase (*The Message*), and made his home with us. He did so in a temple built not of brick and stone but of flesh and bone—in the body of Jesus.
22. Jeremiah 7:9–11, ESV. Notice that phrase "den of robbers" in verse 11. In the Synoptic Gospels, Jesus invokes this phrase to explain his disruptive actions in the temple. This Jeremiah passage thus forms an explicit backdrop for Jesus's actions.
23. Matthew 16:24–25.
24. John 14:23.
25. 2 Corinthians 6:16; 1 Peter 2:5.
26. Ephesians 2:20–22, ESV.
27. Hebrews 13:12.
28. Isaiah 42:25; Jeremiah 6:11; 10:25; Lamentations 2:4; 4:11; Ezekiel 7:8; 9:8; 14:19; 20:8, 13, 21, 33, 34; 21:31; 22:22, 31; 30:15; 36:18; Hosea 5:10; Zephaniah 3:8; cf. Psalm 69:24; 79:6.
29. N. T. Wright, *Jesus and the Victory of God*, 416.
30. Isaiah 51:17–53:12. On the cup of God's wrath, cf. Psalm 75:8; Job 21:20; Jeremiah 25:15; Revelation 14:10; 16:19. On Jesus's understanding of his death as the drinking of this cup, cf. Matthew 20:22; 26:39; Mark 10:38; 14:36; Luke 22:42; John 18:11.
31. This doesn't imply any division in the Trinity. Christ bearing our judgment has historically been understood according to his humanity rather than his

divinity. Because of the unity of the divine nature and will, the cross is a triune act with no division between the Father, Son, and Spirit. Yet Christ bears our judgment according to his vicarious humanity as our representative. In his humanity, Jesus bears our distance from the presence of the Father. In his divinity, Jesus bears the presence of the Father into our distance. For more on this, see Thomas H. McCall, *Forsaken: The Trinity and the Cross, and Why It Matters* (IVP Academic, 2012).

32. "396. Anatrepó," Bible Hub, accessed March 3, 2025, www.biblehub.com/greek/396.htm.
33. John 2:22.

3: BECOME THE BELOVED

1. Lynn Cohick provides a few historical possibilities that don't correspond to what we think of today as co-habitation: "Maybe she had no dowry and thus no formal marriage, meaning her status was similar to a concubine's. Perhaps the man she was currently with was old and needed care, but his children didn't want to share their inheritance with her, so he gave her no dowry document. Perhaps he was already married, making her his second wife. While the ancient Jewish culture allowed it, such an arrangement went against Jesus's definition of marriage as a union between one man and one woman (Matt. 19:4–6)." "The 'Woman at the Well': Was the Samaritan Woman Really an Adulteress?," in *Vindicating the Vixens: Revisiting Sexualized, Vilified, and Marginalized Women of the Bible,* ed. Sandra Glahn (Kregel Academic, 2017), 252.
2. John 4:6–9.
3. Genesis 24.
4. Genesis 29.
5. Exodus 2.
6. Robert Alter, *The Art of Biblical Narrative,* rev. ed. (Basic, 2011), 62. A representative can stand in for the future groom, as in Genesis 24, when Abraham's servant discovered Rebekah for Isaac.
7. John 4:4.
8. John 4:9.
9. See, e.g., Galatians 3:28; Ephesians 2:11–22.
10. John 4:10.
11. John 4:11–12. Both nations—Israel and Samaria—had Jacob as a common ancestor. Now Christ, one greater than Jacob, is here. (The answer to her question "Are you greater than our father Jacob?" is an emphatic "Yes!") If Christ is a new Jacob in this scene, the Samaritan woman is a new Rachel. Christ has arrived to marry his church and bring his divided people back together.
12. Song of Songs 4:15.
13. Infertility was faced by Abraham and Sarah, Isaac and Rebekah, Manoah

and his wife, Elkanah and Hannah, and Zechariah and Elizabeth. See my discussion in *Beautiful Union: How God's Vision for Sex Points Us to the Good, Unlocks the True, and (Sort of) Explains Everything* (Multnomah, 2023), chap. 13.

14. See Galatians 5:22–23. The Samaritan woman's evangelistic "harvest" later in John 4 is also a type of fruitfulness.

15. John 4:13–14. I've rendered "spring" as "well" to highlight that it is the same Greek word (*pēgē*) used earlier for the location where they meet.

16. John 4:16–18.

17. See endnote 1 in this chapter for some possible historical reasons the man she was with currently was not her husband.

18. 2 Kings 17:24–41.

19. While seven deities are listed in this passage, five are male and two are female—the term for the male deities (*ba'al*) can also mean "husband." Brant Pitre, *Jesus the Bridegroom: The Greatest Love Story Ever Told* (Image, 2018), 66–67.

20. Romans 3:23.

21. John 4:26, ESV.

22. John 19:14.

23. Hebrews 13:5; 2 Timothy 2:13.

24. John 3:20–21.

25. "3529. niké," Bible Hub, accessed April 6, 2025, https://biblehub.com/greek/3529.htm, and "1218. dēmos," Bible Hub, accessed April 6, 2025, https://biblehub.com/greek/1218.htm.

26. See chapter 12 for a fuller discussion of "Woman" as a type of the church in John's gospel.

27. John 3:1. John's order of events is not necessarily chronological, but from a literary perspective he places the conversation with Nicodemus immediately after Jesus's actions in the temple.

28. Later in John's gospel, Nicodemus arguably moves from curiosity to defending Jesus (7:50–51) and honoring Jesus at his burial (19:39).

29. John 4:19–20.

30. Mount Gerizim is an important place in the law of Moses, which the Samaritans recognize as authoritative. The blessings of the law were pronounced there, alongside the curses on Mount Ebal (Deuteronomy 11:29; 27:11–26). It is in the later books of the Old Testament, which the Samaritans don't recognize as authoritative (and which paint an unflattering portrait of the northern kingdom), that the temple was established in Jerusalem.

31. John 4:21–23.

32. The next story in John's gospel (4:43–54) will highlight God's blessing going to the Gentiles through faith in Jesus (we'll look at this in the next chapter). So, there is an outward movement in this section of John from Jerusalem (3:1–21), to Judea (3:22–36), to Samaria (4:1–42), and to the

ends of the earth (John 4:43:54; in the next chapter, I will suggest contextual reasons why the "royal official" is best understood as a Gentile and theological reasons why John does not explicitly identify him as such in his telling of the story). This movement mirrors the Great Commission's spread of the gospel in Acts 1:8, "in Jerusalem, and in all Judea and Samaria, and to the ends of the earth."

33. Ephesians 1:23; 2:21–22.
34. John 4:28–29.
35. John 4:42.
36. Shout-out to Tony Kriz, who long ago gave me this analogy.
37. John 4:14.
38. John 4:32–38.
39. The Greek Septuagint translation of Exodus 2:15 uses a form of the same verb and the same preposition (*ekathisen epi*) as John 4:6.
40. Genesis 29:2.
41. Genesis 29:10, my translation.
42. John 19:28, NKJV.
43. Luke 22:42.
44. Romans 5:5.

4: ENDURE THE HARDEST MILES

1. John 4:43, 46. The royal official's encounter with Jesus took place *after* the third day (it likely took Jesus a few days to travel from Samaria to Galilee, and it likely took the official time to hear news of his arrival and travel there). Literarily, however, John includes these references to link this passage with the first sign in John 2. See the appendix for more on how this fits within the structure of John.
2. John 4:46–50. In verse 47, I rendered *katabē* more literally as "come down" (following the ESV).
3. Augustine, *The Confessions of Saint Augustine,* 11th ed., trans. and ed. C. Bigg (Methuen, 1923), 277.
4. As John tells us earlier, Jesus "knew what was in man" (2:25, ESV).
5. Matthew 8:10, ESV.
6. I would suggest John withholds this detail to help set up this sign as a living parable of the gospel, with the royal official as a picture of the Father (naming him as a Gentile would make it harder for his immediate audience to draw this association). I'll make the case for this living parable at the end of this chapter.
7. John 4:44, ESV.
8. Mark 15:39.
9. John 1:11–12.
10. Psalm 46:2.
11. Job 13:15, NKJV.

12. Luke 22:42.
13. Luke 23:46.
14. John 4:51–53.
15. 1 Kings 17; 2 Kings 4.
16. John 4:44, ESV.
17. 2 Kings 4:30, ESV.
18. 2 Kings 4:34–35, ESV.
19. John 19:14. Pilate gives the order at the sixth hour (a number associated with humanity and incompleteness in biblical symbolism), which means the Crucifixion ensues during the seventh hour (a number associated with completeness and rest). On the symbolic flexibility of this timing, given how timing was understood in the ancient world, see Justin Taylor, "What Hour Was Jesus Crucified? Resolving an Apparent Bible Contradiction," The Gospel Coalition, April 18, 2019, www.thegospelcoalition .org/blogs/justin-taylor/hour-jesus-crucified-resolving-apparent-bible -contradiction.
20. Isaiah 53:5.
21. Andrew Wilson, "God Always Heals," Christianity Today, November 2014, www.christianitytoday.com/2014/11/god-always-heals.
22. John 4:54. I'm following the interpretation of many scholars who see this not as the second sign in John's gospel but as the second sign at Cana.
23. John 11:51; 12:33; 18:32.
24. John 10:18.
25. In the official, we see a picture of the Father who receives his dying Son back from the power of the grave. That word "official" (basilikos) connotes royalty in the original language, something "connected with a king" ("937. Basilikos," Bible Hub, accessed December 29, 2024, https://biblehub .com/greek/937.htm). It shares a root with "kingdom" (basileia) and is used elsewhere in the New Testament for King Herod. The royal figure is a picture of the true King of heaven and earth: the heavenly Father.

5: RISE UP

1. John 5:2–6.
2. John 10:7–18. See the appendix for more on this structure of John's gospel.
3. Dwight Peterson, "Visit the Sick," The Work of the People, June 2013, www.theworkofthepeople.com/visit-the-sick.
4. William Barclay, The Gospel of John, rev. ed., vol. 1 (Westminster John Knox, 2001), 210.
5. See the appendix for more on how this section fits within the structure of John.
6. Israel's wilderness was not just a past event but a present reality in Jesus's day. They were under Roman occupation, under the heel of the Gentile powers, awaiting a new exodus to deliver them. When they celebrated the

festivals of Passover (when they entered the wilderness), Tabernacles (when they wandered in the wilderness), and Pentecost (when God met them on Mount Sinai in the wilderness), they not only *remembered* God's past act of deliverance but also *anticipated* God's coming act of deliverance, still longing for him to restore the kingdom and bring them "into the land."

7. John 5:8–9, ESV.
8. John 5:9–10, 16.
9. John 5:17.
10. Numbers 15:32–36; Jeremiah 17:21; Nehemiah 13:15.
11. Matthew 12:8; Mark 2:28; Luke 6:5.
12. See Mark 10:47. This is a version of the Jesus Prayer, popular in Eastern Orthodoxy.
13. Jesus's sermon is structured by his three uses of the words "Truly, truly, I say to you . . ." (John 5:19, 24, 25, ESV). Each is followed by a picture of resurrection illuminated by his raising of the paralyzed man.
14. John 5:25.
15. John 5:28–29.
16. John 5:14.
17. John 9:1–5.
18. This is an allusion to the end of Jesus's famous parable of the prodigal son (Luke 15:25–32).
19. John Owen, *The Mortification of Sin* (Christian Focus, 1996), 28.
20. Barclay, *The Gospel of John,* 210. The word for "mat" in John 5—*krabattos* in Greek—refers to something less like a yoga mat and more like a pallet, which could be used for a bed.
21. "Strong's G964—Bēthesda," Blue Letter Bible, accessed December 27, 2024, www.blueletterbible.org/lexicon/g964/kjv/tr/0-1.
22. This discussion of the angel stirring the waters (John 5:3–4) is in only some manuscripts, arguably to explain for later audiences less familiar with the tradition why the invalid is waiting for the waters to be stirred (verse 7).
23. John 3:5.
24. Barclay, *The Gospel of John,* 209.

6: FEAST IN THE WILDERNESS

1. John 6:5.
2. John 6:7.
3. John 6:9. I've used *little* to render the diminutive in the original language.
4. John 6:1–3.
5. For example, the preceding passage concludes with Jesus saying Moses "wrote about me," and if they believed Moses's words, they would believe him (John 5:45–47, which segues directly into this passage; there are no chapter breaks in John's original text). Immediately after Jesus's miracle,

the people conclude, "Surely this is the Prophet who is to come into the world" (6:14), a reference to Moses's prediction that one day God would raise up "a Prophet like me from your midst" (Deuteronomy 18:15, NKJV). Additionally, John makes sure to tell us "the Jewish Passover Festival was near" (6:4), which associates this story with the Exodus. All these allusions reinforce the Moses motif.

6. John 6:10. "Made" is a more literal rendering of *poieō* than "had," which also makes Psalm 23 echo clearer.

7. Psalm 23:2. The Hebrew word translated "lie down" can also be translated "sit"; "Strong's H7257—Rābas," Blue Letter Bible, accessed December 27, 2024, www.blueletterbible.org/lexicon/h7257/kjv/wlc/0-1.

8. Psalm 23:5.

9. John 6:10; cf. Joshua 8:12.

10. John 6:11–13.

11. Similar to how he first provides actual bread to hungry people, then says, "I am the bread of life" (John 6:35) and invites them to receive life from him.

12. John 6:6.

13. Deuteronomy 8:2–3.

14. John 6:41, 61.

15. "1111. Gogguzó," Bible Hub, accessed December 27, 2024, https://biblehub.com/greek/1111.htm.

16. Numbers 11:4–5.

17. Deuteronomy 8:3.

18. Both these aspects of the law—giving life and bringing a curse—are strong biblical themes.

19. John 6:13, 51. Why is there no similar mention of leftover fish (probably good in an era before refrigeration)? The fish point to the Gentile nations outside Israel. As we'll see in chapter 13, it is *after* Jesus's death and resurrection that Christ's abundance will overflow beyond the twelve tribes of Israel to the Gentile nations, represented by the miraculous catch of 153 fish in John 21. Up to this point, John has highlighted two Gentiles—the Samaritan woman and arguably the (Roman?) official of John 4—possibly alluded to in the two fish with no leftovers. The priority of Jesus's ministry was the Jews, but his death and resurrection would unleash his abundant blessing to the Gentiles.

20. James 1:17.

21. John 6:51.

22. This language of *taken, blessed, broken,* and *given* appears in the Synoptic Gospels (Matthew 14:19; 26:26; Mark 6:41; 14:22; Luke 9:16; 24:30) and is a theme in Henri Nouwen's *Life of the Beloved* (Crossroad, 2002).

23. John 6:49–50.

24. John 6:53–56.

25. With the exception of Huldrych Zwingli and the Anabaptist tradition. Of

course, this doesn't mean most Christians in America today hold to this dominant tradition on a popular level.

26. The early church didn't develop a full-blown theology of *how* it happens but powerfully described the mystery of *what* happens: Christ feeds us with himself. See J.N.D Kelly, *Early Christian Doctrines*, rev. ed. (Harper-SanFrancisco, 1978), 193–99, 211–16.

27. Some question whether John intends this sacramental reading, but I believe it's clear within the literary symbolism of John 6, as well as the broader ethos and design of John's gospel. A few observations.

First, John is writing this gospel to the church on the other side of the Resurrection, for whom the Lord's Supper was a—if not *the*—central feature of their gatherings. John regularly foreshadows themes that are proleptic in the disciples' experience and can be properly understood only retrospectively from the vantage point of the Resurrection.

Second, John gives literary clues that frame this teaching in a resurrection context. Jesus gives the teaching in Capernaum, a location associated with resurrection (where he raised the dying son in John 4). John interrupts the miraculous sign of heavenly bread with a strange interlude—Jesus walking on water, an exodus motif loaded with resurrection overtones—before resuming with Jesus's teaching on what the miraculous sign means. It's as if to say, *It is from the vantage point of Christ's resurrection that you will be able to understand how to eat his flesh and drink his blood, to feed on the bread of his life given for the world.*

Finally, Christ follows up his shocking call to eat his flesh and drink his blood with the greater mystery of his coming ascension: "Then what if you see the Son of Man ascend to where he was before!" (6:62). (That is, to the right hand of God.) John's original audience would have undoubtedly heard this as sacramental theology: the ascended Christ who calls his people to feast on the bread of his body given and wine of his blood shed for the life of the world.

Like the water to wine in John 2 is a sign of his sacramental purifying blood, so the heavenly bread of John 6 is a sign of his sacramental sustaining body. Both meanings are rooted in his sacrifice on the cross.

28. John 6:35, 37.
29. John 6:27.
30. John 6:29.
31. Attributed to Saint Joseph of Optina.
32. Fyodor Dostoevsky, *The Brothers Karamazov*, trans. Andrew R. MacAndrew (Bantam, 2003), 339.
33. Matthew 4:4.
34. Philip Yancey, "God on the Move," PhilipYancey.com, September 2016, https://philipyancey.com/god-on-the-move.

7: BLOW THE DAM

1. "4. Bureau of Reclamation Engineering Achievements," National Park Service, January 13, 2017, www.nps.gov/articles/4-bureau-of-reclamation-engineering-achievements.htm; Calvin Gene Sims, "Hoover Dam Was Test of Engineers' Theories," *New York Times,* October 15, 1985, www.nytimes.com/1985/10/15/science/hoover-dam-was-test-of-engineers-theories.html; "The Hoover Dam," Herbert Hoover Presidential Library and Museum, December 31, 2024, https://hoover.archives.gov/hoovers/hoover-dam; *Britannica,* "Hoover Dam," December 18, 2024, www.britannica.com/topic/Hoover-Dam.
2. John 7:37.
3. John 7:2. Also known as the Feast of Booths.
4. Numbers 20:11; cf. Exodus 17:1–7.
5. John 7:38.
6. Check out the amazing work of leaders like Katherine at the Water Project: www.thewaterproject.org.
7. John 7:39.
8. See Psalm 1:3; Galatians 5:22–23.
9. John 7:37, ESV.
10. Isaiah 55:1.
11. "2896. Krazó," Bible Hub, accessed December 31, 2024, https://biblehub.com/greek/2896.htm.
12. Isaiah 55:2.
13. Tom Brady, "Tom Brady on Winning: There's 'Got to Be More Than This,'" interview by Steve Kroft, *60 Minutes,* CBS, June 2005, www.youtube.com/watch?v=-TA4_fVkv3c.
14. Billie Eilish, "Everything I Wanted," Darkroom/Interscope Records, 2019.
15. This is an allusion to Augustine's famous line in his *Confessions:* "You have made us for yourself, and our heart is restless until it rests in you." Trans. and ed. Henry Chadwick (Oxford University Press, 2008), 1.1.1.
16. Isaiah 55:2.
17. John 7:38, ESV.
18. Whether this refers to Christ's heart or ours hangs on which Old Testament passage Jesus refers to when he says, "As the Scripture has said, 'Out of his heart . . .'" (John 7:38, ESV). Some strong contenders refer to God or the temple, which would correspond to Christ in this passage (e.g., Isaiah 55:1; Ezekiel 47:1). Others refer to the believer, which would correspond to us (Proverbs 18:4; Isaiah 12:3). Some arguably refer to both (Isaiah 58:11; Jeremiah 31:12). There is precedence for this dual agency earlier in John 4:14 (ESV), which highlights both Christ giving the water of life ("whoever drinks of the water that I will give him") and us receiving it so that it flows from us ("will never be thirsty again. The water that I will give

him will become in him a spring of water welling up to eternal life"). Theologically, both readings are true. The phrasing in John 7:38 also allows for both.

19. I offer a fuller exploration of this, and how it connects to the temple imagery of Ezekiel 47 and Ephesians 2, in *Beautiful Union: How God's Vision for Sex Points Us to the Good, Unlocks the True, and (Sort of) Explains Everything* (Multnomah, 2023), chap. 13. The church is the living temple through whom the living water of the Spirit flows.

20. John 7:39.

21. John 12:16, 23, 28; 13:31–32; 17:1, 5.

22. Mishnah Sukkah 4, Sefaria, accessed March 3, 2025, www.sefaria.org/Mishnah_Sukkah.4?lang=bi; Bradley Shavit Artson, "The Ritual of Beating the Willow," My Jewish Learning, accessed March 3, 2025, www.myjewishlearning.com/article/the-ritual-of-beating-the-willow. The Mishnah says there was a wine libation in addition to the water libation; this corresponds to the blood and water that flowed from Christ's pierced side, discussed later in this section.

23. John 7:37.

24. 1 Corinthians 10:4.

25. John 19:34.

26. Acts 1–2.

27. 2 Corinthians 5:21.

28. John 19:28, ESV.

29. Dictionary.com., "damn," accessed January 1, 2025, www.dictionary.com/browse/damn.

30. Galatians 3:13.

31. Ezekiel 47:9.

8: RAISE THE BAR

1. John 8:3–6.

2. John 8:4.

3. Leviticus 20:10.

4. Leviticus 20:10.

5. As we'll see below in the second movement, Jesus's reference to he "who is without sin" and his invitation to "throw a stone" are Old Testament terminology for the eyewitnesses the law requires to have caught the couple in the act.

6. Kyle Harper, *From Shame to Sin: The Christian Transformation of Sexual Morality in Late Antiquity* (Harvard University Press, 2016), 37–61.

7. See my discussion in *Beautiful Union: How God's Vision for Sex Points Us to the Good, Unlocks the True, and (Sort of) Explains Everything* (Multnomah, 2023), chap. 9.

8. Genesis 38; 2 Samuel 11–12.
9. Matthew 7:3–5.
10. John 8:7.
11. Deuteronomy 17:6–7; cf. 13:9.
12. "Witness," Jewish Virtual Library, accessed March 3, 2025, www.jewish virtuallibrary.org/witness.
13. Deuteronomy 19:15–21.
14. As theologian Alastair Roberts puts it, "Jesus' point in challenging the scribes and Pharisees is *not* that the death penalty is wrong *per se*, but that the death penalty could only be unjustly exercised under the current circumstances. Every one of the 'witnesses' is somehow compromised, whether in a conspiracy of entrapment (where's the man?), or through their own guilt of the same sin." "#Luke2Acts—Some Notes on John 3 to 13," Alastair's Adversaria, May 29, 2014, https://alastairadversaria.com/2014/05/29/luke2acts-some-notes-on-john-3-to-13.
15. Bob Dylan, "Rainy Day Women #12 & 35," track 1 on *Blonde on Blonde*, Columbia Records, 1966.
16. Romans 11:32, ESV.
17. See my discussion in *Beautiful Union*, chap. 6.
18. Check out Fight the New Drug for helpful resources on these themes: https://fightthenewdrug.org.
19. See 1 Corinthians 6:18.
20. These are major themes in my book *Beautiful Union*.
21. Matthew 5:27–30.
22. As I put it elsewhere, "When people ask, 'Do you think homosexuality is a sin?' (which as a pastor, I tend to get asked a lot), my first response is usually, 'Well, I think *American* sexuality is sin.' What we look to it for, how we approach it as a whole. From the proliferation of premarital sex to the prominence of adultery, from the skyrocketing rates of divorce to the ubiquity of pornography and hook-up culture, from the prevalence of sexual abuse to the plight of children in broken homes and the cries of the unborn we'll never hear.

"Focusing only on gay sex is like focusing on a leaky faucet on the *Titanic*: Yes, there's water getting into the ship there, but American sexuality is the *Titanic*. We've got a breach in the hull, with water flooding in everywhere. Jesus pulls up in a rescue cruiser saying, 'That ship is sinking, come over here with me.'" (*Beautiful Union*, 105.)
23. Adultery and prostitution are major metaphors throughout the biblical story for idolatry and unfaithfulness to God.
24. John 8:6; cf. verse 8.
25. Alastair Roberts, "The Cup of the Adulteress: Understanding the Jealousy Ritual of Numbers 5," Alastair's Adversaria, February 9, 2013, https://alastairadversaria.com/2013/02/09/the-cup-of-the-adulteress-understanding-the

-jealousy-ritual-of-numbers-5. I'm indebted to Roberts for drawing my attention to the Numbers 5 connection, which is the focus of this section.

26. Numbers 5:15–16; John 8:2–3.
27. Numbers 5:17, 23; John 8:6, 8.
28. Numbers 5:23; John 7:37–39.
29. Numbers 5:26; John 6:5–58.
30. Numbers 5:26–28, ESV; John 8:9–11, NKJV.
31. Exodus 31:18. It's noteworthy that this is the final verse of Exodus 31, which then transitions into the golden calf incident. Remember, there are no chapter breaks in the original text. So in the biblical imagination, Yahweh writing with his finger the tablets of the covenant is immediately followed by the breaking of that covenant by Israel's adultery. John 8 and Numbers 5 are *both* echoing this foundational Old Testament scene.
32. The only two events in the Old Testament where writing with a finger is mentioned are God's writing of the Ten Commandments (Exodus 31:18; Deuteronomy 9:10) and the divine judgment on the king of Babylon (Daniel 5:5).
33. John 8:9–11, ESV.
34. John 3:17.
35. Timothy Keller, *The Meaning of Marriage: Facing the Complexities of Commitment with the Wisdom of God* (Penguin, 2016), 44.
36. John 8:3, NKJV.
37. John 8:9, NKJV.
38. John 8:59, NKJV.
39. The other locations where *mesos* appears are John 1:26, ASV (where John the Baptist points to Jesus as one "in the midst" of them, who will surpass him as the Lamb of God who takes away the sin of the world); John 19:18, KJV (where Jesus is crucified "in the midst" of two criminals); and John 20:19, 26, NKJV (where the risen Christ stands "in the midst" of his frightened disciples, speaking peace).
40. John 19:18, KJV.
41. John 8:1–2.
42. Romans 8:1.
43. Galatians 3:13, ESV.
44. John 19:30.

9: OPEN YOUR EYES

1. Adam Grant, *Think Again: The Power of Knowing What You Don't Know* (Viking, 2021), 33.
2. Gabriel Anton, "On the Self-Awareness of Focal Brain Diseases by the Patient in Cortical Blindness and Cortical Deafness," *Archiv für Psychiatrie und Nervenkrankheiten* 32 (1899): 86–127, quoted in Grant, *Think Again,* 34.

3. John 9:2.
4. John 9:3.
5. John 9:6–7.
6. Genesis 2:6–7. On the connection between water and Spirit in this passage, the "mist" (ESV) or "streams" (NIV) or "fountain" (LXX) came up from the ground to water "the whole surface of the ground" (NIV) or "the whole face of the earth" (LXX). The Spirit, which hovered over the waters of chaos in Genesis 1:2, tamed the waters below to make them life giving to the land. This theme is evident in the river from Eden (Genesis 2:10), which watered the surrounding regions, and in the "river of life" motif that develops throughout the biblical story, in association with the Spirit (see, e.g., Ezekiel 47:1–12; Revelation 22:1–2).

   The word for "breath" (*neshamah*) used here is also associated with the Spirit. "5397. Neshamah," Bible Hub, accessed March 3, 2025, https://biblehub.com/hebrew/5397.htm.
7. G. K. Beale, *We Become What We Worship: A Biblical Theology of Idolatry* (IVP Academic, 2008), 64–70, 127–40.
8. Beale, *We Become What We Worship*, 131–32.
9. Beale, *We Become What We Worship*, 132.
10. "Strong's H6754—Selem," Blue Letter Bible, accessed December 27, 2024, www.blueletterbible.org/lexicon/h6754/kjv/wlc/0-1.
11. Beale, *We Become What We Worship*, 65.
12. Isaiah 6. See Beale's discussion in *We Become What We Worship*, 64–70.
13. On this theme of the image as divine representative, Beale's observations are fascinating in light of the trial element that proceeds in John 9: "Animated by the deity's presence, [the image] mediates revelation from the deity, including decisions about legal or court cases" (*We Become What We Worship*, 67). Israel's leaders persecute the formerly blind man—who now mediates revelation about Jesus (verses 30–33)—yet the man's healing becomes a sign of Jesus's judgment on them (verses 39–41).
14. Isaiah 9:2.
15. John 1:9, 14.
16. John 9:7; Nehemiah 3:15.
17. This pool was used for the water ceremony during the Feast of Tabernacles, associated with the Living Water of John 7 (see chapter 7).
18. John 9:7.
19. Matthew 28:19.
20. Colossians 1:15; cf. Hebrews 1:3.
21. Joshua Ryan Butler, *The Skeletons in God's Closet: The Mercy of Hell, the Surprise of Judgment, the Hope of Holy War* (W Publishing, 2014).
22. John 9:15, 25, 32–33.
23. Revelation 12:11.
24. John 9:8–9.
25. John 9:11.

26. 1 Corinthians 13:12.
27. Hebrews 11:1, ESV.
28. John 20:29, ESV.
29. Hebrews 11:27, NLT.
30. John 9:34, from the verb *ekballō*.
31. John 9:34, ESV.
32. John 9:41.
33. John 9:39.
34. John 9:40.
35. Frederick C. Redlich and Joseph F. Dorsey, "Denial of Blindness by Patients with Cerebral Disease," *Archives of Neurology & Psychiatry* 53, no. 6 (1945): 407–17, quoted in Grant, *Think Again*, 34.
36. This famous quote is frequently attributed to Helen Keller, though I was unable to locate the original source.
37. John 3:19–20, ESV.
38. This does not imply any "break" in the Trinity. The church has historically understood such themes as according to the humanity of Christ, not his divinity. In his humanity, Christ bears our distance from the presence of the Father. In his divinity, Christ bears the presence of the Father into our distance.
39. John 1:5.
40. John 9:1, YLT.
41. Exodus 33:19, my translation; Job 9:11. The Exodus reference is reinforced by the surrounding context, where Jesus has just announced himself to be "I am" (*egō eimi*), the Greek term for Yahweh. The religious leaders understand what he is saying and pick up rocks to stone him for blasphemy (John 8:58–59). Jesus then, in the very next verse, *passes by* this blind man (9:1). Remember, there are no chapter breaks in the original version of John's gospel, so this "I am" scene, where Jesus identifies himself as Yahweh to a resistant audience, bleeds immediately into the next verse, where he *passes by* the blind man, who symbolically represents the stubborn opposition of Israel's leaders to Yahweh in the flesh, whose tabernacling glory stands before them (see 1:14).
42. This line inspired by the Benjamin William Hastings song "Boy on the Moon," track 13 on *Benjamin William Hastings (And Then Some)*, Capitol CMG, 2022.
43. John 9:37.
44. John 9:38.
45. Revelation 21:23–25.
46. John Newton, "Amazing Grace," 1779, Hymnary.org, accessed January 6, 2025, https://hymnary.org/text/amazing_grace_how_sweet_the_sound.

10: DISCOVER YOUR DEFENDER

1. 2 Samuel 5:2, ESV.
2. Psalm 78:72, ESV.
3. Ezekiel 34.
4. Psalm 78:52, ESV.
5. Simon Sinek, *Leaders Eat Last: Why Some Teams Pull Together and Others Don't* (Portfolio/Penguin, 2017), book description, www.penguinrandom house.com/books/311389/leaders-eat-last-by-simon-sinek.
6. Matthew 20:28.
7. John 10:10.
8. John 10:11.
9. Matthew 20:25–26, ESV.
10. Matthew 20:26.
11. "2812. Kleptés," Bible Hub, accessed January 6, 2025, https://biblehub .com/greek/2812.htm.
12. John 12:6.
13. "3027. Léstés," Bible Hub, accessed January 8, 2025, https://biblehub .com/greek/3027.htm.
14. John 10:12.
15. Karen Swallow Prior (@karenswallowprior), "Worse than wolves disguised as sheep are the ones disguised as shepherds," Threads, January 15, 2024, www.threads.net/@karenswallowprior/post/C2IASdYrQuV.
16. I share more of Jeremiah's story, and how I believe God's judgment addresses such horrific realities, in part 2 of *The Skeletons in God's Closet: The Mercy of Hell, the Surprise of Judgment, the Hope of Holy War* (W Publishing, 2014).
17. Ezekiel 34:2.
18. Ezekiel 34:4–5.
19. In 2022, Barna Group reported 42 percent of pastors had considered quitting in the last year. "Pastors Share Top Reasons They've Considered Quitting Ministry in the Past Year," Barna, April 27, 2022, www.barna.com/ research/pastors-quitting-ministry. In a hopeful turn, that number dropped to 33 percent in late 2023. "New Data Shows Hopeful Increases in Pastors' Confidence & Satisfaction," Barna, March 6, 2024, www.barna.com/ research/hopeful-increases-pastors.
20. Ezekiel 34:11–12, 15–16.
21. John 10:30–33.
22. Isaiah 53:4–5, 7.
23. Isaiah 53:5, 12; Luke 23:34.
24. Isaiah 52:13; 53:5–6; cf. Malachi 4:2.
25. John 10:4.
26. Matthew 16:24.

27. John 10:4–5.
28. Michael Youssef, "Listen for His Voice," Leading the Way, July 16, 2022, www.ltw.org/read/my-devotional/listen-for-his-voice.
29. Revelation 11:15, ESV.
30. If you're looking for some good places to start, BibleProject has great resources for studying Scripture (https://bibleproject.com); 24-7 Prayer has great resources for experiencing the power of prayer (www.24-7prayer.com); Adele Ahlberg Calhoun has a great introduction to other practices in *Spiritual Disciplines Handbook* (IVP, 2015).
31. Kenneth E. Bailey, *The Good Shepherd: A Thousand-Year Journey from Psalm 23 to the New Testament* (IVP Academic, 2014), 21–22.
32. The quotations and paraphrases in the preceding paragraphs are from Psalm 23, ESV.
33. John 11:43–44. I've used NIV for the first half of this passage (to highlight Jesus's dramatic call) and ESV for the second half (to highlight the Exodus overtones in the original language).
34. John 10:3–4, 7.
35. In John's gospel, Jesus's raising of Lazarus is the final catalyst for his own execution (11:53). From here, the leaders plot to kill him. Jesus knows raising Lazarus will send him to the cross, yet he lays down his life for his lamb. Similarly, on a broader level, Jesus will lay down his life on the cross for all his sheep, that he might raise them—as he has here raised Lazarus—from the grave.
36. John 10:10, 15, 28.
37. Luke 7:47.
38. My friend Célestin Musekura has powerfully lived such forgiveness in the wake of the genocide in Rwanda; see his excellent book co-authored with L. Gregory Jones, *Forgiving as We've Been Forgiven: Community Practices for Making Peace* (IVP, 2010).
39. For a great resource on forgiveness, see Lysa TerKeurst, *Forgiving What You Can't Forget: Discover How to Move On, Make Peace with Painful Memories, and Create a Life That's Beautiful Again* (Nelson, 2020).
40. Micah 5:4, ESV.

11: WALK FREE

1. Lorraine Boissoneault, "A Brief History of Presidential Pardons," *Smithsonian*, August 2, 2017, www.smithsonianmag.com/history/brief-history-10-essential-presidential-pardons-arent-watergate-related-180964286; "The Man Who Refused a Pardon," CBMC International, February 9, 2015, www.cbmcint.com/the-man-who-refused-a-pardon; United States v. Wilson, 32 U.S. 150 (1833).
2. John 18:38–40.

3. John 18:38; 19:4, 6, ESV; cf. 19:12.
4. "3027. Léstés," Bible Hub, accessed January 8, 2025, https://biblehub .com/greek/3027.htm.
5. John 18:36.
6. "912. Barabbas," Bible Hub, accessed January 8, 2025, https://biblehub .com/greek/912.htm.
7. John 3:16, NKJV; 10:30; 14:11; 17:24.
8. Exodus 4:22; Isaiah 43:6; Jeremiah 31:9; Hosea 1:10; Revelation 21:7.
9. *Lēstēs* in Mark 11:17 (and John 10:1) is the same word used for Barabbas here in John 18:40.
10. John 18:39.
11. Luke 15:11–32.
12. John 10:18.
13. Mark 10:45.
14. Joshua Ryan Butler, *The Pursuing God: A Reckless, Irrational, Obsessed Love That's Dying to Bring Us Home* (W Publishing, 2016), 90–91.
15. John 19:11.
16. Revelation 13:8.
17. Butler, *The Pursuing God,* 91.
18. J.R.R. Tolkien, "On Fairy-Stories," in *Tree and Leaf* (HarperCollins, 2001), 72.
19. C. S. Lewis, "Myth Became Fact," in *God in the Dock: Essays on Theology and Ethics,* ed. Walter Hooper (Eerdmans, 1970), 63–67.
20. Kate Bush, "Running Up That Hill (A Deal with God)," track 1 on *Hounds of Love,* EMI Records, 1985.
21. 2 Corinthians 5:21.
22. Ephesians 5:2.
23. *United States,* 32 U.S. at 160–61.
24. Aleksandr Solzhenitsyn, *The Gulag Archipelago: An Experiment in Literary Investigation,* trans. Thomas P. Whitney, vol. 2 (HarperPerennial, 2007), part 4, chap. 1.

12: ANTICIPATE SURPRISE

1. John 20:1.
2. John 19:30.
3. John 19:41; 20:15.
4. This is an allusion to the *protoevangelion* of Genesis 3:15, the first foreshadowing of the gospel in the biblical story, which pointed forward to that day when the serpent would strike the heel of the Messiah (as Satan did on the cross), but he—the Seed of the woman—would crush the serpent's head (as Christ did in his victory).
5. 1 Corinthians 15:22.

6. John 20:1.
7. John 20:11–13.
8. John 11:36.
9. John 20:12.
10. In his institution of the Lord's Supper, Jesus refers to his death as "the new covenant in my blood" (Luke 22:20; 1 Corinthians 11:25).
11. John 20:15. "Who is it you seek?" is my translation of *Tina zēteis,* which is also translated "Who is it you are looking for?" (NIV) or "Whom are you seeking?" (ESV).
12. John 18:1–7. Jesus asks the mob this same question twice for emphasis.
13. Luke 8:1–3.
14. See Matthew 12:43–45.
15. John 20:15.
16. John 2:4.
17. John 4:21, 23.
18. John 8:10, ESV.
19. John 19:26, ESV.
20. Ephesians 2:19–22; 1 Peter 2:4–7.
21. Romans 8:1, 34–39.
22. On the beloved disciple being brought forth from Jesus's side, see my discussion in the conclusion on the "bosom" (*kolpos*) passages in John 1:18 and 13:23; cf. 21:20. On the mother and disciple being joined, many translations render John 19:27 with something like "this disciple took her into his home," but the more literal translation is "this disciple took her into his own [*idia*]," a more personal term with a sense of their lives being joined.
23. This likely echoes "the woman" of Genesis 3:15, whose Seed would crush the serpent. In other words, John's use of the term "Woman" to highlight these archetypal realities draws our attention to the fulfillment of the *protoevangelion,* the overcoming of the curse, and the establishment of new creation through Christ and his church.
24. John 20:15–16.
25. Matthew 18:3; "4762. Strephó," Bible Hub, accessed January 10, 2025, https://biblehub.com/greek/4762.htm.
26. "4462. Rhabbouni," Bible Hub, accessed January 10, 2025, https://biblehub.com/greek/4462.htm.
27. John 20:17.
28. "680. Haptomai," Bible Hub, accessed January 10, 2025, https://biblehub.com/greek/680.htm. To cling, hold fast, or hold on to is an image with covenantal associations in the Bible (see Genesis 2:24; the word used here in the Septuagint is *proskollaō,* yet the imagery is similar, and the covenantal associations are arguably present with *haptomai* in John 20:17, given the typological associations of Mary with the church in the surround-

ing passage). *Haptomai* can even refer to carnal intercourse; this usage is not dominant but does occur in context with the term *gynē* ("woman"), used here in verse 15 (see 1 Corinthians 7:1 and the Septuagint for Genesis 20:6; Proverbs 6:29). Such marital allusions in this scene are obviously analogical, not literalistic, but they underscore the typological associations for this resurrection encounter with the marriage of Christ and the church.

29. Revelation 21:9.
30. Revelation 22:20.

13: CHANGE THE WORLD

1. John 21:3.
2. John 21:2.
3. John 21:4–6.
4. Luke 5:1–11; cf. Matthew 4:19. True, this story is recounted in Luke's gospel rather than John's. Yet David Ford offers a fresh defense for the classic position that John wrote his gospel later than the Synoptics, was deeply familiar with their circulated traditions, and alluded to them at regular points in his gospel, in *The Gospel of John: A Theological Commentary* (Baker Academic, 2021). In the words of commentator C. K. Barrett, "John collects scattered synoptic material and synoptic themes, welds them into a whole, and uses them to bring out unmistakably the true meaning of the synoptic presentation of Jesus." *The Gospel According to St. John: An Introduction with Commentary and Notes on the Greek Text,* 2nd ed. (Westminster, 1978), 196.
5. Psalm 144:7; Isaiah 17:12–13.
6. Herman Bavinck, "Common Grace," trans. Raymond C. Van Leeuwen, *Calvin Theological Journal* 24, no. 1 (April 1989): 59.
7. 2 Chronicles 2:17. The precise number is 153,600, but it would be awkward for the disciples to count 153 fish and three-fifths of a fish. The symbolic use of numbers in Scripture can be aesthetically evocative without being scientifically precise.
8. This abundant catch of fish likely explains why, earlier in John 6, there are twelve leftover basketfuls of bread but no leftovers of fish mentioned. The twelve basketfuls of bread correspond to the twelve tribes of Israel and Jesus's priority of mission to his own people, Israel (see my discussion in note 19 of chapter 6). Upon his death and resurrection, however, the mission overflows abundantly to the Gentiles, represented here in the miraculous catch of fish corresponding to the Gentile nations.
9. Ezekiel 47:9–10.
10. See the respected theologian Richard Bauckham's detailed argument in "The 153 Fish and the Unity of the Fourth Gospel," *Neotestamentica* 36,

no. 1/2 (2002): 77–88, www.jstor.org/stable/43049111. One hundred fifty-three (153) is the triangular number of seventeen (17), connected to the Hebrew gematria for *Gedi* (17) and *Eglaim* (153). This interpretation leads to a similar conclusion as the 2 Chronicles 2:17 reference: that the number 153 represents the totality of the children of God—including the Gentile nations—drawn into the new creation.

11. John 21:11.
12. Luke 5:6–7.
13. Matthew 16:18.
14. Ephesians 2:10.
15. Revelation 12:11, NKJV.
16. John 21:9, ESV.
17. John 18:18, 25–27.
18. John 21:15–17.
19. John 21:17.
20. Isaiah 9:6.
21. John 21:17.
22. The image of *fisherman* in this passage speaks to Peter's evangelistic calling; the image of *shepherd* speaks to his pastoral calling. These images also speak, by extension, to the church's calling.
23. The Pentecostal pastor Giovanni Traettino shared this saying with me when we met with Pope Francis in 2017 (recounted here: www.joshuaryanbutler.com/blog/meeting-pope-francis-2017). The saying may be inspired by Pope Francis himself, who has referred to the need for priests to have "the smell of the sheep." Robin Gomes, "Pope to Priests: Be 'Shepherds with "the Smell of the Sheep,"'" Vatican News, June 7, 2021, www.vaticannews.va/en/pope/news/2021-06/pope-francis-priests-students-church-louis-french.html.
24. John 21:18–19.
25. John 15:5.
26. John 15:5.
27. The vineyard is a significant biblical image for God's people (see Isaiah 5 and 27, which form a backdrop for Jesus's declaration of himself as the Vine and his disciples as the branches).
28. John 15:9, 12–13.
29. Colossians 1:24. When Paul refers to "what is still lacking in regard to Christ's afflictions," he doesn't mean something was lacking in Christ's atonement on the cross but is rather speaking to a participatory dimension of the body of Christ in his sacrificial love, which bears his redemptive power through his Spirit to the world.
30. 1 Corinthians 4:7.
31. John 21:19.

CONCLUSION: BE THE BELOVED

1. John 21:20. Some scholars dispute whether this disciple is someone other than John, like Lazarus. I'm not convinced, however, and take the traditional identification of John with the beloved disciple.
2. John 13:23; 19:26; 20:2; 21:7, 20.
3. John 13:1.
4. John 15:12, ESV.
5. Thanks to my fellow pastor Jon Furman for the insights of this paragraph.
6. Song of Songs 6:3.
7. Matthew 3:17, ESV.
8. David Brooks, *The Road to Character* (Random House, 2015), xi.
9. John 21:20.
10. John 13:23, my translation.
11. "2859. Kolpos," Bible Hub, accessed January 4, 2025, https://biblehub.com/greek/2859.htm.
12. John 1:18, NKJV.
13. For a philosophical perspective on this phenomenon, see Byung-Chul Han, *The Burnout Society*, trans. Erik Butler (Stanford University Press, 2015). For a sociological perspective, see Jonathan Haidt, *The Anxious Generation: How the Great Rewiring of Childhood Is Causing an Epidemic of Mental Illness* (Penguin, 2024).
14. John 20:31.
15. Karl Barth, quoted in Roger E. Olson, "Did Karl Barth Really Say 'Jesus Loves Me, This I Know . . .'?," Patheos, January 24, 2013, www.patheos.com/blogs/rogereolson/2013/01/did-karl-barth-really-say-jesus-loves-me-this-i-know.
16. Wyatt Houtz, "The Life of Karl Barth: Early Life from Basel to Geneva 1886–1913 (Part 1)," PostBarthian, April 18, 2018, www.postbarthian.com/2018/04/18/life-karl-barth-early-life-basel-geneva-part-1.
17. I heard this quote from a scholar who did his PhD in Barth studies, but I was unable to locate the original source. It is also recounted here: Taylor Mertins, "On the Impossible Possibility of Karl Barth or: Why God Is God," *Think and Let Think* (blog), September 1, 2016, https://thinkandletthink.com/2016/09/01/on-the-impossible-possibility-of-karl-barth-or-why-god-is-god.

APPENDIX: AN ELEGANT DESIGN

1. Between these two verses, verses 44–45 highlight Jesus being rejected in his home country and accepted by the Galileans, who—like the Samaritans just prior—welcome him. This reinforces the section's theme of Jesus's rejection by the Jerusalem insiders and reception by many outsiders. It also echoes and expands John's earlier statement in his introduction that

"his own did not receive him. Yet to all who did receive him . . . he gave the right to become children of God" (John 1:11–12).

2. John 2:11; 4:54.
3. John 3:29, ESV.
4. John 3:29.
5. John 2:6.
6. On John's status as the greatest prophet under the old order of things yet outshone by the new order inaugurated by Christ, see Mark 1:1–3, quoting Malachi 3:1 and Isaiah 40:3; and Luke 7:28.
7. John 2:23–25.
8. Isaiah 9:1.
9. John thus mirrors, in his own unique and poetic way, Luke's description of the Great Commission in Acts 1:8.
10. John 5:2.
11. John 10:7.
12. Psalm 78:52, ESV.
13. John 11:44, ESV; Exodus 5:1; 9:13.
14. John 12:1; 19:42. On the latter reference, the word "Passover" (*pascha*) isn't used—arguably as this would disrupt the seven prior uses in this section, with their numerological significance. Instead, John uses "the Jewish day of Preparation," referring to the day on which the Passover lambs were slain. This term also forms an *inclusio* with John 19:14 ("It was the day of Preparation of the Passover"), which inaugurates the crucifixion of Christ.
15. John 11:55 (two times); 12:1; 13:1; 18:28, 39; 19:14. I'm including the two uses at the end of John 11, as they segue directly into John 12 and John's original text didn't include our modern chapter breaks. See also allusions to Passover in John 19:36 (cf. Exodus 12:46; Numbers 9:12) and 19:42.
16. John 1:29, 36; cf. Romans 5–8.
17. John 2:13, 23; 6:4. This isn't to say crucifixion imagery is absent from the other signs (we've seen throughout this book how present it is) but rather to say there is a stronger emphasis on Christ's sacrificial death in the tearing down of the temple and the breaking of the bread, while there is a stronger emphasis on his resurrection in the third-day wedding, the healings of the official's son, the paralytic, and the blind man, and the raising of Lazarus.
18. John 20:1, 19.
19. John 21:4.
20. The early chapters of the Gospels emphasize this theme, for example, when Christ goes down into Egypt (like Israel of old), is baptized and then tempted in the wilderness (like Israel passing through the Red Sea into the wilderness testing), and inaugurates his kingdom ministry (like Israel entering the promised land).

JOSHUA RYAN BUTLER is a teaching pastor with the Willamette family of churches in the Portland area and the author of *The Party Crasher, Beautiful Union, The Skeletons in God's Closet,* and *The Pursuing God.* Josh loves shifting paradigms, to help people who wrestle with tough topics of the Christian faith by confronting popular caricatures and replacing them with the beauty and power of the real thing. He and his wife, Holly, along with their three children, live in Portland, Oregon. They enjoy spending time with friends over great meals and exploring the scenic beauty of the Pacific Northwest.

DISCOVER THE LIFE-TRANSFORMING TRUTH THAT GOD IS FOR YOU.

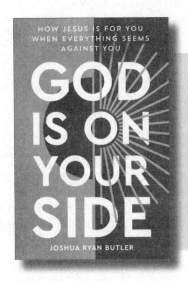

This book is for those haunted by a nagging sense that God is indifferent or disappointed in them. Learn that our greatest comfort is not what we've done to win God's love but all God's love has done to win us.

This practical, illuminating, author-curated companion guide to *God Is on Your Side* encourages exploration of the goodness of God in a confusing world.

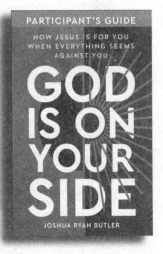